LEO ZAKUTA

Reminiscences, Rants, and Raves

LEO ZAKUTA

Reminiscences, Rants, and Raves

compiled by Annette Zakuta

IGUANA

Copyright © Annette Zakuta, 2013
Published by Iguana Books
460 Richmond St. West, Suite 401
Toronto, Ontario, Canada
M5V 1Y1

All rights reserved. No part of this publication may be reproduced, stored in a retrieval system or transmitted, in any form or by any means, electronic, mechanical, recording or otherwise (except brief passages for purposes of review) without the prior permission of the author or a licence from The Canadian Copyright Licensing Agency (Access Copyright). For an Access Copyright licence, visit www.accesscopyright.ca or call toll free to 1-800-893-5777.

Publisher: Greg Ioannou
Book layout and design: Sharlene Hopwood, Stephanie Martin
Cover design: Jane Awde Goodwin
Author photo: Annette Zakuta

Library and Archives Canada Cataloguing in Publication

Zakuta, Leo, 1925-2008
  Leo Zakuta : reminiscences, rants, and raves / compiled by Annette Zakuta.

ISBN 978-1-927403-30-3

  1. Zakuta, Leo, 1925-2008--Anecdotes. 2. College teachers--Ontario--Toronto--Biography. 3. Jews--Ontario--Toronto--Biography. 4. Authors, Canadian (English)--20th century--Biography. I. Zakuta, Annette II. Title.

PS8599.A429Z58 2012   C818'.5403   C2012-907569-8

This is the original print edition of *Leo Zakuta: Reminiscences, Rants, and Raves.*

IN MEMORY OF
LEO ZAKUTA

1925 — 2008

Foreword

Leo and I were born and raised in the same milieu: the secular, intellectual circles of pre-WW2 Jewish Montreal. For both our families, culture and literature were the important values. We first met at the "Y" Summer Camp, where we were both counselors, in 1950. I was 21 and he was 25.

At the time, nothing happened. But six years later, when he had started teaching in the University of Toronto's Sociology Department, we reconnected. On a trip home to Montreal to visit his parents, he asked his friend Leonard Levine for the names of some congenial girls. Leonard gave him three names. Leo phoned me. Six weeks later, we were married and on our way to Toronto.

Throughout our 52 years of marriage, we enjoyed a loving and dependent relationship. After Leo's death, I found that one way of living without him was to put together a memoir of Leo. I realized that it could also serve another purpose as well. Leo had asked to be cremated, and did not want a gravestone. A memorial book would be a place we could visit instead.

Leo had already written some autobiographical essays, compiling them in a booklet along with tributes to some of his friends and 'letters to the editor' he had written over the years. Leo's booklet would, I decided, serve as the basis for my own memorial compilation. I then collected the eulogies that had been read at the memorial service for Leo held in the Hart House Music Room at the University of Toronto on October 24, 2008. About a year later, Leo's friends from the Rosedale Tennis Club installed a bronze plaque in his memory on courts 7 and 8, where he had played tennis almost daily for many years. The unveiling of this plaque was, for us, like the traditional Jewish unveiling of a tombstone. Several people spoke spontaneously in remembrance of Leo, and I was able to gather their remarks in writing afterwards.

In addition, I have included a few pieces reflecting Leo's research on his maternal and paternal family history.

I am indebted to Jeremy Harman for giving me the confidence and the courage to undertake this project, and my friend Margie Golick for suggesting the title. I would also like to acknowledge the support I received from: Sylvia Angell, Margaret Cockshutt, Mary Elder, Beatty Endler, Marie-Claude Gatineau, Airie Giffen, Margie Golick, Michelle Gorry, Rose Katz, Bernice Krafchik, Sylvia Lustgarten, Mayta Markson, Roberta Markus, Anne Palayew, Gina Shochat, Bea Zakuta, and Shannon Hodge (archivist at the Jewish Public Library in Montreal). My cousin Sylvia Angell was particularly eager to read this book, but sadly, she died in November 2011, before it was finished.

Shiona Mackenzie-Morrison, a friend of Silvie's, undertook some early work on the manuscript, and I would like to thank her for her enthusiasm and assistance. At a later stage, Nessa Olshansky-Ashtar provided further editorial input, for which I am grateful. I want to thank Greg Ioannou, the publisher, Jane Goodwin, Sharlene Hopwood, Stephanie Martin, Emily Niedoba, and Meghan Behse of Iguana Books for their expertise and patience. I am also thankful to Warren Sheffer, my copyright lawyer, for his confident knowledge, reliability, and sensitivity.

Finally, I want to thank my daughter Silvie for her unstinting help and generous contributions to every aspect of this project, and my son Jamie for his good-natured support and encouragement. I am grateful to them both. Jamie and Silvie shared my conviction that the project would be a worthy testament to their father, and a valuable legacy.

Annette Zakuta
September 2012

The following three vignettes — an essay, a posthumous tribute, and an anecdote — will give the reader a preliminary glimpse of Leo's character.

I

This essay, written by Silvie when she was 14, appeared in the 1979 Slogan, the yearbook of her high school, Branksome Hall.

My Favourite Relative

There is a word in the Yiddish language that has always been one of my favourites. The word is 'mishugas.' Its literal translation is 'something which is a bit crazy,' but in Yiddish the word implies that it is not to be taken seriously. Everybody has some 'mishugasn'; some are charming, some are bizarre, some are childish, some are insane, but none of them really makes too much sense.

My favourite relative is my father, who is blessed with many a 'mishugas.' He is tall with hazel eyes and brown hair. One of his 'mishugasn' is that he has kept the same haircut for the past twenty-five years, no matter how the styles have changed.

Although he likes nice clothes, he is rarely seen in anything but a t-shirt and jeans. He also wears slip-ons, like the kind worn by children who haven't learned how to tie their shoelaces. This has nothing to do with laziness; it is just because he finds them more comfortable than anything else. If this is not a 'mishugas,' I don't know what is.

Whenever my parents go out, no matter where they are going, what they are doing, and who they are seeing, my father always has to complain a little before they leave. He has been doing this for so many years, it has become habit, so now he does it without even thinking.

My father is a perfectionist, which explains much of his 'mishugas.' Although he sometimes has a bad back, he will never hesitate to pick up even the most microscopic piece of paper or dust from the floor. He also goes about turning off lights, turning on lights, closing curtains and blinds at night, opening them in the morning, and generally straightening up any little thing that is out of place.

He even has a whole garbage system worked out; there is a place for everything. Old newspapers go in their own special cupboard; other papers have their own can as well. Kitchen garbage has its own bag, and cans and small bottles have theirs. Twice a week, he makes his rounds, collecting the garbage from all over the house. Then he puts it in its own special bag, in its own can, in our garbage box. When our cleaning woman comes once a week, he leaves strict orders with her NOT TO TOUCH THE GARBAGE! When the garbagemen come, of course they just take it out and dump it in the truck. I am sure that if they could see the amount of work that goes into organizing that garbage, they would be much more careful with it.

However, because he is a perfectionist, he also feels that he has to be a perfect father, and he is very devoted to his family. Although he is very demanding of me, he gives me a lot more than he asks in return. He is always there if I need him. No matter how much work he has, he will always put me before it. My father is the most fair-minded and honest person I know, and even with all his 'mishugasn,' I would never trade him for any other.

Silvie Zakuta
Grade 9

II

After compiling this memoir, I asked Jamie to write a short introductory sketch of his father.

The stories, tributes, letters, and poems contained in this book reveal many things about my father. Throughout his life he was a generous, loving, and supportive man. As you'll discover, his early years were shaped by the Jewish community of 1930s and 1940s Montreal, where he made the important transition from 'corner' to 'college' boy. Despite growing up during the Depression, his life was rich in many ways. The friendships he formed at this time endured for life.

During his teaching years and beyond, he was forever eager to express his views on various subjects. He wrote numerous letters to editors of various publications, which he entitled "Exercises in Futility"–a reference to how few actually appeared in print. If he were alive today, he surely would have his own blog or Twitter account–who knows how many followers he would've had? Quite a few, I suspect.

His dedication to family, friends, and teaching was matched only by his passion for tennis. He derived great pleasure and camaraderie from the inimitable 'tennis gang'–the letters in the tennis section of this work speak volumes. As his son, however, I would like to share a story about the kind of man he was.

It's about an event that occurred during my elementary school years. I was the unfortunate recipient of teasing and bullying, and often came home in tears. Dad would comfort me and encourage me to stand up and fight even if it meant a bloody nose, or worse. I never quite summoned up the courage to do so, but I'll always remember his sage words regarding cowardice and sticking up for oneself.

What I most cherish and miss about dad was our friendship. He was always just a phone call away. Whether it was to discuss the day's hockey or tennis match–had I seen that magnificent shot of Federer's?–or just to see how I was, Dad always made time. I'm forever touched by the words in a card he gave me for my 44th birthday. It reads, "In celebration of the journeys that make us who we are." In addition, Dad had inscribed it with the words, "to a great and companionable son." To this day, I keep it to remind me of him–my father, my friend.

As a final thought, the plaque at courts 7 and 8 of the Rosedale Tennis Club will forever honour his memory, as will this book.

Jamie Zakuta
April 2011

III

According to his mother Keile, when Leo was a very young child, he had "beautiful golden curls and a silver tongue." One family friend used to have long conversations with him (in Yiddish) when Leo was 3 or 4 years old. This friend was so impressed with Leo's conversation that it prompted him to say to my mother-in-law, *"a bord, a boich, un a veib, un er iz a rov."* Loosely translated, this means that at all he needed was a beard, a large belly, and a wife, and he could be a rabbi.

Annette Zakuta

Table of Contents

I MUSINGS 1
   1. An Old Man's Memories 7
      i. Coming to "America" 7
      ii. "Tough Guy"? 15
      iii. Adventures with the Outremont Police 18
      iv. Becoming a "College Boy" and After 27
      v. Our Tennis Group 35
      vi. Canada Day Talks at the Garbers 51
      vii. For Better or Verse 56
      viii. On Our 50th Wedding Anniversary (Sept. 4, 1956–2006) 58
      ix. Moving Day: A Song Of Celebration 63
   2. Tributes to the Living and the Dead (compiled 2006) 65
    (a). Tributes to the Living 65
      i. Arthur Axelrad 65
      ii. Ida Berk 66
      iii. Bryce Bosnich 68
      iv. Margaret Cockshutt 70
      v. Harold Files 72
      vi. Eileen Garber 73
      vii. Margie Golick 77
      viii. Rose Katz 82
      ix. Marjorie Kennedy 83
      x. Yelena Kalacic 86
      xi. Bernice 86
      xii. Johannes Pretorius 89
      xiii. Helen Hutchison 90
      xiv. Gina Rakoff 91
      xv. Marianne Stein 92
      xvi. Roy Wolfe 92
      xvii. Annette Zakuta 93
      xviii. Valentine Day in Barbados, 1991 93
    (b). Tributes to the Dead 95
      i. Bill Alexander: Eulogy 95
      ii. Marc Allodi 97
      iii. Ethel Bernstein 98
      iv. Ellen Clark 98

    v. Ruth Cooperstock 99
    vi. Betty Dales 99
    vii. Sheila Eastman 99
    viii. Harry Eastman 100
    ix. Norman Endler 104
    x. Fritzi Frankel 107
    xii. Jim Giffen... 108
    xiii. Bernard Goldstein.. 113
    xiv. Oswald Hall 116
    xv. Tannis Lee 123
    xvi. Leonard Levine.. 124
    xvii. Rex Lucas 128
    xviii. Peter Lustgarten... 130
    xix. Diego Marin... 132
    xx. Lou Sherman... 133
    xxi. Stefan Stykolt 134
    xxii. Gerry Wise.. 146
    xxiii. Keile and Hershel Zakuta (my parents)..................... 147

II   WRITINGS.. 150
    i. Membership in a Becalmed Protest Movement 150
    ii. The Radical Political Movement in Canada 172
    iii. Equality in North American Marriages 196
    iv. "We Distinguish — They Discriminate":
        Observations on Race Relations 211
    v. On 'Filthy Lucre' 228

III CORRESPONDENCE.. 245
    1. Exercises in Futility: Complaints and Occasional
        Commendations 245
      i. Letters to *The Globe and Mail*.. 246
      ii. Letters to *The Globe and Mail* Columnists 269
      iii. Letters to the [University of Toronto] *Bulletin*............ 275
      iv. Letters to *The National Post* 284
      v. Letters to Other Publications 287
      vi. Letters to CBC Radio, CBC TV, and TVO 295
    2. Personal Letters 322
      i. To Jim Richardson, President, Canadian Sociology
         & Anthropology Assoc., 19 May, 1983........................ 322

    ii. Exchange of letters with my friend Myer Katz + attached memo 323
    iii. To my friends Chris and John Furedy, 16 March, 2000 324
    iv. To my friend Brian Bixley, 22 March, 2003 326
    v. To Beryl Donaldson Langer, 5 December, 2005 327

IV   TRIBUTES TO LEO 331
  1. Memorial Service for Leo Zakuta 332
    i. Abba Lustgarten 333
    ii. Silvie Zakuta 338
    iii. Jamie Zakuta 341
    iv. Jacob Lustgarten 345
    v. Margie Golick 347
    vi. Margaret Cockshutt 351
    vii. Norman Dyson 353
    viii. Judy Hellman 354
    ix. Deborah Heller 355
    x. Chris and John Furedy 356
    xi. Stephen Ain 358
  2. Unveiling of Plaque in Honour of Leo at Rosedale Park 362
    i. Sean Miller 363
    ii. Judy Hellman (read by Anne Lenchak) 364
    iii. Peter Goering 366
    iv. Barry Sessle 367
    v. Peter Moon 368
    vi. Shirley Harris 370
    vii. Deborah Heller 371
    viii. Richard Nicolson 372
    ix. Annette Zakuta 373
    x. Norm Dyson 373

V FAMILY DOCUMENTS 375
  1. The Zakuto Trail 375
    i. *Yiches* 375
    ii. Lineage 380
    iii. Abraham Zacuto (b. Salamanca, Spain, ca. 1450, d. Portugal, ca. 1522) 382

   iv. Zacutus Lusitanus (b. Lisbon 1575, d.
       Amsterdam 1642) 385
   v. Rabbi Moses Zacuto (ca. 1620-1697) 386
2. The Ain Family 398
   i. Svislocz in Our Time 398
   ii. Letter to Keile Zakuta from her Father, Aaron
       Isaac Ain 406

*Keile and Hershel at their wedding
Montreal, 1924*

I MUSINGS

Vanity of vanities, saith the Preacher ... all is vanity (Eccles. 1:2).

Old age has some strange effects, and here is one of them.

The introduction to the first piece tells why it was written, but I cannot explain why the pieces continued, or where I got the *chutzpah* to send all of this to my family and friends. I'm tempted to blame Annette for her constant encouragement, but that would be unchivalrous. So I must take refuge in the frailties of age and the words of the Preacher in Ecclesiastes.

Leo Zakuta

Acknowledgements:

To Annette, who was my advisor, editor and constant consultant
To Silvie, who was always there when I freaked out at the computer
To Jamie, who helped me unwind by watching baseball and tennis on TV with me

Reminiscences, Rants, and Raves

Leo, 4 years old
Montreal, 1929

Hershel, Leo, Kenny, and Keile
Keile's brother Joe Ain, and sister Sarah Ain (behind)
Montreal, 1930

Keile, Kenny, and Leo
Laurentian Mountains, 1935

Kenny, Hershel, Sarah, Keile, and Leo
Montreal, 1928

Kenny, age 10 and Leo, age 12
Montreal, 1937

Leo and Kenny playing street hockey
Montreal, 1940

*Kenny and Leo, High School Cadets at Strathcona Academy
Outremont, Montreal, 1942*

1. An Old Man's Memories

i. Coming to "America"

Introductory Note: This piece, the first of a series entitled "An Old Man's Memories," was written for the annual Canada Day garden party of our old Montreal friends, Eileen and Ralph Garber. Guests are always asked to present a short piece on a specific theme. It can be a poem, a skit, a brief talk, or whatever the presenter fancies. These efforts turn out well; I can't recall any that didn't. There is no pressure to perform, and many guests do not. Only those who have signified their willingness to do so beforehand are called on.

Although reluctant at first, I have always participated, because I enjoy doing so. The theme this year was to imagine the experience of an immigrant to Canada who has just arrived from a very different society. I interpreted that instruction freely, indeed, too freely, because my topic ran away with me, so that the completed piece was much too long for the occasion. I cut it in half for the garden party, but it appears here in its entirety, with some recent additions.

Leo, Hershel, Keile, and Kenny
1933

I thank Eileen and Ralph for giving me a captive audience once again. I had such audiences regularly in my previous existence, but, unlike them, you need not pay any attention to what I say, and I can talk about my family and myself. And talk I will, since old men are notoriously garrulous, and the subject is so close to home.

*Keile at the window of the Zakuta's
3rd floor cold-water flat, Montreal*

I was tempted to use Zimbabwe as my example, in order to achieve the most dramatic contrast, but decided instead to adhere to the venerable principle of staying with what one knows best. So we will travel along a familiar and well-beaten path — leaving the *shtetl* for "America," in this case my parents' coming to Montreal, where my brother and I were born and grew up. I feel that I have the shtetl in my bones — so much has been written about it — mostly because my mother talked about hers so often and with such feeling.

My parents came from Svislocz, a shtetl near Bialystok. My mother's father had been touched by a movement known as the "Enlightenment," which had emerged in certain parts of the Pale, and encouraged interest in the world beyond the shtetl. Thus, he was a secular Jew, a Zionist, and a teacher who advocated teaching the Russian language. All of these were near-heresy in the pious shtetl of his time. My mother was fortunate that both her parents died before the war began in 1939.

My father was less lucky. His family was poor, his father devout, and at the age of twelve he was sent away from home as an apprentice to a carpenter, where typically he slept in the barn. He was conscripted into the Russian army in 1914, was wounded and, like so many Jews, "escaped" and made his way home. Later in the war, he worked in an aircraft factory in Dresden. In the 1940s, he lost his aged mother, his sister, and her family to the Nazi murder machine. Ironically, of the shtetl's many masters during the First World War — the Russians, the Germans, the Bolsheviks, and finally the Poles — the most humane and civilized, especially in their treatment of the Jews, were the Germans. (My mother was an office worker for them during their occupation of Svislocz.) The memory of that relatively humane occupation was to prove costly to the many Jews in the next war who refused to flee before Hitler's advancing armies, because they couldn't believe the tales of German atrocities. Now, minus Jews, Svislocz is in Belarus.

My parents arrived in Canada in their mid-twenties. My mother taught at the Jewish orphanage in Montreal until I came along. Thus I eventually became a third-generation teacher, and my daughter Silvie, who teaches Bar Admission courses to law students, a fourth. When my mother arrived in Montreal in the early 1920s, she knew no one but her *landsleit*,[1] the Lewises, the parents of David and the grandparents of Stephen. She spoke on David's behalf, in Yiddish of course, at large public meetings at the time of the famous 1942 Cartier by-election. Where they differed was in assessing the chances of the Communist candidate, Fred Rose. My mother thought he was a real threat, and suggested to David that he campaign accordingly. David, however, dismissed him as a mere "nuisance, like a mosquito." Fred Rose did win, and afterwards, my mother liked to tell the story about the "mosquito." She was one of the many women dismissed by the poet Ida Maza (Massey), whom she knew well, as "*veiber* (women) of the sink and stove," a phrase that aroused my mother's scorn. She was also a strong feminist long before that cause became popular again.

My father worked as a carpenter for others and, at some point, went out on his own as one of the numerous small-time — microscopic would be more exact — contractors around. We lived, like so many, in a cold-water flat. Soon the Depression arrived and robbed my parents of what small fragment of security they had. Work for my father was scarce, and profits even scarcer. Besides, he had no stomach for the inevitable hard bargaining and other cost-cutting efforts of his customers. That was a trial for my mother, who was itching to take them on. (Later, her brother handled these difficulties with ease.) Our parents tried to shield us from their worry about where the next meal and rent payments would come from, but since so

---

[1] Fellow immigrants from the same shtetl.

many others were in the same boat, we had no sense of deprivation. The war in 1939 ended the Depression for most people, but not for house builders, because the "war effort" claimed materials until about 1944.

But if financial times were hard indeed, social life was just the opposite — warm, lively, and comfortable. Montreal had a large, vibrant Jewish population, most of whom lived close together, re-creating the shtetl on the streets of the city. Among them was a sizeable group of secular Jews, many of whom were socialists or communists, a community in which my parents were enmeshed and thoroughly at home. Annette's family, while non-political, also belonged to that same community. Although not close friends, our parents knew one another and had many mutual friends. (Exactly the same was true of Annette and me.) My father had been a Bundist, i.e., a socialist, back home, and remained one here, though eventually more from sentiment than conviction, while my mother was amused by the Bundists' gravity about their nearly invisible "party."

The division between socialists and communists was often bitter, a bitterness we also felt; but oddly, friendship and kinship often transcended those divisions, usually because of a tacit agreement not to talk about politics. When that agreement was violated, the results could be explosive. For instance, a Communist couple was visiting us one day in 1941. The Germans had not yet invaded Russia–the Stalin-Hitler Pact was still in effect–but they had long since overrun Poland, including Svisloch, and my father was terribly worried about his family "at home." When the subject came up, the Communist couple repeated the party line of that period–the talk about Nazi atrocities was just imperialist propaganda designed to support the war against Germany and thus not to be taken seriously. My father, a quiet man not given to expressing his feelings, exploded, shouting at them to get out of his house. Frightened, they fled, running down the stairs with him on their tail, still shouting, and my mother running after him, calling him by name to calm him down. I watched the whole thing at close hand, entirely in sympathy with my father.

After the war, following two decades of harrowing economic times and a warm and lively social life, great changes began to occur, which is a good place to leave this lengthy narrative, but not before telling one more story.

The setting is Alfred Joyce Public School in 1935. The school was part of the Protestant School Board system. Thus, our school day always began with recitation of The Lord's Prayer; we then saluted the flag, and finally, sang *God Save the King*. All of this was alien and worse for the child of a family that was Jewish, non-religious, socialist, and therefore certainly not royalist. I remember finding it difficult to participate in these sacred rites. Annette has just reminded me that I may have had plenty of company. I was first strapped in Grade 5 for leaving the classroom without permission to get a drink of water from the nearby fountain. I had a cold and was uncomfortable. I was still enough of a baby to go home blubbering to my mother. She had been in Canada only twelve years. But she promptly put on her best housedress–her interest in fashion was non-existent–and marched off to let the principal know that she opposed corporal punishment. He, in today's language, was straight out of central casting–a strapping man (the pun is unavoidable), an ex-cavalry Lt. Col. who bestrode the halls in his riding boots with frequent references to "the beggahs." (I used to wonder whether he meant "buggahs.") Perhaps they didn't know what to do with former World War officers and installed them in the schools to deal with boys.

As young as I was, I recognized the incongruity of this encounter, and was surprised when my mother returned obviously pleased with the meeting. They had apparently hit it off, and he had even given her a reading list for me. Of course, it featured G.A. Henty, the imperialist's imperialist. Thus began my feast with the Henty books.

They all had the same plot, but they were extraordinarily educational as they followed the embattled Union Jack to Khartoum, the Khyber Pass, and the farthest reaches of the Empire, and hence encompassed much more history and excitement than one ever got in school.

By the time I, along with some friends, got strapped again, two years had passed. We were strapped for "talking in line"; we had become wise guys and joked sneeringly about the teacher's "Van Mungo windup" (Van Mungo was a pitcher for the Brooklyn Dodgers.) Naturally, I never told my parents. But the scene of the doughty immigrant woman marching off to confront Lt. Col. James E. Sampson, late of His Majesty's Cavalry, has remained with me for life.

Leo Zakuta
7 August, 2005

> Epilogue: What follows was not part of this piece originally, but it completes much of that story.

After the war, my family's economic fortunes took a sharp turn. In 1944, my father formed a partnership with his brother-in-law, my mother's much younger brother, a civil engineer, who worked as an airport engineer for the federal government. Not having any resources of their own, they sought a third partner to provide financial backing for their new construction firm. They initially approached the "rich" relative that every family has, but he was too wary to get trapped in such a quagmire. They finally did find such a person, but he soon backed out. (My uncle used to say that he got writer's cramp whenever he had to sign a cheque.) Those failures turned out to be an extraordinary piece of luck. Dismayed, they continued on their own as AIN & ZAKUTA. They could not have foreseen how propitious their timing was, and how effectively and harmoniously their respective interests and skills fit together. My mother played a central role in maintaining that harmony.

The war's end unleashed an explosive demand for new housing, pent up by a fifteen-year drought of depression and war. My father, no longer needing to be a businessman, was now comfortable supervising construction. His partner, though an engineer, had little interest in construction, but developed a remarkable talent for lining up work, including large projects with the federal government, and was very skillful in dealing with people. The company grew rapidly and eventually left house-building for industrial and commercial work, specializing in building the newly-emerging shopping centres. When my father retired and my uncle became increasingly involved in philanthropic work in the Jewish community and in Israel, the company remained in the very competent hands of my brother for many years, until his retirement.

The picture on the social side was different. My mother had lost much of her eyesight in the early 1940s, and my father became more reclusive, especially after he retired. His main activities–reading, walking, listening to opera, and watching sports on TV–required no company, while my mother, with her quick wit and sharp tongue, thrived in company and social activities. But her poor eyesight prevented her from going out by herself, and my father had little appetite for such affairs. Nevertheless, she had learned to read Braille, which helped — she too liked reading — and remained adept at her domestic chores, especially in the kitchen. In their last three decades, they lived in a kind of compound of four houses which they had built themselves on a dramatic site without fences. Also included were my uncle's house, my brother's, and that of one of the project's architects. Thus, my parents' social life was mainly familial during this time. As they aged, my brother looked after them with singular devotion. Late in life, my father told my mother, "I had a hard youth but a very good old age." My parents both died at home, their care organized meticulously by my brother and his wife, my mother in 1982 at the age of 85 and my father in 1986 at 92.

Leo Zakuta
1 February, 2006

ii. "Tough Guy"?

Preparing for the Garbers' annual garden party has left me in a reminiscent mood, aided, perhaps, by my imminent eightieth birthday. The previous story ended with my two strappings at Alfred Joyce Public School. Now I recall a third one between the others, which resulted from teasing — not by me, but of me. I was often teased about being fat and redheaded. *Redhead piss in bed; five cents a cabbage head.* (Could it have been carrot head originally?) and *Fatty and skinny walked down the street....* Skinny referred to my brother. Photographs of that period show a boy who may have been slightly chubby, but certainly not fat. Unfortunately I didn't know it then.

Eventually I beat up the smallest of the teasers on the way home from school. He reported it to the teacher who, after hearing my defense, recited this bit of folk wisdom: *Sticks and stones will break your bones, but names will never hurt them.* "Go get the strap." But the teasing stopped. Four years later I had become the gang's "tough guy," the one they pushed to the forefront when trouble loomed. Mercifully, it seldom did, and that position didn't last long. I left the gang suddenly two years later for a different life. But becoming a "tough guy" was a major turning point in my life, and it involves another tale, which must be preceded by a passage from Shaw's "Man and Superman" (the Don Juan in Hell act).

> Don Juan (talking to The Devil): ... Your weak side, my diabolic friend, is that you have always been a gull: you take Man at his own valuation. Nothing would flatter him more than your opinion of him. He loves to think of himself as bold and bad. He is neither one nor the other: he is only a coward. Call him tyrant, murderer, pirate, bully; and he will adore you, and swagger about with the consciousness of having the blood of the old sea kings in his veins. Call him liar and thief; and he will only take an action against you for libel. But call him coward; and he will go mad with rage: he will face death to outface that stinging truth. Man gives every reason for his conduct save one; and that one is his cowardice. Yet all his civilization is founded on his cowardice, on his abject tameness, which he calls his respectability.

The setting: the corner of Hutchison and Fairmount Streets on a summer evening in 1940. Our assembled "gang" was seeking justice. One member had allegedly "squealed" on another, and the victim had to beat up the "squealer" to right the balance. Since neither party displayed any enthusiasm for the task, we urged them on. Suddenly we heard a voice saying, "If you like fighting so much, why don't you fight with me?" It emanated from a tall, skinny fellow at the top of an outside staircase, and he was clearly pointing at me, perhaps because I was the tallest. Several things became clear to me on the instant. First, anyone who would challenge a boy who was surrounded by his gang to a fight had to be a Golden Glove boxer, and thus I would be beaten to a bloody pulp. Second, none of my friends would lift a finger to help me. But, finally, my brother was there and he would certainly help. So, awful as it would be, there would be a limit.

Thus, I somehow managed to emit a reluctant "OK." The fight took place in front of the Chevra Kadisha shul at the corner. It was mercifully brief, because the white wall of the synagogue was soon splattered with blood. To my astonishment, it was not mine, and the sight of all that blood somehow ended the fight. He was obviously not a boxer but a foolish boy. I must have grabbed him by his bow tie and punched him in the nose, hence all that blood. I remembered nothing about the fight itself except handing him his bow tie afterward in an unnatural calm with the words, "Here, this must be yours."

The gang adjourned in triumph to a local "candy store," and while they talked about my courage, toughness, and calm, I sat on a crate shaking uncontrollably. While I was shaking and listening to my friends' praise, I suddenly understood why I had consented to a certain and painful beating. It was because of an even greater fear — that my friends would consider me a coward if I had refused. Thus, what the others saw as courage was really cowardice, that is, giving in to fear. That thought didn't trouble me; what had happened was too splendid and dramatic, and I was thrilled to accept my friends' interpretation of it and the instant skyrocketing of my standing in the group. But an awakening had begun — the realization that one could not necessarily know people's motives from external appearances. That when actors weigh alternatives, they often make complex judgments involving self-esteem and the anticipated judgments of others, which are not easily apparent. All of that came much later, of course, but it originated in the "candy store."

By the time I was a Ph.D. student, I had it figured out. Such things, for instance, as altruism and selfishness, generosity and courage, kindness and brutality, are not parts of acts, but judgments passed on them by the actors themselves and others. In the jargon, they are value judgments, which doesn't denigrate them — life without value judgments is unimaginable — but they are separate from the acts themselves. If one wishes to explain behaviour, instead of judging it, one must ascertain the actors' "inner life," including their value judgments and those which they anticipate from others as they weigh alternative lines of conduct. It is what Prof. Herbert Blumer of the University of Chicago called "the actor's definition of the situation." I owe this approach to his teaching, and its development and application have been my chief interest as a sociologist. It was a long journey from the 15-year-old sitting on a crate and shaking uncontrollably.

Leo Zakuta
24 August, 2005

iii. Adventures with the Outremont Police

Outremont was until recently a small, independent city on the side of Mt. Royal in the heart of Montreal. Its counterpart was Westmount, also a small, independent city, on the other side of the mountain. Both were incorporated unwillingly into Montreal about fifteen years ago. Westmount was the home mainly of well-to-do Anglo-Saxons, whereas the upper parts of Outremont housed the most prosperous French-Canadians, a smaller group, including the Trudeaus. The residential pattern was the same on both sides of the mountain — altitude and wealth roughly corresponded as the streets sloped downward, more steeply in Westmount, until they reached the flatland at the bottom and met the boundary of Montreal. In our time, many Jews had penetrated far into Outremont, though not to the upper heights, and had begun to move into Westmount.

We lived on Hutchison Street, the lowest and last street in Outremont. The boundary between Outremont and

Montreal ran down the middle of our street. Although the people and the houses were no different on either side — mostly cold-water flats with Montreal's unique outside staircases — the boundary was, nevertheless, important. The children on one side went to the Outremont schools; those on the other side to the Montreal schools. So we had little contact with each other.

We had lived on the Outremont side, probably by chance, since 1931, when I was 6 years old. Our street was a mixture of Jews, French-Canadians, some Anglo-Saxons, and a few Irish, in about that order. Education in Quebec was divided along religious lines. The French-Canadian and Irish children went to schools in the Catholic school system, so we hardly knew them. Everybody else, including the many Jewish children, belonged to the Protestant School Board.

Our "gang" was all Jewish with one significant exception, Gordie, an Anglo-Saxon, a superb athlete in every sport, much superior to the rest of us. He was fast, powerful, and elusive, with remarkable hand-eye coordination. His family may have been more prosperous because he was the one who always owned the equipment — baseball gloves, bats, balls, and footballs, whatever. In exchange, he demanded the first choice when we picked teams or else he would go home with his equipment. He got his way. Gordie was something of a natural leader. He was the one who gave many of the kids nicknames, usually after star professional athletes. He probably taught me how to read a baseball box score at an early age.

Gordie and I were classmates from Grade 1, where he "won the medal" for finishing in first place at the end of the year. I was second. Next year we reversed those standings. His academic performance began to slip gradually, and by the time we entered high school, still in the same grade, something odd had happened to him. He began making cheerful but accurate predictions about how badly he had failed each exam. I think he repeated Grade 9 three times and then dropped out of school, but not out of our daily sports activities. My brother, who is slightly younger than I and who remained in the "gang" after I left, managed to keep track of Gordie's path long after the "gang" was dissolved. The last word was that he was on Skid Row, though no one knew how he got there.

I referred to our group as a "gang" and so did others. But it was not a "gang" in the contemporary sense. We almost never fought with other groups and seldom got into serious trouble. We were a group of friends, all from the same street, who "hung out" on that street in the evenings and who were united mainly by our passion for sports. In high school, a number of us made the long walk together to and from school four times a day. (We went home for lunch.) Sports consisted of softball in the summer, touch football in the fall, and hockey in the winter, every day after school, on the weekends and, if possible, in the evenings. Spring in Montreal was not our best time. It was too late for hockey and still too cold and wet for baseball. What few scrapes we got into tended to occur in the spring, when there was little to do.

Our gang lived for sport, and my parents encouraged that interest. I have a vivid memory of my father taking my brother and me to Omer de Serres, a large hardware company with which he did business, in about 1938, and buying us all kinds of hockey equipment that was far beyond his means and our expectations. As we were leaving, I saw a pair of hockey gloves that were expensive but irresistible. We had never had any before. He bought them without a murmur, and although not a word was said about them at home, I have always seen them as a symbol of youthful greed. My mother was dismayed by how much he had spent, but didn't have the heart to reproach him. She was so determined that her sons not resemble the gaunt and pale yeshiva boys whom she had known in her shtetl that, although a fastidious housekeeper, she would sometimes permit Kenny and me to come in for supper without removing our skates, so that we could go right back to the rink. We both grew up to be "jocks" of a sort and have remained so.

We began playing at an early age, probably at about 6 or 7, initially on the sidewalk and street in front of our houses and in the lane behind them. Ball hockey was played in front with a tennis ball and, of course, without skates. The earliest softball games were played in the lane. From there we graduated to nearby vacant lots, including two adjoining ones which had no vegetation and were ideal for baseball and football. For hockey (now called "shinny"), we moved nearby to "O'Connor's." Mr. O'Connor built and maintained a large ice rink by himself on an empty lot where all were welcome. In high school, we played real hockey, in an organized league, on the city's good rink in Rockland.

The boys organized that league themselves, booked the rink at the Outremont City Hall, arranged the schedule and even got some companies to sponsor the teams by providing sweaters with the firm's name, and stockings. One sponsor was Kik Cola, a cheap soft drink popular in Montreal. Our Grade 9 teacher, a martinet whom we all feared, apparently liked hockey, because he encouraged us to post our league standings on the classroom walls, something unheard of at the time. The few of us who stayed in school long enough also played for our high school teams, sometimes at the Montreal Forum. Our Saturday morning practices at the Forum preceded the Canadiens' game-day skate, so that some of them came on before we were through, which was exciting. Once, foolishly, I deliberately bumped into one of their smaller forwards; it was like hitting a steel fence.

At my very first turn at bat in softball, I recall someone sneering "Babe Ruth." I was holding the bat cross-handed. So much for natural athletic ability. One of our very early softball ventures in the back lane included Looie, a kid from the Montreal side of the street, which was unusual. At his turn at bat, Looie managed to hit the ball; it rolled softly to one of the infielders, who, of course, threw it wildly to first. The shouts of his teammates sent Looie to second base, where the same thing happened, and on he went to third. Still another bad throw. "Run home! Run home!" his teammates shouted, which Looie promptly did, streaking across the plate and continuing at full speed down the lane until he was out of sight. Not surprisingly, perhaps, he never rejoined us.

In the later years of elementary school, we played another game on the street, which we called "American baseball." The bases were laid out in the conventional diamond pattern on the road, where the infielders stood. The object of the game was to drive a tennis ball against the sharp point of a cement stair; that was the equivalent of being at bat. If the ball landed on the other side of the street without being caught, it was a home run. It was a great game for the reflexes, learning to stab a line drive with one hand.

The great shadow over this seemingly idyllic existence was the Outremont Police. They were our constant nemesis. We understood why they chased us off the road; it was dangerous. But it didn't stop there. They haunted us everywhere, except, of course, on the hockey rinks, where we were beyond their reach. But on the vacant lots we were fair game. They not only chased us off the fields, but confiscated our bats and balls. These could be retrieved from the police station simply by signing a book. So we hiked up there regularly; there was never any hassle, no threats or even lectures. Just sign the book, get the equipment and leave. And back to the playing fields. Why did they invariably chase us off the vacant lots? Neighbours' complaints? We never heard any. Broken windows? There weren't any near enough to break. The police didn't bother with reasons and we never thought of asking. It all seemed natural in that era. They often told us to go to "Rockland," the city's large park, but it was much too far away. Our "theory" was that Outremont was such a safe and quiet place that they had nothing better to do. And, who knows, maybe we were right.

Our special nemesis was large, beefy Constable Smith. Once, much later, we were playing touch football on the vacant lots when the police car was spotted from afar. "The cops" was the shout, and someone had the presence of mind to throw the football over a high wood fence so that it disappeared from sight. The police car pulled up and Constable Smith came over. What he saw were two teams obviously lined up for a touch football game, but no ball. He stood silently for a long time; none of us moved. Finally, one of the more daring kids got his bike — we all had bicycles by then, piled up on the side of the field — and rode slowly in a large circle around everyone, including Smith, who was in the middle. Another followed him and then another until we were all riding slowly in the same large circle around Smith. He neither moved nor spoke until he finally exploded: "Get the hell out of here!" Music to our ears. We retreated jubilantly to the nearby "candy store," and I recall first tasting that heavenly new treat, the Coffee Crisp chocolate bar. After that brief timeout, we returned to the field, retrieved the ball, and resumed the game. Life did have to go on.

My next major adventure with the Outremont Police, in the summer of 1942, was much more serious. In the early evening I went to join my friends in a game of softball. Just as I arrived, the ball landed on a garage roof right in my path so I went up and threw it back. The police arrived at that moment and, as I came down, they opened the car door and ordered me to get in. I panicked and ran down an adjoining lane. It was a terrible mistake. The police knew exactly how to handle that. One got out of the car and blocked one end of the lane, the other drove the car down the other end and soon caught up with me. He got out of the car and I faced a drawn revolver. Exhausted and terrified, I was thrown into the back seat of the car and taken to the station. They let me sit and stew for some time before asking me for my phone number in order to call my parents. That scared me even more, so I lied. I told them that my mother had a serious heart condition and the shock could kill her. For whatever reason, they didn't call. I sat there trying to figure out how I could get out. Finally, I suggested a plan — would they let me go if I promised to keep the gang from playing on that field again? Surprisingly, they agreed. (Why? I never knew.) But I was frightened enough to take my end of the bargain seriously, especially because there were threats if I failed. How could I accomplish that? If I told my friends about that "deal," they would surely be back there next day. And what would happen to me? I lied again, telling the gang that someone had "squealed to the cops" giving them all our names and addresses, and they said they would "pull in everybody" if anyone played there again. But I had little confidence in that ruse.

What saved me was something totally unexpected — the federal government's great "harvesting" fiasco. Within a few weeks, I was among the many boys in our class who went west to help with the harvest because so many of the young men on the prairies were away in the armed forces. I will save that story for my next essay, but shortly after our return, I left the gang completely and forever, so that where they played was no longer my concern.

One might have thought that would end my adventures with the Outremont Police, but it didn't. A year or two later, early on a summer evening, I was standing alone on a nearby street corner waiting to meet my friend Leonard, as we had arranged. A police car pulled up and a familiar face growled at me, "Move along." "Why?" I asked. "You're blocking traffic," came the reply. It was broad daylight and there wasn't a soul in sight. I moved along.

My final encounter with the Outremont Police occurred in 1948.

Several of us were at Buddy's house when Gerry, a charter member of the group, appeared, very upset and very drunk, which was most unusual. (We were all non-drinkers at that stage of our lives.) He told us that his girlfriend had just "given him the shoes," as our phrase went, and he was soon sick. We decided that what he needed most was a cold shower to clean him up — it was a hot, muggy summer evening — and then sleep. But how could we get him into the shower when he couldn't even stand? So we had to get in with him to hold him up, which meant removing our clothes. The therapy seemed to work. He had his shower, was put to bed and promptly fell into a deep and peaceful sleep. The rest of us returned to the living room and to dry off in the heat by just sitting there naked for a while. It seemed as if nothing special had occurred except that we had helped Gerry. What we forgot was to close the blinds.

Before long, there was a knock on the door; it was the Outremont Police Morality Squad. We rushed to get dressed, but they forbade it. So we were totally naked throughout our session with them. I was our spokesman only because my French was the least wretched; our bargaining position made the use of English out of the question. They began by taking our names, addresses, and phone numbers, all the while repeating, "Vous êtes des mauvaises hommes" and "Vous êtes des hommes-à-hommes." I explained what happened and even got them to come in and see Gerry fast asleep. After we left the room, one of the policemen told me that our story would never work in court and that we should get a better one. I replied that we couldn't because that was exactly what did happen. They shrugged their shoulders and, as they left, told us we would hear from them soon.

To say that we were worried is an understatement, even though nothing had occurred while they were peering through the window. We were all sitting far apart, but so what? Bernie was the most frightened, because he had applied to several rabbinical colleges, and the publicity could destroy any hope of becoming a rabbi. His two older brothers were very successful rabbis in the U.S.

Time went by — weeks, months and years — but we never heard from the police again. Gerry married that girl after all, and they had a long and, I believe, happy marriage. Bernie went to rabbinical college and became a rabbi in the U.S., where he still practices on occasion. Buddy went to graduate school in the U.S., and became a psychologist and then a professor in Minnesota, where he still lives. Frank became a lawyer and practiced in Ottawa, where he eventually worked as a senior lawyer for the federal government. Hershy, who was not really part of our group, became a successful businessman.

Why did the police not pursue the case? Did the others give it much thought? I did. Initially, I took some credit for refusing to change our story. I also knew that they had seen nothing incriminating. Not until much later did I realize that that obstacle could be overcome. But, from the start, I believed that the main reason was something else. Buddy's house was in a prosperous part of Outremont, as were the other boys'–even mine by then, though not in Outremont — which meant that prosecution would almost certainly involve defense lawyers in what the authorities perhaps saw as a weak case. For me, that remained a satisfactory explanation for 50 years. In 1998, on one of Buddy's infrequent visits to Toronto, we returned to that event, and I cited my "theories" about why the police had never pursued the case. Buddy just laughed and said, "My father used to play chess regularly with the head of the Morality Squad."

Leo Zakuta
30 December, 2005

iv. Becoming a "College Boy" and After

In his excellent book, *Street Corner Society* (1943), the sociologist William Foote Whyte studied a working class Italian community in Boston during the Depression. He distinguished between two groups of young men — "corner boys" and "college boys." The distinction was acute. The "corner boys" hung out in groups, which they called gangs, on the street corners, in nearby restaurants, and the like. The "college boys" were more solitary, occupied with making their way out of that community and "up" in the world, using a college education as their main vehicle. That distinction proved valid for most of our society then, and still is, though the details have changed.

I was 6 when we moved to Hutchison Street in 1931, and until November 1942, I was a "corner boy." I have described our lives in my preceding essay, "Adventures with the Outremont Police." This piece is about how I became a "college boy," and its aftermath. I had wanted in a rather diffuse way to go to college, and my parents certainly hoped I would. What blunted my ambition was uncertainty about whether we could afford it, and perhaps what is now called the "absence of role models." That is, I hardly knew anyone who was or had been in college. None of the boys in our gang had any interest in going; most of them did not complete high school, but went to work as shippers and the like in the Jewish-owned clothing and textile factories. Indeed, not one of them ever did go to college. So it all seemed somewhat remote, though I had become an avid fan of Dickens and Dumas, and of foreign correspondents such as William Shirer. When I graduated from high school — Strathcona Academy — in June 1942, I had the choice of McGill (or "Sir George") or Grade 12 at our high school, which was the equivalent of first year university. I chose the latter, because the fees were much lower ($100 instead of $250), and perhaps because it was more familiar.

My life changed radically in Grade 12. I began as a "corner boy" and was a confirmed "college boy" several months later. The change began with our "harvesting" trip out west, though I didn't know it then. That federal government project was ill-conceived. Although we were asked to replace the men who had gone off to war, we city boys were useless on the prairie farms. We had to wake up before dawn and harness the horses, though we hardly knew one end of the creature from the other. What we could do well was eat, and the farm meals were substantial and excellent. The farmers could hardly believe that they had acquired such a distinct liability instead of the promised help. Our class wound up on several adjoining farms in Alberta. Luckily for us, the snow arrived almost immediately and ended harvesting for that year. Now the question was what to do with us. The federal government paid our fare out (by train, coach class, no sleepers) and we were to pay for our return from the $5 per day we had been were promised. But we found ourselves with no money, a contingency that had not been envisioned. So we were all sent to the nearest small town, where we were housed in the empty town jail. That was a lark.

I don't remember how we were fed. Some of the boys boasted of having a good time with the local girls who missed their men. Our arrangement could not continue long. So we were shipped off to Edmonton, the provincial capital, where we stayed at the Salvation Army. I only recall that we loathed its food and spent what little we had to get something palatable. We were now desperate to get home, but how? Somehow the Premier of Alberta, William Aberhart, met a small delegation, three members of our group. When they entered his office, he picked up the phone and called his second-in-command, Ernest Manning, the father of Preston and later Aberhart's successor, saying, "I've got a bunch of Frenchmen here." None of the group could speak more than a few words of broken French, but all were from Quebec, and that was enough. The upshot of that meeting was that our return fare was looked after. By whom, we never knew. We were on our way home.

How was all of this related to my becoming a "college boy"? During this episode, I became friendly with Frank, a boy in our class who had come over from England with his mother and sister in the early years of the war, as had so many others. Shortly after our return, he invited me to a meeting of something called the "Current Events Club," which met every Sunday evening in a different member's home. I was more than eager to accept. I knew several club members; some were in my current class; others had been my classmates previously; the club consisted of boys and girls in about equal numbers; all seemed college-bound or were there already; all were from more prosperous parts of Outremont. Thus, the group was clearly a distinct rung up the social ladder. Finally, coming from my politically-engaged family, "current events" were meat and drink to me. In fact, poor as we were, we had a subscription to TIME magazine by then (1942). It seemed perfect.

And indeed it was. I went to the meeting, found it completely comfortable, discovered it was a formal shell for a large clique of boys and girls whom I found very appealing, and I stayed in the group forever. In some sense, I have never left it. Some of its members, and others who entered soon after, are still my friends today, sixty-three years later. That is how I became a "college boy" all at once and with both feet.

I now spent all my leisure time with these new friends. We gathered in several homes, where such gatherings were welcome. I acquired a girlfriend (from the group) for the first time in my life. Indeed, most of us participated rather little in campus social life; ours was in this group instead. Besides, some of our members were at Sir George Williams, which made social life on either campus less appealing. My undergraduate education at McGill, now that

I was rid of the math and science courses that had almost prevented me from getting there, was a treat, and I thrived.[2]

Sometime in 1943, about half a dozen boys in our group became fervent CCFers. It was not a large step for most of us. (The CCF, Cooperative Commonwealth Federation, was the predecessor of the NDP.) We grandly called ourselves the Outremont-Woodsworth Unit, held weekly meetings attended mainly by members of the larger group but by others as well, and participated vigorously in several election campaigns. We had some self-appointed mentors, who were a little older, who tried to lead us to a "harder" kind of socialism, Trotskyism, but with a total lack of success.

In 1945, a new obsession swept the group — bridge. We played endlessly; two of our members were so caught up in it that they no longer played with us, but only at the McGill Student Union, to the point where both failed their last year at McGill and had to take courses later to obtain their degrees. On one occasion the head of the CCF Youth Movement in Quebec, a minuscule body, came to one of our meetings to find out what had happened to us, once the largest and most active "unit" in the organization, and now seemingly dead or dormant. It was a strange event, because no one had the heart or perhaps the courage to tell him that bridge had swept socialism away.

Our group had shrunk somewhat during those last few years. Many of our original girls did not go on to university and dropped out of the group. And after 1946, some of the group's original members left to attend graduate or professional schools in the U.S. Nevertheless, chiefly thanks to Leonard, there was new blood. Leonard was one of the first members of the original circle of friends that I met. He and I became fast friends, mainly because we were

---

[2] I took my B.A. and M.A. at McGill, and my Ph.D. at the University of Chicago.

taking the same English courses at McGill. (I acquired his taste for Aldous Huxley.) He worked as a librarian at the YMHA, a vantage point from which he plied his considerable social skills. He was the epicenter of our group, knew everyone and everything, and had a special knack for bringing new people into the group, male and female alike.

He and I have kept in close touch throughout the years. On visits to my family in Montreal during the Christmas and Easter breaks, I always spent time skiing at the houses he and his friends rented every winter in the Laurentians. But I owe him one immeasurable debt. In the summer of 1956, I came for a long visit with my family in Montreal, and naturally turned to him to find out if any of the girls I had known were still in town. He, of course, gave me several names. The one who most appealed to me was Annette. I had not seen her since 1950, when we were both counselors at an urban day-camp, though in different parts of the city. I had known her slightly before that, again through Leonard, and we had a number of mutual friends. I called her, and six weeks later we were married. Soon after our return to Toronto, Annette became a founding member of what was to become a well-known group, Five Potters. (I had come to teach at the University of Toronto in 1952, after a year at the University of Manitoba, and have lived in Toronto ever since.)

In 1967, Leonard, having become a Community Liaison officer at the newly established Department of Psychiatry at McMaster University in Hamilton, moved to Burlington. He was now an hour's drive from Toronto, so we saw each other often. Shortly after his arrival, we took him to a neighbour's party in Toronto to introduce him to our friends. Of course, he knew more people there than we did. After he retired, he gradually moved back to Toronto. In the meantime, McMaster had awarded him an honorary degree. He now, due to severe incapacity, lives in a nursing home in Toronto. I see him regularly, going with Rhoda, a mutual friend of long standing. Leonard, who had been at the centre of our web of communications, is able to understand what people say to him, but unable to communicate with them.

Bernard, Buddy, and I spent the summer of 1949 together in Chicago. (We had a 'Bernard' and a 'Bernie' in our group. Both had been in my class from Grade 6 right through high school, and both were in the Current Events Club when I arrived.) Bernard and his wife, and Buddy and I, lived in tiny adjoining apartments near the University of Chicago that sweltering summer. Both remained academics in the U.S., and both made their way to Toronto occasionally after visiting family in Montreal. Buddy and I speak to each other on the phone often. He phoned me while I was writing the last piece, which enabled me to verify details of the Morality Squad episode. Bernard died in 1996.

Annette and I owe some of our closest and most enduring friendships to the nationalist/separatist turmoil in Quebec in the late 1960s and 1970s. The children of these friends came to Toronto as part of the mass exodus of English-speaking Montrealers in those years. Subsequently, their parents, Rose and Myer, Margie and her late husband Peter, and Vivian, have come here regularly to see their children and grandchildren, and we have been able to spend time together. (Vivian is the sister of Eileen, whose garden party launched this series. Her husband Sam, who died young, was also a good friend of ours.) All of these people were close friends of each other in Montreal. Other couples are more scattered — Hazel and Leo in Sarnia and Anita and Arthur in New York State — but family ties and visits to Leonard have brought them to Toronto as well. We have other friends, such as Ruth and Morrie and Annette's cousin Sylvia and her friends, who still live in Montreal, whom we see when we are there, and occasionally, in Toronto.

Lou, a close friend and another of Leonard's recruits, was transferred by his company in the early 1960s to supervise their expansion to Toronto. We resumed our friendship, though by now we both had families. He died at the age of 58, but his wife Harriet remains a friend.

Several individual reunions occurred in 1998, each after a fifty-year interval. All were by chance, except the reunions with Bernie and Ellie, both members of the Current Events circle. They had heard through Buddy that we were in Fort Myers staying in the unit next to our Sarnia friends, who had also been their friends. So they drove over from Naples. Leonard was visiting us at the same time, which made the occasion even more special.

The second occurred on a tennis court in Montreal. I heard my name called questioningly. I turned to see a man who identified himself as Gerry Wise (from the Morality Squad episode). We had a long and noisy reunion with endless hugging. I doubt that he recognized me; he must have heard my name. I certainly would not have recognized him. His most distinctive feature in the distant past was an enormous shock of hair. Now he was as bald and shiny as the proverbial billiard ball. Sometime later he and his wife visited us for lunch in Toronto. She had been in Annette's class in high school. Gerry died in 2002.

The last of these reunions, with Frank (the one who had originally invited me to the Current Events Club meeting), also occurred by chance. Unlike the rest of us, he left Montreal after Grade 12 and went to Queen's in Kingston, then to law school in Toronto, and finally, to Ottawa. I had last seen him in 1948; Leonard maintained contact with him for perhaps another decade. Then we lost track of him completely for endless years until my niece, Sharon Zakuta, a lawyer working for the federal government, told me that her boss had asked if she was related to Leo Zakuta. Thus did we re-establish contact with Frank. It was not long before the first of our three group reunions, which he attended eagerly, as he did the other two. There were also visits to Toronto, and we phone each other after long intervals. Recently, he told me about a forthcoming trip to the Far East, and when the great tsunami struck I seemed to have a vague recollection of him saying that he and his wife might be in Phuket, Thailand. Phuket had been hit very hard, and I scanned the newspapers for days for the lists of Canadian survivors and known dead, without results. But many were still unaccounted for, so the worry remained. I knew no one whom I could contact for news. Eventually, I thought of sending a faint-hope email. The reply came in a few days: "Safe and almost sound. My wife's inherent snobbery ruled out Phuket." They had been far away. Perhaps curiously, although most of us have email addresses, our communication is mainly by phone.

Arthur's story is different. He was not part of that group, though he eventually knew most of them. Also an Alfred Joyce student, we did not become friends until the late 1940s at McGill, when our girlfriends were best friends and we spent much time together. He married his, briefly; I did not, though I wanted to. (Leonard was responsible for my meeting her.) Arthur arrived in Toronto not long after me to pursue a career as a teacher and researcher in the medical faculty, which he did with distinction. He and his second wife, Barbara, are our friends, and he and I have had many long phone conversations, sometimes after long intervals.

Roberta's story is also different. She came to Montreal as a war orphan after the war and was adopted by a well-to-do family. I knew her slightly at McGill. We became friends, mainly through Annette, when she and her husband moved to Toronto. He died young; since then she has become one of our closest friends.

We often saw Norman, Annette's cousin, and his wife, Beattie. He was also an original and committed member of our tennis group until his death in 2003. Finally, Annette's sister, Sylvia, and her husband, Peter, moved from Montreal to Toronto in 1965 and have lived here since. Peter died just a year ago. Our families, including the children, have been very close and have spent much time together.

I mentioned our three group reunions. Bernard organized the first one, in 1990, a small get-together at a Montreal restaurant, mainly of the original Current Events Club members. Despite the background noise, it was so successful that we decided to do it again soon. The other two were large reunions at our house in 1991 and 1997. Both were two-day affairs, dinner the first evening and brunch the next day. I certainly enjoyed them. Age, frailty, and distance make it unlikely there will be any more. I have confined this long list of friends and relatives to Montrealers and former Montrealers, because all of these relations, including my marriage, grew out of a single event and a single day in 1942. The event was Frank's invitation to the meeting of the Current Events Club (Frank has had a special place in my heart ever since), and the day was when I went to that meeting. It transformed my life.

Leo Zakuta
4 January, 2006

v. Our Tennis Group

Our tennis group is certainly unusual and perhaps unique. It is an entirely informal body, but it is large — about twenty-five members; it has endured for thirty years; and we play outdoors almost every day, far beyond the conventional tennis season. Above all, everyone who comes out gets to play, which accounts for the group's size and longevity.

It all began quite improbably for me in the summer of 1974. Our son, Jamie, was going to summer camp and needed a tennis racquet. Having bought him one, we of course had to buy one for our daughter, Silvie, who was slightly younger and not going. Once she had it, what was to be done with it? I would have to play with her. I had an ancient racquet gathering dust in the basement, which I had used seldom and ineffectually many years before. It had playing instructions inscribed on the frame, and it had been in a press and was still ok. Annette washed it, and Silvie and I went to hit balls against an adjacent garage wall. We spent the next few weeks looking for the perfect wall.

When Marjorie, an officer of the graduate school, with whom I worked closely, heard about my tennis venture, she invited me to join her and her friends at the Rosedale Tennis Club. I was apprehensive, but she and her friends were kind and patient, and I became an instant convert and soon an addict. I was able to play regularly, although I could not become a Club member for a long time. The tennis boom was under way, and in addition to the residential requirement, which I met, the Club had a long waiting list. (That boom has since receded, and all the clubs hunger for new members.)

Marjorie, her friends, and several others were a group in the loosest sense, but, as we continued to play together, they became the nucleus of the later, more cohesive body. Before long, I was doing the phoning for our daily arrangements, perhaps because only I worked mainly at home. After a few seasons, we took the first step towards becoming distinctive — we continued to play after the Club season ended early in October. The Club, of course, took down its nets and screens and shut the Clubhouse, but by then we had acquired some old nets which it had discarded and I had mended. We set one up and continued to play.

The Rosedale Tennis Club, though private, operates — like many others — in a city park. The City of Toronto's rules governing its relations with these private clubs, which pertain to court maintenance and public accessibility, are a workable compromise between the interests of both parties. The Club looks after the courts during its season, but the greatest maintenance problem, which we must cope with annually, occurs after the Club season, when the overhanging trees shed their many leaves. In our first few years either the Club or the City locked the courts each fall. Thus, we had two problems in the post-season — access to the courts and keeping them clean. We dealt with the first briefly by climbing over the low points in the fence, but then found other, unlocked places to play. Since we had our own net(s), that was manageable, though many phone calls were required. I have a "tennis phone" with speed dialing for many of the members. I used to refer to our game as "the oldest established permanent floating tennis game in Toronto."

One winter day, in the mid-1980s, I was driving by our locked courts and noticed activity inside. City workers were cutting branches off some of the overhanging trees. I must have told them that this was our home because one of them asked if I would like to have a key to the courts. Would I like to! It was like asking if I would like to win the lottery. After I got the key, the courts were never locked again for the winter. Not that the Club Executive didn't toy with that idea, but that's another story. Leaf removal was the other major problem. I made it mine. I had good equipment because we had a long driveway at home with large, overhanging trees, and I liked buying that equipment. So I accumulated blowers, rakes, and large brushes, some of which I had repaired myself from discarded pieces, and became our group's janitor in the off-season. It helped that I lived near the park, and I sometimes went to inspect the courts to let the others know whether they would be dry enough to play in the afternoon. Early retirement from the University of Toronto facilitated my activities.

Something much more important had occurred in the interim. I spent much of the summer of 1982 in Montreal with my dying mother and my family. On my brief returns to Toronto, I found some of our newer members playing doubles. They did not invite me to join them, which was understandable — people played either singles or doubles — but still painful. The original members were not around, so I was left sitting, racquet in hand. I resolved that no one should have to endure that unpleasant experience again. Out of that adversity came the first and most important of our unique arrangements — "Server out." When there is an extra player, each server sits out the next game and the person sitting out comes in. (It can be applied to additional players if there is no vacant court to accommodate them.) This device was not universally welcomed at first, because it eliminated sets of doubles, with all their suspense and tension, as soon as an extra person arrived. But, bit by bit; it was accepted, and before long, accepted unquestioningly. In time, when anyone spotted an extra player arriving, the call went out "Server out" or "Server out on two courts" if we were playing doubles on two courts.

We have developed a few more minor arrangements. When we occupy two or more courts, we rotate the teams after four games, everybody having served, so that every team gets to play against all the others. When we have three or seven players, one court plays "American doubles" (it goes by other names in other countries), in which the server takes on the other two, defends only the singles area, and the serve rotates. After four games on the other court, the teams rotate, to give everyone equal doubles time. Occasionally the turnout is so large that we have to figure out how to manage. The largest turnout was 14, but 11 or 12 are not uncommon. What has helped is that two of the courts are separate from the rest and even further from the street. During the Club season we live there, and the accommodating Club "pros" have usually turned a blind eye to our "double booking," presumably because of our numbers. We constitute a large portion of the most active members and play every day.

Some additional arrangements, all of which evolved gradually. We have set hours of play which everyone knows, so phoning is seldom necessary. People simply arrive at or near the designated time, though late arrival is no deterrent to "getting a game." Another is that when the Club removes its nets in the fall, it leaves two courts for us to put up our nets, which we leave up until the Club reopens in April. Finally, tennis balls. During its session, the Club provides new balls to every court each day. What we now do in our off-season, which often extends to the end of December and resumes in March, is that I buy balls by the case (24 tins) and we share the costs. In some years we have held a Christmas party at the courts during a session. We have many photographs of these affairs — often with snow from an adjoining ice rink in the background — for which Sheila bakes cupcakes and Don provides eggnog and brandy. (Traditional roles are not entirely dead.) In cold weather, racquets can be handled just as adroitly with thin gloves, though playing often renders them unnecessary. Sometimes we play to the accompaniment of music for the skaters.

*Some members of Leo's tennis group in the early years
Sheila Smith, Bill Alexander, Nenagh Hanly, Norman Endler,
Marjorie Kennedy, and Leo
Rosedale Park, Toronto, c. 1980*

Reminiscences, Rants, and Raves

*Some members of Leo's tennis group in the mid-1990s
Peter Goering, Leo, Jane Avery, Barry Sessle, and Bob Knight
Rosedale Park, Toronto, c. 1995*

*Don Williams, Sheila Smith, Norman Endler, and Leo
on the tennis court
Rosedale Park, Toronto, c. 2002*

Our group grew chiefly by members bringing friends. Two entered our group differently, months apart in the mid-1980s. Each sat alone in the stands beside our court, racquet in hand, looking as if he was eager to play. None of us knew them and we probably assumed they were waiting for their partner(s). Eventually, I invited each one to join us, and we thereby acquired two stalwarts. Both have been "regulars" ever since and both have brought in others. I sometimes refer to them and some others as "new boys." A few have invited themselves. That's how we got an ex-Argonaut football player, who appeared at the gate and asked if we wanted a fourth. He was a welcome addition, a large and powerful player with cat-like reflexes, and a gentleman. Eventually he moved to a distant part of the city and we lost him. Some people have phoned me, upon the urging of the pro, to ask about joining us. My stock reply is, "Of course, come and try it and see if it suits you." It's always a worry that the caller's level of play may be too low. If it's too high, they won't stay. During the early 1990s, our group grew so rapidly that I worried if it could survive, but some peripheral members left and restored the status quo.

Who are we? Originally, we consisted of about 8-10 members, most of whom were academics at the University of Toronto or York University, and equally divided between the sexes. Of that original group, only two of us remain. Several moved to distant places; two others, both professors, died during the last few years; two are in nursing homes, an original member who became old and infirm and a younger, later arrival. As the group grew, it became predominantly male, but lately the gender balance has been restored. We range from just under age sixty to just over eighty, so that most members are retired. Academics still predominate — seven professors and three retired teachers. The occupations of the remainder are too diverse to list, and no two the same, although all are or were professionals or white collar workers. Ethnically, we are over half Anglo-Saxons; about one-quarter Jewish; two Japanese; one French-Canadian; one Serb, and a few whom I would have to ask. My son Jamie, a strong player, joins us occasionally. When he and I team up, I think of the old joke about the flea that rode across a suspension bridge on the back of an elephant and remarked afterwards, "We sure shook that bridge, didn't we"?

A "club," which in effect we are, within a Club, I have always felt, is a potential source of trouble. I have therefore taken pains to maintain cordial relations with the Club's Executive, and especially with the "pros," who manage the Club's daily activities and on whose goodwill we are dependent. They overlook our double-booking and find us a court when there seem to be none. Fortunately, establishing such relations with a series of "pros" has been easy and pleasant. I recall no instances of friction. It has been almost as easy, though occasionally more complicated, with the Executive. Some of our group have occasionally suggested that I complain at the next AGM (Annual General Meeting) about the "pros" scheduling too many private lessons during Club hours and thus tying up courts. I have never done so, figuring that we had more to lose than to gain by antagonizing the "pros."

I always go to the AGM to protect the interests of our group and to show our interest in the Club. In most years, that Meeting consisted only of the Executive and me, which became a kind of standing joke. They have treated me cordially, and latterly, with increasing respect, viewing me as the repository of the Club's memory. The Executive turns over every few years, so it has no long-term memory. For instance, several years ago, the Executive discussed a proposal to lock the courts for the winter. I was, of course, alarmed, and told them about the last time that had been done, many years before. Locking the courts was tantamount to turning them over to the ball-hockey players, who had no difficulty scaling the low point of the fence. They left their goalies' nets on the courts undisturbed all winter, and their shoes may have damaged the surface. Far worse, for their own safety, they removed the posts for the tennis nets. An audible gasp accompanied that part of my narrative. But the denouement was my account of helping the Club's Equipment Manager (now one of Ontario's most senior judges) re-install the posts the next spring. Someone had inserted empty pop cans into some of the post-holes, where they fit so tightly that they were almost impossible to remove. There was no further talk about locking the courts, but it strengthened my resolve not to miss an AGM.

On one occasion, a new Executive devised a plan to put us in our place. (This was the only time it ever happened.) It was crude and transparent. A fee of $25 for the season would be required to reserve only courts 7 and 8, which was where we played, a day in advance. We discussed our options at length. Some wished to fight it at the AGM. My response was that we could win every battle with the Executive, but not the war. Accordingly, I wrote a cheque for $25, which gave me the useful privilege of reserving the court a day in advance. The Club received no other payments, and mine was never cashed. That was the end of that, and we eventually reached an *entente cordiale*. It was never even mentioned at the next AGM.

And now back to "Server out." It began simply as a device to ensure that no one felt left out. What I did not foresee were the far-reaching consequences of inclusion vs. exclusion, though they may seem obvious in hindsight. First, exclusion would have impeded the group's growth. More important, those excluded would have made their own arrangements with others in the same position, and we would soon have splintered into sub-groups, which have a much shorter life span. Many twosomes and foursomes play together, sometimes for years, but eventually collapse when someone is injured, becomes ill, moves, or for some other reason. Some players then give up tennis permanently. Our attrition rate is neither as high nor as damaging. Discouragement about finding partners and making arrangements does not enter into it. One simply comes out and plays, even after a long absence. By being inclusive instead of exclusive, "Server out" provides an assured game without having to find partners and make arrangements, and thereby has been chiefly responsible for our size and endurance.

What have these thirty years of tennis meant to me? Many satisfactions, obviously, but life seldom grants unmixed blessings, so there is much on the other side as well. Among the former, exercise is perhaps the most obvious, though I regard it as a bonus rather than as the main reason for playing, which is for the sheer pleasure of the game. The camaraderie and predictable banter that go with playing every day for years with the same friends ranks high. So does the competitive intensity of a close doubles match and the speed with which we forget afterwards who won. Welcoming back long absent members is always agreeable. Then there is, curiously, tennis as therapy. No matter what worries and aggravations one brings to the court, once play begins, one can think only about that little yellow ball — where is it going and what can I do with it? There are also particular treats, such as the rare days when I can do no wrong and feel young again; the occasions, all too few, when I hit the ball exactly where I want to and hear "great shot"; a special treat is when I hit a left-handed winner — I never fail to call the others' attention to it — and once when I played a full session and never needed a second serve. The most striking such high point occurred in 1999 in George Connell's moving eulogy, before a large audience, for Harry Eastman, who had been his good friend and close colleague (Vice-President), when George was President of the

University of Toronto.[3] Talking of Harry's natural athletic ability — they had often skied together — he said that although Harry didn't take up tennis until he was in his seventies, he did so well that he "was admitted to Leo Zakuta's elite circle at the Rosedale Tennis Club." (George had played with us several times years ago, and Harry had been my friend [and Annette's] for forty-five years.)

However, for every satisfaction there must be an equal but opposite reaction, and these are abundant. The chief annoyances are the almost constant feeling that I should be playing much better — I don't have good hand-eye coordination — and the days, more numerous than the opposite, when nothing goes right. It helps that we all have such days, but they are still painful. The struggle to correct one's "errors" only makes things worse. On those days I have often wanted to go home or thought about giving up tennis altogether, but that's just not done. The only solution is to keep playing until one "bottoms out" and things begin to improve. There is also the sharp but short-lived dismay of "blowing" an easy put-away shot or the mortification of missing it completely without having the excuse of being blinded by the sun, or of ending a long and exciting doubles rally with an error. Worse is the immobility following a serious injury or illness, when I can hit the ball when it comes to me but can't run it down. No one ever says anything, but I wonder what they think. But the greatest pain is the awareness of advancing age relentlessly taking its toll. Thus my personal motto is "Slow the slide."

If the pains appear to outweigh the pleasures, they are counter-balanced by one overriding sensation which outweighs them all — how easy and comfortable I feel in

---

[3] George Connell was President of the University of Toronto from 1984 to 1990.

the group. All the while trying to push aside thoughts of how much longer can it last.

Leo Zakuta
9 January, 2006

List of Players: Past & Current (2005)
P = Past; C = Current; O = Original Member; R = Retired

ACHESON, John	civil engineer and teacher, died 2004	P
ACHESON, Frances		PR
ALEXANDER, Bill	professor, Univ. of Toronto (OISE), died 2001	PO
AVERY, Jane	tax lawyer (nursing home)	P
DYSON, Norman	judge, Ontario Superior Court	C
DYSON, Rose	media consultant	P
EASTMAN, Harry	professor, Univ. of Toronto, died 1999	PR
ENDLER, Norman	professor, York University, died 2003	PO
FUREDY, Chris & John	professors, York & Univ. of Toronto (Australia)	PR
GOERING, Peter	architect	CR
GRIMES, Catherine	psychologist	POR
HANLY, Nenagh	high school teacher	POR
HARLEY, Birgitta & David	professor, Univ. of Toronto (OISE) and lawyer	CR
HARRIS, Shirley	elementary school teacher	CR
HELLER, Deborah	professor, York University	C
HELLMAN, Judy	professor, York University	C

HEMREND, Bernie	orthodontist	POR
IMAIZUMI, Haneko & Takashi	marketer and executive, Nikon	CR
KALACIC, Yelena	masseuse	C
KENNEDY, Marjorie	administrator, Univ. of Toronto (Vancouver)	POR
KIRKPATRICK, Mike	former Argonaut and Toro football player (moved)	PR
KNIGHT, Bob	contractor	C
KOVAC, Mike	ophthalmologist	CR
LEMAGUER, Lorie	architectural designer	C
LEVY, Josh	psychoanalyst	C
MADONNA, Lou	designer	C
MILLER, David	businessman	CR
MOON, Peter	investigative reporter, *Globe & Mail*; Canadian Forces Ranger	CR
ONDRACK, Dan	professor, Univ. of Toronto	PO
ROWE, David	professor, Univ. of Toronto	PR
ROWE, Una	human resources director, law firm	CR
SCHABAS, Ezra	professor, Univ. of Toronto	CR
SCOTT, Ken	business magazine editor	PR
SCULLY, Peter	lawyer	C
SESSLE, Barry	professor and former Dean of Dentistry, Univ. of Toronto	C
SHEPARD, Ken	management consultant	C
SHUTE, David	writer	C
SLOMAN, Leon	psychiatrist, Clarke Institute, Univ. of Toronto	C
SMITH, Sheila	high school teacher	COR
STEAD, Lorna & Geoff	Victoria BC	POR

THURSTON, Grace & John	Australia	POR
WEISER, John	professor, Univ. of Toronto (OISE)	CR
WILLIAMS, Don	high school teacher	CR
WOLFE, Roy	professor, York University (nursing home)	POR
ZAKUTA, Leo	professor, Univ. of Toronto	COR

Leo's tennis group drew the attention of Gillian Cosgrove, a local reporter. The resulting article was published in the *National Post* on January 15, 2000. [AZ]

Leo and the gang in the winter
Don Williams, Peter Goering, Leo, and Barry Sessle
Rosedale Park, Toronto, c. 2003

Christmas party on the tennis court, 2003

*Leo climbing the fence of the Rosedale Tennis Club
(kept locked in winter to keep people out)
Rosedale Park, Toronto, c. 1985*

GOING TO EXTREMES IN SNOWY ROSEDALE

Freezing for Love: They've been called crazy, foolhardy, and driven by an unusual passion. They do it every day for hours, often with different partners, no matter what the weather. Most of these dedicated, determined, and unflagging lovers are in their 60s and 70s. And they are at it again this week, bundled up in parkas, sweat pants, ski hats, ear muffs and gloves, drawn by an irresistible force to Rosedale Park to indulge their addiction. They brave wind-chill factors of minus 15, snow squalls and freezing rain, and even shovel away snow banks — all to "play" (make that "survive") what surely qualifies as an extreme sport: winter tennis.

Dismissed as eccentric old coots by skaters on the adjacent hockey rink, this hardy band of tennis aficionados pitches up at 1 P.M. each day for a bracing game of doubles. There are 20 of them in total, but on any given day, anywhere from four to eight players warm up in the icy air with baseline strokes, lobs and smashes.

The ritual began back in 1974 when a group that played together all summer resolved to continue through the winter. "It's like the oldest floating crap game in the world, except it's tennis," says Leo Zakuta, 74, one of the founders along with fellow Rosedale residents Norman Dyson, Sheila Smith, Catherine Grimes and Bill Alexander.

Mr. Zakuta and Mr. Alexander are retired University of Toronto professors, Mr. Dyson is an Ontario judge, Ms. Smith is a retired high school teacher, and Ms. Grimes is a psychologist. Relative newcomers include Barry Sessle, Dean of Dentistry at U of T, Josh Levy, a psychoanalyst, Chris and John Furedy, psychologists, and Peter Goering, a retired architect. With so much brainpower on the sub-Arctic courts, one wonders why they don't have their heads examined.

Rosedale Tennis Club, a private club that uses public courts after 5 P.M. during the season, closes Thanksgiving and the nets go down. But that doesn't stop these intrepid competitors. They simply bring their own nets and string them up after sweeping away the leaves or shoveling off the snow.

Mr. Zakuta actually prefers tennis in winter. That's because he can play for two hours and barely work up a sweat, whereas in the summer heat, he "goes home panting like a dog on all fours." In true-grit fashion, he disdains gloves. "My hands are very cold for the first few minutes and then I don't feel them anymore."

"Along the way, we discovered that the human body has a better tolerance for cold than the equipment does. If it gets too cold, the balls go hard and the racket strings go brittle. Then we have to quit. But that hasn't happened in many years."

vi. Canada Day Talks at the Garbers

2001 *On July 1 Annette and I were at a "Canada Day Celebration" on Ralph and Eileen Garber's lawn. The invitation said, "Please bring a short, pithy toast to Canada." I did not intend to speak, but changed my mind at the last moment. Many of the speakers, especially the younger ones, had been highly critical of Canada. The one before me called her toast "a lament for Canada." Here is mine.*

Mine is not a lament. I am not enthusiastic about public expressions of patriotism. But when I think of the place from which my parents came, I feel lucky to live in a country that is free, peaceful, prosperous, and tolerant, a rare combination in this troubled world.

And that's how I got launched as an active participant in this annual event. My talks in succeeding years follow.

2002 An Old Liberal's Lament

I beg your indulgence, good folks all
For departing from the call.
For so feeble is my verse
That I could only fear the worst.
(See what I mean.)
Thus I chose
To stick to prose.

I am doubly grateful for Eileen and Ralph's invitation. Not only did it invite us, but it specified that "the theme is AGAINST (from mild disdain to spleen-venting ire)." Completely wide open. That certainly cheered one cantankerous old bugger. So call it disdain or call it spleen-venting ire or anything else along that wide spectrum. Indeed, what you call it will depend on how strongly you disagree with me, but I am going to inveigh against goodness. Yes, against goodness.

Not against personal acts of kindness or generosity — though even here let's remember the maxim that *no good deed goes unpunished* — but against institutional goodness. For instance, against foreign aid, which has been described as a system that taxes the poor in rich countries and gives the money to the rich in poor countries or, if that's too strong, to supporters of that madman Mugabe. Or charity. We a.k.s[4] (sanitized translation: old has-beens) — by the way, do any of you recall the line in the ancient Kaufman and Hart musical "Of Thee I Sing," when all the U.S. Supreme Court judges prance onto the stage and sing in chorus: "We are the a.k.s who give the o.k.s"? — we a.k.s remember how our Trotskyite and other Marxist comrades knowingly revealed to us that charity, like FDR's New Deal, was a capitalist trick to anesthetize the poor and stave

---
[4] For the Yiddish *"alte kakers."*

off the inevitable revolution and final reckoning.[5] Such a long time ago that was. There is a delightful treatment of that theme in Bernard Shaw's essay "Death of an Old Revolutionary Hero." It's in his collection of essays "The Black Girl in Search of God," another highly entertaining piece.

And what could politics conceivably have to do with goodness? Well, every party claims that its chief interest is the public good. But three of ours have been so busy tearing themselves apart that mercifully they cannot even think about the public good, while the fourth and biggest is threatening to outdo them all in the art of *hara-kiri*.

But enough of being less than serious. To illustrate that no good deed goes unpunished, I am about to bite the hands that feed me and respond to their kind invitation by probably raining on this parade. (The clichés run wild.) I will devote the short time that remains to a new misguided form of *goodness* — *that branch of political correctness that includes such euphemisms as affirmative action, equity, diversity and role models.* These are no trifling matters. Political correctness in general has become a formidable foe of free speech, especially on the campus. And *equity*, which sounds so unassailable, no longer means equality of opportunity, long sacrosanct, but equality of outcome. So instead of ending the age-old practice of judging people by the colour of their skins or by what lies between their legs rather than between their ears, new practices have arisen on behalf of an ideology just as pernicious as its predecessor.

And *diversity* only means diversity sometimes. For instance, does anyone suggest that medical research would be improved if the seemingly disproportionate number of Jews and Chinese in that field were diluted? Better still, the ranks of professional football and especially basketball

---

[5] See "Post-Partum Note" immediately below.

players consist entirely of males and mostly of blacks. Where are the proposals to achieve *diversity* and thereby strengthen these teams by hiring women and more whites? What these examples show is that diversity is not the issue. That word, like the current use of *equity*, is a euphemism and smokescreen for a patronizing program of social engineering.

As for *role models*, many of us are academics. How many of us ever encountered a Jewish professor when we were students, at least in Canada? And you will recall the joke, "What's the difference between the International Ladies' Garment Workers' Union and the American Psychiatric Association?" The answer is "one generation." *Role models*, indeed! (That was where the talk ended.)

Post-Partum Note (*written later*):

The Comrades were big on "the final reckoning," but no more so than their coreligionists, the Christian theologians, whom they despised for deluding "the suffering masses" with the "opiate" of a perfect afterlife. Nevertheless, they unwittingly embraced the Christian vision of history, though they stood it on its head, or, more precisely, reversed it. Instead of beginning with "the word" — with "the flesh" as the derivative — their foundation was Marx's "material conditions of existence," and ideologies ("the word") were the emanation. For both, the derivative mattered less.

History began for both the Christians and the Marxists with an earthly paradise, soon lost, and continued seemingly forever as a set of struggles — for one, between "the word" and "the flesh," and for the other, the "class struggle." Both, of course, also offered a message of hope, a shared vision of how these struggles would end in ultimate triumph — in a "final conflict" (the opening words of the *Internationale*) or Armageddon, in which good would prevail over evil, the righteous and the wicked would go to their just rewards, paradise would be regained, and history would come to an end.

2003 My All-Purpose Political Address

Politics being the subject, can anyone remind me who said: "A politician is an arse upon whom everyone has sat except a man"?

So here we are again, with the irresistible opportunity to harangue a captive audience. I'm calling this My All-Purpose Political Address, equally suitable *or not* for any office, political or other, because the only issue here is my impeccable, nay, perfect credentials. They constitute my platform. Everyone knows what a platform is — a device to hoist a candidate or party to a winning position, whereupon it disappears, except for the opposition's reminders. They, of course, forget that they did exactly the same thing. But I digress. What can perfect qualifications be? And how does one achieve them?

I learned what they are the hard way, slowly and painfully, as is my wont. And of all places, at the University of Toronto, where I was once a bureaucrat in the graduate school. One of my duties was to be on many Search Committees — for chairmen (now chairs — I once asked in an angry moment, "If X is the Chair, is Y, his Associate, a Stool?"), deans and the like. You might think that interesting work, and for a while it was. In fact, if only it had been left at that, the discussion of the shortcomings of the candidates would never have been less than interesting. But every Search Committee wanted to warm up for that job — the only one that mattered — by first discussing what they called "criteria." Indeed, one committee undertook to "prioritize our criteria," a phrase then so new to me that it left my mouth agape. It was at OISE, of course.

As you may imagine, the discussion of "criteria" stretched to a limitless horizon without encountering any useful landmarks. And yet, tiresome and time-wasting as those discussions were, I did learn something from them. I eventually realized that all the criteria — everything the members wanted — could be boiled down to one simple, perfect qualification, the one which I solemnly offer you as my platform today — the ability to walk on the water. Nothing more. It explains why every Search Committee fervently wants an "outsider": they know all too well the walking-on-the-water capabilities of their own colleagues, but never lose faith in a miracle-worker out there somewhere. I will conclude by not telling you something; I'll desist from repeating the ancient joke in which one great religious prophet tells another, who is sinking out of sight, how to do it. His message is, of course, "Fool, walk on the rocks!"[6]

vii. For Better or Verse

RELATIVITY

Said Bernard Shaw's aunt
Of a contemporary cutie:
"The least plain sister

---

[6] Afterthought: the mocking tone above overlooks something important. The desperate search for "miracle-workers" reflects the scarcity of skillful administrators, at least in the universities, where gifted teachers and researchers far outnumber gifted administrators. Why the latter are so scarce and get so little recognition is beyond the scope of this brief footnote.

Is the family beauty:
I sometimes think
How good that advice is:
The least pleasing matter
Is the family crisis.

August 1988

SUPERFLUOUS ADVICE (A title with one superfluous word)

It's senseless to sigh
And pointless to plead
For one gentle word
Which you desperately need.

August 1988

THEY SAY THAT GROWING OLD HAS ITS OWN SATISFACTIONS

Now I lay me down to sleep
Beside you warm and soft I keep
Closely pressed until you wake
And then again my pleasure take.

August 1988

ODE TO THE FART

O, lowly, shameful, furtive blast
In polite parlance you're the last.
Breaking wind and passing gas

Are euphemisms with more class.
But here where bowels are repaired
And their contents must be aired,
Of such import is that act,
Why not opt for simple fact?
Shun delicacy; eschew all art.
Just ask the patient "Did you fart ?

Mount Sinai Hospital
June 1994

LONG NIGHTS

Now I lay me down to sleep,
Instead a watchful wake I keep
With thoughts and worries I can't forsake
Can I fix that lamp or my child's heartbreak?

How agreeable to work with the hands,
No matter how trifling the job's demands.
But how hopeless and helpless to try to mend
Life's broken promises and our children defend.

September 1997

viii. On Our 50th Wedding Anniversary (Sept. 4, 1956–2006)

As a supposed student of the family, I thought that I should prepare an exhaustive and definitive disquisition on what it takes to survive such long proximity. In this arduous investigation I have stumbled across the secret of marital longevity. One clue, though not the answer, is contained in the birthday card which She Who Must Be Obeyed gave me years ago. On the front page it says

> Lots of women marry a guy
> and then they try to change him,
> but not me.
> I love you just the way you are.

Leo and Annette at their wedding reception
Montreal, September 4, 1956

Well, that's nice, but let's see what's on the inside. On the inside it says

"But don't get any worse."

And now for the real secret of marital longevity. Surprisingly, it can all be wrapped up in one short word, a familiar four-letter one. No, it's not "love," agreeable as that is. Indeed, the last three letters are "uck" and (*Honi soit qui mal y pense*) the first letter is the same as in the word "love."

בס"ד

This Is To Certify

That on the 3rd day of the week, the 28th day of the month Ellul in the year 5714 A.M. corresponding to the 4th day of September 1954, the holy Covenant of Marriage was entered into, in Montreal, P.Q. Canada between the Bridegroom MR. LEO ZAKUTA and his Bride MISS ANNETTE SEGAL.

The said Bridegroom made the following declaration to his Bride: "Be thou my wife according to the law of Moses and of Israel. I faithfully promise that I will be a true husband unto thee. I will honor and cherish thee; I will work for thee; I will protect and support thee, and will provide all that is necessary for thy due sustenance, even as it becomes a Jewish husband to do. I also take upon myself all such further obligations for thy maintenance as are prescribed by our religious statute."

And the said Bride has plighted her troth unto him, in affection and sincerity, and has thus taken upon herself the fulfilment of all the duties incumbent upon a Jewish wife.

This Covenant of Marriage was duly executed and witnessed this day according to the usage of Israel, and the laws of the Province of Quebec, Canada.

Rabbi   Witnesses

Spanish and Portuguese Synagogue, Montreal P.Q. Canada

Reminiscences, Rants, and Raves

ix.   Moving Day: A Song Of Celebration[7]

On moving to the Manulife.
A sonnet + 1
Based on "No more pencils, no more books, No more teachers' dirty looks."

No more planting, no more weeds
No more mowing, no more seeds
No more gardeners, no more leaves
No more roofing, no more eaves
No more coon crap, no more tar
No more digging out the car
No more plumbers, no more drains
No more worry about the rains
No more dread of peeling paint
No more estimates that leave you faint
No more ants and no more creaks
No more mopping up the leaks
No more stairs so you'll think twice
No more snow and no more ice
No more thoughts about the price.

Leo Zakuta
20 September, 2006

---

[7]   Of limited applicability to owners of summer houses, farms, or condos, or those who miss their gardens and "the great outdoors."

Reminiscences, Rants, and Raves

*Leonard Levine and Leo at Peter and Mary Elder's Christmas dinner
Dundas, Ontario (c. 1990)*

2. Tributes to the Living and the Dead (compiled 2006)

(a). Tributes to the Living

i. Arthur Axelrad

*Written for a celebration of **Arthur Axelrad's** 70th birthday*

MIGHTY ARTHUR

He plucked the sword from out the stone
And thus ascended to the throne.
And by his deeds he gained great fame
And mighty Arthur was his name.

Untold ages since have passed,
And deeds today are most half-assed.
But one doth play a different game
And mighty Arthur is his name.

Some set their sights on the Holy Grail,
While most just chase a bit of tail.
For some it's a gene and for others a dame,
And which will mighty Arthur claim?

His Table Round is called a lab,
His Knights gather round in a setting drab.
Though low is the ambience, high is the aim.
And mighty Arthur is his name.

This Knight sets off to investigate
And Nature's mysteries penetrate.
A Monster dread he hopes to tame,
And mighty Arthur is his name.

So, to this great prof and greater researcha
(Or should we state that vice versa?)
A happy birthday we all proclaim.
To mighty Arthur; *vaksen zol zein* [*zein*] name.[8]

Leo Zakuta
Dec. 1993

ii. Ida Berk

Written for a celebration of Ida Berk's 94th birthday

IDA BERK

Thank you for the opportunity to talk about my favourite student. I talk about her at every opportunity, but this occasion is special. When I saw her in my first class again a week ago, I told the students that I wanted to share with them my extraordinary delight to have her back once more. I told them that she had come to the university about 7 or 8 years ago and that she and I have been going steady ever since. They quite appropriately applauded her presence.

Words cannot convey my pleasure on that occasion and on this. Perhaps you will understand my feelings better if I tell you about our first meeting. It was in September 1977 when I met my first class after a year's sabbatical. Before the sabbatical, I had been a bureaucrat for some years in the graduate school and so had done little undergraduate teaching for a long time. As it always does, the sabbatical year had magnified the usual end-of-summer jitters about getting back to teaching into something approaching panic. The class was located in the most remote corner of

---

[8] May his name increase.

the campus, even beyond it, at the Banting and Best Institute. The room was quite the worst I had ever taught in — dark, much too large, and I was imprisoned by one of those large desks for demonstrations that stretched across the width of the room. The students were somewhere on the other side far off in the gloomy distance. To get closer to them, I had to make a ceremonious parade around that barrier, and then back again whenever I wanted to use the blackboard. But most intimidating of all was that sea of such young faces, which made me feel inexpressibly old, irrelevant, and out of it. It was not an auspicious start.

When the class ended, an elegant and elderly lady approached me and introduced herself. It was of, course, Ida Berk, whom I had heard of but never met. After a moment or so, she put her hand on my arm — John Turner should have learned about tactile politics from Ida Berk — and said, "Young man. ..." What else she said I have long forgotten; only those inspired words remain. It was the magic formula for instant rejuvenation.

So, for me, it was love at first sound. The succeeding years intensified it as Ida Berk came back over and over again to grace those classes — lively, alert, and elegant. To have her back again this year after another sabbatical is thrilling. I am not sure what she gets from her association with the young students in these classes, but from listening to them and seeing them, I know how much they enjoy her presence.

I used to talk about her to my mother, who was of a roughly comparable age. She always shook her head in wonder and admiration; it was just the kind of thing she would have loved to do had it been possible. I too share that wonder and admiration, and have in addition the extraordinary pleasure of her continued presence in my classes.

If I may adapt a venerable toast for a venerable lady, I salute Ida Berk with the wish, "Next year in Sidney Smith Hall."

Leo Zakuta
29 September, 1984

Ida Berk died in 1990 at the age of 100. She was 87 when we first met.

iii. Bryce Bosnich

Written in great haste for a dinner marking the departure of Bryce Bosnich, Department of Chemistry, from the University of Toronto to the University of Chicago. He was a star performer at the "Long Table" in the Faculty Club for many years, and delighted in referring to many of us as "liberal pinkos."

Seating at the dinner at Le Trou Normand
July 16th, 1987

	Richard Gregor	Sheila Eastman	John Munro	Ed Safarian	Peter Russell
Harry Eastman					
	Anthony Poe	Leo Zakuta	Bryce Bosnich	Jack Macdonald	Kelly Gottlieb

A LIBERAL PINKO SOCIOLOGIST'S LAMENT

It is a not so ancient Chemist,
And he stoppeth three of three.

Leo Zakuta

"By thy long sharp tongue and glittering eye,
Now wherefore stopp'st thou me?"

"The Faculty Club's doors are opened wide
And I belong therein;
The guests are met, the feast is set:
May'st hear the merry din."

He holds him with his skinny hand,
"Hold off! unhand me, grey-clad loon!"
"Not till you tell me," sayeth he
"What do you think of my man Muldoon?" (Mulroney)

He holds him with his glittering eye–
The Luncheon-Guest stood still.
"Hey, pinko," that dread voice goes on,
"Now, what do you say about my boy Ron?" (Reagan)
"His faith is great" his masters said,
"Beyond compare his zeal
But so loose a cannon on the deck
We never could conceal."

"We've sent him here, we've sent him there,
We've urged him to lie low.
But everywhere that Bosnich went
His cover he did blow."

Now comes a turn that's little known
His devotion melts those hearts of stone
Reluctantly, they keep him as their own.
Though every impulse cries "Disown!"

"One last chance," they all agree.
"There's still one place for such as he.
In the distant Peaks of Gullibility.
There's a strange spot known as the U of T."

"Liberal pinkos everywhere
And no two thoughts in synch.
A home at last for him," they said
"Amidst sociologists and shrink."

But even there the same fate him befell.
Those two Irish clowns he tried too hard to sell[9]
So, now as he parts from the U of T,
We shall miss his sallies of fiendish glee.
All of us bid him a sad farewell
And salute the Man from the KGB.

Leo Zakuta
16 July, 1987

iv. Margaret Cockshutt

For the retirement dinner of Prof. Margaret Cockshutt, Faculty of Library and Information Science. Read by Prof. Katherine Packer.

MARGARET

I am painfully disappointed that because I am overseas I cannot share fully in this evening for Margaret. She is so close and valued a friend that I am grateful to be permitted to participate in this indirect way.

Margaret and I first met 20 years ago as fellow bureaucrats — she in your faculty and I in the graduate school. Our first association was as members of the Degree Committee of Division II, where I was unhappily cast in conflicting roles — Committee Chairman by statute and "chief advocate" by necessity. When Margaret spoke for the first time, I knew we

---

[9] Brian Mulroney and Ronald Reagan.

had struck gold and that my dilemma had ceased. The Committee's mandate was to uphold the academic standards of the graduate school, but most of its members cared little beyond their own departments. Margaret, like the outstanding lawyer she would have made, saw the university, like the law, as a whole, and applied her high and unyielding standards equally to all departments. She expressed her views lucidly, without any of the common hesitation about how her colleagues might receive them. But what impressed me most was that no matter how diligently and carefully I thought I had studied each case, I would discover that she had done her "homework" better, and had a clearer appreciation of its particular nature and wider significance. I naturally turned to her increasingly for advice in all aspects of my work, and always found the same extraordinary capacity for work, excellent judgment, and concern about the Division and the School.

These qualities were so obvious that Margaret was called on to represent the Division and the university in various capacities. Indeed, Prof. Safarian, then Dean of the School of Graduate Studies, told me several times that she was the best Graduate Secretary he had met. He was, of course, familiar with all four Divisions, and was not one to bestow praise carelessly or extravagantly.

In the many years since, I continued to consult Margaret about my own academic life and career. The temptation was irresistible. I could count on an impeccable and fearless judgment, and the comfort of knowing that I would get an honest opinion even if she knew that, at the moment, I might find it unwelcome. That courage of her convictions, together with her intelligence, are perhaps Margaret's most distinctive and remarkable qualities. She always understood how much grief comes from saying "Yes" when one ought to say "No." Thus she did not seek or enjoy confrontations with colleagues. Some of you may not be so sure of that, but I learned long ago how much she agonized over that prospect, because her instincts are humane and compassionate, and her style is thoroughly civilized. Above all, it has been so much fun to work with and talk to Margaret. But I have not told you a thing about her that most of you don't already know.

Leo Zakuta
8 May, 1992

v. Harold Files

Letter to the Harold G. Files Gift Fund Committee, McGill University

HAROLD G. FILES[10]

To the members of the committee

I am very grateful to you for having undertaken something that expresses my feelings so well, for, of course, my essential gratitude is to Prof. Files. I took all of his courses, "loved" them, and admired him immensely personally. He was by far my favourite teacher at McGill.

    I remember clearly my apprehension on entering his office for the first time. My trouser leg was rolled up; my leg was painted green, and I was ornamented in still other ways, which my memory has mercifully obliterated. All because I was too timid to defy the freshman initiation committee. His kindness and courtesy on that occasion and on many subsequent ones are unforgettable. They did much to make the change from high school to university little short of ecstatic, and his courses maintained that feeling long beyond its normal life span.

---

[10] Department of English. The occasion was presumably his retirement.

Many thanks, therefore, for enabling me to participate, however indirectly, on this occasion.

Leo Zakuta
31 March, 1964

vi. Eileen Garber

My first poem — for Eileen Garber's 60th birthday

Ralph phoned to extend the invitation. He told Annette that a poem or sketch or something of that kind would be welcome. She replied, "Leo will be glad to do that. He loves to do that kind of thing." Leo, however, froze in fear, never having done "that kind of thing" in his life. But the commitment had been made, and the wheels began to turn. As I wrote in the preface to another poem, "Chopping ice and shoveling snow / That's what makes the verses grow."

FOR EILEEN ON THE OCCASION OF, OR
"QUEEN FOR A DAY"

"Come," said Eileen to her friends
And another invitation extends.
With Seders and birthdays,
Kids' visits and mirth days,
Hospitality there never ends.

So we'll offer a song to Eileen
To show our collective esteem.
With a digression or two
To include me and you.
But today she's meant to be Queen.

Reminiscences, Rants, and Raves

An Outremont lass named Eileen
Married some guy from Lachine
There were progeny seven
All created in Heaven
Nudge nudge wink wink, if you know what I mean.

This near-ballerina Epstein
And the still nameless lad from Lachine
Both turned to good works
And surrendered some perks
Of the world's more conventional scene.

A *farbrente*[11] feminist Garber
Men's traditional place couldn't harbour
Be it ever so humble
It still requires a tumble
"The kitchen's their place, not the parlour."

In a world which lived under a pall
Where the bombs would supposedly fall
To save it from Reagan
And Nixon and Begin
She marched to save us all.

I will say in advance of the following pair:
As verses, they're doubtless less than fair.
Both were composed
While I reposed
Solidly froze in the dentist's chair.

J. stands for Jessica and Jeremy too,
Jill, Jody and Judah — to mention a few.
Add them together; they make up a min.

---

[11] Yiddish for 'ardent, fiery, impassioned.'

(That's half a minyan[12]).
But how did Naomi and Daniel get in?
    OR
Ask not what the Garbers, Ralph and Eileen,
Have done to enliven their very own scene.
For they have left more Jays in their wake
Than on Toronto's team by the lake
Plus Naomi and Daniel in-between.

And now for something completely different:

I will not render Auld Lang Syne,
But Ancient Days With Each Epstein.
Norman was first. I met him as a fan
Of some outlandish socialist plan.
Vivian was next, from well before Sam,
A no-nonsense maiden with an aversion to sham.

I last met Eileen in those days of yore
A vibrant doer of Camp Escobar lore.
You may think I'm done, but I tell you there's more,
As we turn the clock back to long before,
When I encountered their parents
In the Bernard Street store.
A half century's fled, as the calendar rules,
Since we bought our books there for the Outremont schools.

For the next part of this saga, we skip more than a decade. The words of an old hymn have been slightly adapted to waft us along to the Y Urban Camp where Annette and I met in the summer of 1950.

---

[12]   Hebrew for 'prayer quorum.'

CHORUS (Sung to the tune of "40 Years Ago" by Burl Ives)

Forty years ago; nigh forty years ago.
I wish I were a boy again as in the long ago.
Forty years ago; nigh forty years ago.
Bless the Y for old camp meetin' times of forty years ago.

Oh, for one day of those past years, and of that day one hour,
When good old Eileen filled with good was shoutin' with the power.

And campers, counsellors laughed and cried
As she went down the aisle
A-shakin' hands and blessin' all in old camp meetin' style

CHORUS

Oh, praise the Lord, I'm glad to see we're comin' back again.
The Holy Garber's here today, so let us say Amen.
New-fashioned ways we don't approve; some may call us slow.
We like the good old-fashioned ways of forty years ago.

CHORUS

The Garbers were my leaders then.
I could not be moved.
They patiently bore with me when
They must have disapproved.
Stip was our section head.
With six-year olds to vie
Came Debbie, Bill, and Barbara

As well, of course, as I.
And surely, we must not forget
Arthur, Chippy, and Annette
All at the other Y.
To say nothing of Leonard in the Library.
The moral of this history, it's plain for all to see,
Is that cronyism is older than Mul-ro-ney.

And now it's time to say farewell.
And on the maudlin cease to dwell.
And, what the hell,
My verse won't jell.
So, finding no familiar strain
I'll just say in language plain
We all share this brief refrain:
New Jersey's loss we count our gain.

Leo Zakuta
1 February, 1987

vii. Margie Golick

Written for Margie Golick's 60th birthday. Her "maiden" name was Schwartz, which in Yiddish means dark or black. There is a Yiddish idiom which, translated literally, means "Black is [to] me before the eyes," or translated freely means "Woe is me!"

Reminiscences, Rants, and Raves

BLACK VERSE OR SCHWARTZ IS [TO] ME BEFORE THE EYES

I

So, this one's a biggie
But what can that mean
When to me she has always
Remained seventeen?
Our very first meeting
Is fresh in my mind
With two sassy chick-lets
That Leonard did find
Margie and Vivian, pert as could be
With tongues that were sharp
And wondrously free
Their brightness and sureness
The boldest would daunt
Les Demoiselles d'Outremont.

II

There's a universal fascination
Shared by every tribe and nation
As the calendar quickens
And the gait grows slow
Our thoughts turn back
To a long time ago
So, I picture us then
And look at us now
As if the lifetime between
Had vanished somehow
For generations have gone
And others have come
Since the days when this story
Had just begun
As time, that most implacable thief
Has taken so many
And left us in grief
And in their place
Brought other lives
Children, their children
Husbands and wives
Pointless to ask
If on balance it's good
Has the universe unfolded
As it should?

III

How did we alter?
Let me count the ways
Since those trips to the altar
And still more distant days.

So we'll fly through the years
With a gasp and a wheeze
With that daring old fool
On the flying trapeze.

Bye, bye, bitchiness
(Though now they call it PMS)
But call it glad tidings
Or call it the curse
It's long since departed
For better or worse
And bye, bye, perpetual rise
Hello, backs and legs
And ears and eyes
Bye, bye, command
Of endless details
Hello to a memory
That predictably fails
Farewell to the visions
Of a perfect romance
Where worries dissolve
In a soft loving glance
Welcome instead
To the six p.m. plight
They're tired and hungry
And no supper's in sight.

IV

Look round the kitchen,
What catches your view?
Cookbooks and Cuisinarts
And a microwave too
Domesticity's vanished
Or has it been shared?
And the old ways are banished
Since we were paired
And work by committee
Is always impaired.

For the girls that we married
Had to be
Sharp and tough
And curse so free
Once fearful of parents
We still thought we were wild
Now afraid of our children
We know that we're mild.

V

The decades disposed of
In a manner so glib
We return to our Margie
With no need to fib
For her talents are many
Her skills so diverse
I feel it's beyond me
To set them to verse
Her mind is inventive
And playful to boot
In manifold manner
It's borne its fruit
Globe-trotting expert
In constant demand
Books in a steady stream
Flow from her hand
Her poems delightful
Are a treat for the ear
Microcomputer pioneer
In the midst of all this
For fitness sake
She ran each day
Up to Beaver Lake
And as a measure for leisure
While the mother of three
She casually picked up a
PhD

(Thirteen years of my life
To acquire that ticket
Is it true that she merely
Appeared at the wicket?)

VI

So here's the lesson for
today
Based on this brief resume
Lives of great men
All remind us
That those times
Are far behind us

In the present
Unlike then
There are just superwomen
And no supermen.

Footnote:

Can estrogen explain it all?
Or does the Avis slogan get
the call?
It's an old Canadian story
Repeated countless times
The very highest flyers
Come from the Maritimes.

Alas, I must add
A footnote ill-bred
So do very many
Whose wings never spread
Of Maritime folks
Thus can it be said
Either they're quick
Or live off the Fed.

VII

Reflections after Ivry

If you think you are fit
Full of vigour and starch
You have never gone with her
On her famous Death March
(Credit that mot juste to
Marianne Stein
I've hidden another in the very first line)
Across the dock
The people come and go
Talking of absent
Friends we know.

Though Margie in work
Seems totally bound
She misses no word
That's bandied around.

With Peter we embarked
On a grand tour du lac
And slowly, so slowly
We rowed our way back
Alone on the dock
Our Margie remained
Her attention by work
Entirely claimed
But as the hours went by
Without us in sight
I in her place would
Have succumbed to fright
In matters of this kind

VIII

We now reach a matter
That often is shady
How have the years
Affected the lady?
First, my conclusion
And then explanation
A little like sinning
Après expiation
So, in today's vernacular
"Together" is the word for her
That conclusion,
Now it's stated,
All that's left is–
Substantiate it.

Who could have pictured
A woman serene
In that feisty young filly
Of seventeen?
The edges retracted
A softness revealing
And showed us an aspect
Still more appealing
But the core of that kid
Remained intact
Including the sparkle
Which first did attract.

Now at last my tale is told
Now no further words unfold
Some little talk a while of me and thee there seemed,

How well I know
My threshold of panic
Is distressingly low
But what did we see
When so late we drew near?
Margie quite tranquil
No victim of fear.

But more of me as I prattled
and preened
And all I can say in my
defence
Is another and another cup
to drown
The memory of this
impertinence.

Leo Zakuta
August 1988

viii. Rose Katz

A sonnet plus, for Rose Katz because ...

ROSE

Run around ran Rosie,
A pocketful of posies.
Easily she'll run a mile,
And garden in a pleasing style.
A lady without shtick or guile,
As straight an arrow, it is true,
As anyone I ever knew.
What you see is what you get,
Ancient pal of my Annette.
Cook and baker with the best,
Mistress sure of her inviting nest.
Endless strength in tribulation,
Source of the phrase "She's not my nation."
Many a friend has crossed my door,
But not a one that I love more.

Leo Zakuta
27 July, 2006

*Rose and Myer Katz with Leo
Barbados, c. 1995*

ix. Marjorie Kennedy

*Read at a party for **Marjorie Kennedy** before her move to Kingston*

MARJORIE KENNEDY, F.M.,
O.E.P.F.T.G.i.T.(m.a.R.T.C.)

It is written that some people will do anything for a game. This occasion therefore is to protest and lament Marjorie Kennedy's decision to abandon her old and true friends in her search for the more perfect tennis match. Perhaps we ought not to be too surprised. Her game is excellent; she is indeed the most disciplined player I know. And I must admit to my share of guilt in her departure. Have I not, after she tucked another perfect volley away at the net, cried, "Move her up to a higher division," little realizing how literally she would take those words.

In leaving us, Marjorie has torn herself from her roots, not only as a long-established member of our group, but as the one with perhaps the best claim to be regarded as its founder. I owe my membership in the group directly to her, and thereby hangs a tale, which, since I have you here, I cannot and will not resist telling.

In 1974, when my son Jamie went to summer camp, the required equipment included a tennis racquet. Having bought one for him, how could we do less for Silvie, and once she had a racquet, what was to be done with it? So I fished my ancient racquet out of the depths of the basement. It hadn't been touched in about 25 years — and seldom before that — and had become so encrusted that Annette restored it by washing it. (Behold it!) And Silvie and I began to look for walls against which to hit ancient tennis balls. We spent that summer looking for the perfect wall.

By then Marjorie and I had worked together closely and cordially at the U of T graduate school for many years, and when I told her about these goings-on with walls and balls, she invited me to join her at the Rosedale Tennis Club where real players played real games. It was an intimidating prospect. I got there eventually, and played with Marjorie and her friends, which meant mainly Lorna and Geoff Stead and Grace Thurston. Sometimes Sheila Smith, Nenagh Hanly and Catherine Grimes played with us, as did Bill Alexander and Roy Wolfe. Looking back now, I am astonished and grateful at how cordially they all treated that totally inept newcomer with his washed racquet with its onboard instructions.

Over the years the group coalesced and grew. Perhaps the chief catalyst was our stubborn refusal to recognize the appropriate span of the tennis season, so that we persisted after more reasonable people turned to other things. When the Rosedale courts were locked for the winter, we climbed the fence and played to the skaters' music. And when we grew tired of climbing, we set up winter quarters happily at Bennington Heights for some years. I have played with members of this group at Moore Park, Davisville, Riverdale, Branksome Hall, Victoria and Trinity Colleges, several times at Wycliffe College (with Marjorie, Lorna and Geoff) in that quaint court at the corner of Queen's Park and Hoskin, and even on those strange sloping courts at Ryerson. We have played indoors at the Winter Tennis Club, Harbourfront, York University, and even in Burlington.

Throughout those years Marjorie was a central and valued member of the group. We will miss her skill, her cheerfulness and her imperviousness to the weather. To say Au revoir, I present her, on behalf of all of us, with this reminder of those many convivial and energetic times. It is — or should be — inscribed: Marjorie Kennedy, Founding Member, Oldest Established Permanent Floating Tennis Game in Toronto (mainly at Rosedale Tennis Club). Alas, the words "Founding Member" were inadvertently omitted, but by a cunning but secret method the omission will be rectified and the natural order of the world restored.

Leo Zakuta
17 May, 1990

x. Yelena Kalacic

A toast I made at the wedding of Yelena Kalacic, a member of my tennis group. The verse is from The Rubaiyat of Omar Khayyam.

Ah, fill the Cup — what boots it to repeat
That Time is slipping underneath our Feet:
Unborn Tomorrow and vanished Yesterday,
Why fret about them if Today be sweet!

Leo Zakuta
21 January, 2003

It is said that there is no fool like an old fool, so here are some verses composed in haste (on a bus to Sun City, South Africa), which I will repent at leisure.

xi. Bernice

Ballad for Bernice or Krafchik's Caravan or Skin Deep[13]

A dynamic derm named Bernice
With energy that required release
And talents abundant
Collected colleagues redundant
And carted them all off to Greece.

(All right, it was South Africa, but that doesn't rhyme. And since this is about poetry, not real estate, rhyme is more important than location. That rhyme was just a little

---

[13] The group consisted mainly of dermatologists.

premature. Eight years later she did lead many of us to Greece to attend Gillian's wedding in Crete.)

Refrain

Bernice is our leader,
We shall all be moved
Hither, thither, yonder,
Just as she approved.

Her friends she was eager to please,
So into the group she did squeeze
A privileged few
Though their numbers grew,
And she became our Mother Terese
Or like the guy who guided the geese.

Refrain

Bernice is our leader,
We shall all be moved
From early in the morning
Until we flop to roost.

As we traversed the South African veld
With Bernice in the lead as our "held,"
(Held is Yiddish for hero.)
Our obstacles melted to zero
And the many into one she did weld.

Refrain

Bernice is our leader,
We shall all be moved
By bus, by plane, by minivan,
By land rover and helicopter

And almost by choo-choo. (Outeniqua Choo-choo: trip foiled by Helen Hutchison)

To conduct a remarkable tour
Her arrangements were many and sure.
So, for the leopard's claws, the lion's jaws and the elephant's paws,
It's hats off to our baas
For the memories that are bound to endure.

Leo Zakuta
12 February, 1998
Riempie Estate Hotel
Oudtshoorn, South Africa

Remarks on behalf of "The Dermatology Group" on February 18, 1998 near the end of our South African tour (Buitenverwachting Restaurant, Cape Town)

Leo and Annette on safari in Africa
Mala Mala, South Africa, 19981

xii. Johannes Pretorius

What a splendid setting for our "last dinner" together. This occasion is about expressing our appreciation for (our guide) Helen (Hutchison) and (our bus driver) Boris (Johannes Pretorius). This time I cannot blame Bernice (Krafchik) for thrusting the responsibility for this task upon me. I volunteered for it; I even asked for it. Strange as that may seem, you will be able to understand why on the basis of your own academic and professional careers. Students inevitably must come to you for letters of reference. Sometimes the very best ones preface that request with the statement, "I'm sorry to bother you, but . ..." The reply is of course, "Bother! That's no bother at all. It will be a pleasure to write that letter for you." The more highly one regards the student, the more agreeable that task is. That is why I sought the privilege of saying something about Helen and Boris.

First, that fine gentleman who bears the proud name Johannes Pretorius, usually known as Boris, because of his remarkable resemblance to the great tennis star, Boris Becker. Boris's mettle was tested almost immediately after he met us in Port Elizabeth. Shortly after we began the drive to Tsitsikamma, his windshield wiper broke. It was dark and raining all the way. He breathed not a word of it to anyone but continued to drive. Had I not been in the front seat, I would not have known about the wiper; the others did not. I didn't think it could be done, and, at first, I watched with stiff apprehension, then with amazement, and eventually with relaxed admiration. So we knew from the outset that we were in very skilled hands. That was confirmed over and over again on the mountain roads and high passes. Boris's handling of the bus inspired relaxed confidence.

His conduct was equally impressive. Always cheerful, good humoured, unfailingly courteous and punctual. We were constantly off the bus and on again, and it was, "Boris, can you wait a minute, I forgot something in my room" and "Boris, can you hold on, I forgot something on the bus." Nothing ever seemed to try his patience, not even the repeated loading and unloading of the luggage, and our requests to check that our own had been put on board. His only response was always a cheerful wish to be helpful. His performance was the very model of what one might hope for. And for that, Boris, we say "Thank you and well done."

xiii. Helen Hutchison

(Helen, our guide, sat in the front seat of our bus right behind Boris. Annette and I occupied the front seat on the other side.) From my perch, to which I clung selfishly, guiltily but tenaciously, I could hear the endless questions zinging towards Helen. "Helen, what is ...? Helen, why is the ...? Helen, what happened at ... ? Helen, where are we going tomorrow? Helen ... Helen ... Helen. ..." Many of those questions were mine. And back came the answers, so knowledgeable, on such a wide variety of subjects, and so full and cheerful that one would never have guessed that she had probably heard those questions many times before. Her prepared remarks were equally informative and sophisticated, and she understood what would interest us.

Equally impressive — perhaps even more because it seems harder — was the way in which she shepherded her potentially wayward flock. It was done firmly, but gently and good humouredly, no matter how late or lost the stragglers were. How she rounded us all up after our countless descents from the bus, especially in and around Cape Town, where the crowds were always large, I never could figure out. It reminded me of those films of a skilled sheepdog working a flock of sheep.

"Departure tomorrow morning will be at 8" (for example) she would announce in a voice that did not invite debate. Eventually, I realized that if we got underway at 8.15, she would be well satisfied. She always had the schedule and itinerary clearly in mind, and knew not only where we were going, but why, and, equally important, when, and thus she kept our schedule from spiraling out of control. These indomitable qualities were doubtless required for her membership in the Black Sash.

In trying to summarize Helen's performance, my many years as a teacher made me think inevitably of grading. Many years ago I was casting about for the ultimate compliment to a student for a piece of work. The conventional superlatives seemed inadequate. Finally, I wrote on her paper, "I'm only sorry that there is no grade higher than an A+ that can be awarded to this paper."

That is how we all feel about Helen's performance. And not from a distance.

In this very short time, she has become a friend to all of us. And, on behalf of us all, I thank her.

Leo Zakuta

xiv. Gina Rakoff

For Gina Rakoff at a celebration of her 60th birthday

GINA

I only want to venture a small, you should excuse me, sociological observation. I have been to a number of these occasions marking entry into a new decade, and have heard about many more.

This is the first one I have ever heard of that isn't for a man. So perhaps it represents one small step for womankind.

Leo Zakuta
3 March, 1996

xv. Marianne Stein

On receiving my first ever Valentine (at the age of 62.5, from Marianne Stein)

MARIANNE

Hail to thee blithe Moosie (nickname derived from M. Roos)
Nerd thou never wert
What thou wert was Roosie
Maiden not and quite impert.
Thoughts of late
I've had to goose thee.
But, cunning thing,
Thou dids't seduce me.
And now I have a Valentine,
For little else in life I pine.

February 1988
A Secret Admirer too

xvi. Roy Wolfe

For the ageless Roy Wolfe, an original member of our tennis group, on his ? birthday (to the tune of "It Ain't Necessarily So")

ROY

A toast we now offer to Roy.
He tears round the courts like a boy.
And though no gal will give in,
He says "I call this living.
My opponents I'll seek and destroy."

Now, Roy, he is small but so spry,
Now, Roy, he is small but so spry.
His years he defieth,
Others lay down and dieth,
Now, Roy, he is old but oh my!

Leo Zakuta
14 November, 1987

xvii. Annette Zakuta

A non-swimmer before and after this event.

On Bajan beaches swimmers grow
Between the breakers row on row
Years of fears are cast aside
As Annette surrenders to the tide.

Leo Zakuta

xviii. Valentine Day in Barbados, 1991

*Response to **Margie Golick's** Valentine poem to Annette*

I suppose you think it's good and fine
That you fain would be HER Valentine.

But I prefer the days of yore
When 'twas much more meet to be a whore.

The above ungracious lines were written, alas, before Lady Bountiful returned from The Pastry Shak. So ...

In penance shamed I hang my head
While scarfing still her bounteous bread.

Leo with Peter and Margie Golick at the Pastry Shack Barbados, c. 1995

To Peter Golick

Peter, Peter, dolphin eater
Had a wife and wouldn't beat her.
In Barbados made her dwell
Where he kept her (ending to be supplied by the audience).

Leo Zakuta

(b). Tributes to the Dead

i. Bill Alexander: Eulogy

HE'S JUST OUR BILL

Who has not thought while listening to a eulogy, "If only he could have heard these words while he was alive"? Bill had that rare opportunity, as he listened to the tributes of his friends at a gathering to mark his 60th birthday. That's why I want to repeat now what I said in his presence on that light-hearted occasion 6 years ago.

~~~~~~~~

Bill, 60? Who can believe it? I seem to be the self-appointed representative this evening (as I am again today) of the jock element in Bill's life, a small minority in this gathering of learned educators. How can these two groups find happiness together here? Perhaps by talking about Bill while trying to re-educate anyone who subscribes to that unfortunate phrase: "Tennis is just a game." Some of us know it as a way of life, but time permits only the briefest reconnaissance of the evidence.

Bill is a core and original member of a large and unusual tennis group which inhabits the park just around the corner. Membership tallies in unofficial groups are seldom precise, but ours is now about 20, and we have been together for almost 20 years, with, of course, inevitable comings and goings. Bill's membership in the original group has long puzzled me. The rest all had prior ties with someone else in the group. Bill, as far as I can tell, had none. Asking him — the logical step — has been no help. He simply says, "I don't know. I can't remember." So I must guess. The main qualifications were always skill and congeniality. Bill was so generously endowed with both that we probably just enveloped him at the outset.

Nearly all of my time with Bill has been on the courts, leaving them, or in cars going to and from our winter habitat. That pattern is typical for nearly all of us. Still, we have come to know each other well, learned much about each other's families, and have developed considerable camaraderie. Bill epitomizes that. His good humour, friendliness, warmth, and openness have made him especially accessible, and have generated a particular affection for him. When a shoulder injury sidelined him for several months recently, I was asked repeatedly, "How's Bill?" "Have you spoken to Bill?" His return was an occasion for celebration.

Now for the serious stuff — the game itself. Bill's play is skillful and powerful, and its strongest suit is his lethal net game. Its quickness and precision are unparalleled. Being his partner is a treat, but dread combines with grudging admiration when he's on the other side of the net. If you still think, "It's just a game," you would not if you could witness one of our doubles matches that has gone to, say, 6-6 or 8-all. There might be some signs that you were not at the Wimbledon finals, but the intensity of emotions and the grim determination not to lose would not be among them. Bill is a competitor; he loves to win. Who doesn't? And yet, the next day we might find it hard to recall exactly who had played with whom the day before.

Finally, a note of warning to Bill's colleagues at his other place of employment. We mean to do all we can to wrest him from your domain so that we might have him exclusively for our own. That's why I have titled this "He's just our Bill."

21 January, 1996

That was where it ended. What a lovable, courageous and impressive man.

William Alexander, PhD
February 2, 1936–December 11, 2001
His smile brightened our lives.

Leo Zakuta
14 December, 2001

ii. Marc Allodi

Letter to the Allodi family after MARC ALLODI drowned, at the age of 15, in a canoeing accident while on a wilderness camp expedition. He was our son Jamie's age, and was his friend.

Dear Fred, Mary, and Jimmy,

Your letter in Monday's *Globe and Mail* was excellent. Your capacity to write a letter that was so composed, considerate, and constructive so soon after Marc's death has our admiration. Fred, your words about Marc, at the Newman House service, displayed the same kind of remarkable courage.

You and Marc are constantly in our thoughts. We feel that we knew him so well. His extraordinary abilities in so many directions were well known. But what we chiefly associate with his memory were his enthusiasm, vitality, cheerfulness, courtesy, and consideration. He was so thoroughly engaging that the single most striking memory of all is simply the pleasure of his company. We were privileged to have that pleasure many times, most recently at the tennis courts this summer. It is unbearable to think, as we often do, that Marc with his winning smile and cheerful greeting is not on another court.

The Zakutas
20 September, 1978

iii. Ethel Bernstein

Letter to Al Bernstein after the death of his wife Ethel

Dear Al,

I have just been re-reading Ethel's poem "Too Soon." When I was home recently to see my father, I copied it from Fay's copy, because it is so beautiful and moving. It reminds me again of how terrible your loss is.

    I also want to tell you that my mother knew all about Ethel's illness and, although dying herself, was dreadfully shaken and upset about Ethel, whom she liked and admired so much. She worried about you too, because she knew how close you and Ethel were to each other. Annette and I talk and think of you often.

Leo
22 May, 1983

iv. Ellen Clark

To Del and Rosemary Clark on the death of their daughter Ellen

Dear Del and Rosemary,

We are sad to hear of your tragic loss, the fate that every parent dreads. We remember Ellen chiefly from the gatherings at your home in the 1950s. She was an attractive, bright, lively, and thoroughly charming girl. Her interesting career indicates that she made effective use of these assets and her heritage from both of you.

Annette and Leo Zakuta
27 May, 2002

v. Ruth Cooperstock

To Henry Cooperstock on the death of his wife Ruth

We have known about Ruth's illness and followed her battle against its ravages with ever-growing admiration. Nevertheless, it is hard to believe that someone so extraordinarily bright, vital, and courageous is no longer with us. Your loss, and that of your children, fill us with sorrow.

Annette and Leo Zakuta
2 February, 1984

vi. Betty Dales

To John Dales after the death of his wife Betty

BETTY DALES

Although we knew about Betty's illness, the news of her death was a dreadful shock. Her warmth, serenity, and sparkle will be missed by all who knew her. We think often about your indescribable loss.

Annette and Leo Zakuta
July 1984

vii. Sheila Eastman

To Harry Eastman, long-time friend and colleague, after the death of his wife, Sheila

Reminiscences, Rants, and Raves

Dear Harry,

Annette and I were saddened by your great loss, and that of Julia, Alice, Harriet, and their families. Sheila's friends will miss her kindness, her intelligence, and her lively inquiring mind.

Affectionately,
Annette and Leo
January 1992

viii. Harry Eastman

To Julia, Alice, and Harriet after the death of their father, Harry Eastman

HARRY EASTMAN

Harry's intellect, wit, elegance, and courtesy were all remarkable in themselves.

Together, they made him the exceptional friend we so admired and now will sadly miss and long remember. (Yesterday's moving memorial service was so in keeping with Harry's style.)

Annette and Leo Zakuta
27 April, 1999

To: the members of our tennis group

April 20th marks a year since **Harry Eastman's** sudden and unexpected death. Most of us knew him only as a tennis player during his brief time in our group. He had a distinguished career as an economist and administrator at the University of Toronto and beyond. At the University of Toronto, he was Chairman of the Dept. of Political Economy, a very large and prestigious department, and later was the university's Vice-President (Planning and Research). The Government of Canada appointed him Commissioner, Commission of Inquiry on the Pharmaceutical Industry, and he was Chairman of the Patented Medicine Prices Review Board for some years. I wrote the short memoir below recently for his daughters and their families. With their permission, I am circulating this to our group to present brief glimpses of his academic life.

HARRY

Harry is often on our minds. Annette and I talk about him frequently. He and Sheila were our friends since the mid-1950s. Sometimes I see men entering the park who, from a distance, remind me of him. Two particular episodes involving him have stayed with me. Neither is about tennis; they go back much farther, to our university days, the first to the mid-1960s and the other to about a decade later. They have something curious in common. Besides showing two different sides of him, they involve the two most fateful turning points in any academic career — the Oral Defence of the PhD thesis and the meeting of a tenure committee. The first episode was a trifle; the second was deadly serious.

One must know that, at the University of Toronto, at both of these turning points, the candidate's fate is in hands of a small committee, usually of about 6 to 8 members, whose verdict may well mean the extinction of the candidate's academic career. In both cases, it takes only two negative votes to turn the candidate down. (Abstention, even if permitted, counts as a negative vote.)

The first episode occurred at lunch in the Faculty Club. Harry and I and two others whom I can't recall were at a table. It was before the era of the "Long Table," and so must have been in the mid-60s. At the time, Harry was Associate Dean of the graduate school and therefore ultimately responsible for every PhD Oral Defence in his Division. Most difficult or messy cases would have landed on his desk. They may not have been numerous, but each could have been troublesome. No one could have been more aware of the pitfalls of an Oral Defence. On this occasion, he mentioned that right after lunch he had to participate in a PhD oral exam about which he was uneasy. One of our colleagues at the table, who should have known better, asked, "Why are you worried, Harry? Aren't these occasions just a formality?" "Yes," Harry answered with a smile, "when they are."

The second episode, about tenure, occurred in his department when he was chairman. The responsibility for organizing and conducting a tenure "hearing" falls directly and heavily on the departmental chairman. It's a troubling business. The procedures are many and complex. He is ultimately responsible for all of them, and any error of commission or omission is almost certain to result in an appeal if the candidate is turned down.

Furthermore, the chairman must conduct the meeting himself and is a voting member of the Tenure Committee. He must, like everyone else, express his evaluation of the candidate before the vote. (After the vote, the signed ballots are opened and each member's verdict is disclosed.) All in all, not an enviable task. Silence is not an option for committee members. It would have been my own preference as an outsider. I was there because the graduate school had to be represented on the committee, and it fell to me as the Associate Dean of the Division.

The meeting was difficult. Although the candidate had strong support, one senior member of the department was adamantly opposed. He was a "heavyweight," well known and respected throughout the university, articulate and outspoken. He seemed unshakeable. A single negative vote is not critical, but another committee member let it be known that he was undecided. The discussion and debate continued as usual while the evidence was presented, but the issue remained in doubt. Eventually Harry pitched in. He had read the candidate's major work, he said, in preparation for this meeting, and found that its calibre supported a motion for tenure.

The "leader of the opposition" then began to question Harry about that work. Harry answered his questions patiently and, I thought, thoroughly. But the questioning persisted until it seemed to imply that perhaps Harry knew less about the work in question than he claimed. I saw the corners of Harry's mouth draw back in a grimace and his clenched teeth showed. "Are you suggesting that I'm lying?" he asked quietly, as everyone caught his breath. "No, no, not at all," the questioner replied. What else he said, I can't recall. It didn't matter. It was game over even though the meeting continued for a while. I don't remember how the adamant colleague voted, but the candidate was granted tenure, so the confrontation obviously dislodged the undecided member from the fence.

Is it any wonder that Harry was so widely admired throughout the university?

Leo Zakuta
4 April, 2000

ix. Norman Endler

Norman Endler: Eulogy, Memorial Service, York University

NORMAN

I am a participant today at my own request, since I am not a member of either the York University or the psychology constituencies. As you know, alas, it is not unusual on such occasions for the speakers to talk more about themselves than about the person to be honoured. So, even if you won't forgive me, I will adhere to that tradition momentarily. My connection to Norman was a close one. He was my wife's cousin and my friend. He and Annette grew up near each other in Montreal, and the family ties were always close. When Norman completed his graduate work in the United States in the early 1960s, he visited Annette and me in Toronto on his way back home to Montreal. He was looking for a teaching position, and I mentioned that there was a new university just organizing in Toronto that might be worth looking into. Thus began Norman's long and distinguished career at York as one of the original founders. He was among the very first and probably the youngest to be hired.

I want to touch on only two aspects of Norman's life. The first is his interest (to put it mildly) in tennis. A small group of us began to play together in Rosedale Park in 1974, and I invited Norman to join us. He remained a member of that group until the end. It still exists and has grown large, but Norman was always a regular participant, even though the club was quite far from his home. His style of play was unusual; he was a masterful retriever. He seldom hit winning shots, but he won more points than he lost. He just returned everything — over and over and over — almost always softly, often lobs — until his opponents lost patience and tried to put an end to it with a big smashing winner. That shot naturally mostly went into the net or out of the court. His serve was equally unusual — soft and looping, and, as any tennis player knows, therefore frustrating. Rocket-like serves are easier to handle. The temptation to murder the soft serve is both foolish and incorrigible.

Newcomers who might have thought that Norman would be easy pickings usually wound up shaking their heads like the rest of us. It was better to be his partner. *(I wish I had included the next 2 sentences in my address but unfortunately thought of them only afterwards: He liked to say, "Age and guile always beat youth and impatience." And, you know what — occasionally they do.)*

My other theme is his book, *Holiday of Darkness*, subtitled *A Psychologist's Personal Journey Out of His Depression*.[14] It was an important and courageous book. Perhaps some of you, like me, gave copies to friends or referred them to it to help them through sombre periods. It was courageous because of its honesty, and because it told how, when all other remedies failed to alleviate Norman's deep depressions, he turned in despair to ECT (electroconvulsive or "shock" therapy), even though so many knowledgeable associates advised strongly against it. For Norman, the ECT worked like a magic wand. Here is how Graham Reed[15] described the book and its author in his preface:

> This book describes one of the most harrowing afflictions to which human beings are heir. It is the journal of a man struggling in the grip of a severe depressive illness, of the onset and course of that

---

[14] Norman Endler, *Holiday of Darkness* (Toronto: Wall & Thompson, 1982).

[15] Graham Reed was Norman's colleague in the Dept. of Psychology and Dean of the Graduate Faculty, York University.

illness, and of his ultimate triumph over it. The account is detailed and written with sincerity, yet laudably free of over-dramatization, morbidity, or self-pity. As such, it is a most moving testimony. But it is more than that. It provides us with insights to the experience of a disorder that, directly or indirectly, affects most of us at some time. Interleaved with the story is a richly informative and sophisticated study of the affective disorders and their treatment.

This combination of personal saga and scientific exposition reflects nicely the qualities of the author; and the effectiveness of the book is a tribute to his vigor, resolution, and intellectual power. Norm Endler's personality shines throughout the book. He is an honest, pragmatic man, notably immune to pretentiousness, self-regard, or neurotic hang-ups. He is, in fact, an eminently stable person. His warmth, sociability, and good cheer account largely for the affection and respect with which he is regarded by a wide circle of friends. His life revolves around two axes, one of which is his family and friends; the other, his profession as a university teacher and researcher. He is an unusually gifted man whose superior intelligence is rendered productive by unflagging energy and a capacity for organization. It is not surprising that in his chosen area of academic expertise (personality/social psychology) he is a distinguished scholar with an international reputation.[16]

---

[16] Endler, *Holiday of Darkness*, vii.

Finally; who can forget Beatty's formidable strength and devotion throughout their terrible ordeals? Norman's dedication of the book says it perfectly — "for Beatty ... forever."

Leo Zakuta
19 September, 2003

x. Fritzi Frankel

Letter to Saul Frankel on the death of his wife Freda (Fritzi)

Dear Saul,

Fritzi's death saddened us greatly. We think of her vitality, laughter, of the pleasure of her company, and of your immeasurable loss.

Annette and Leo Zakuta
20 August, 1997

xi. Peter Golick

To Margie Golick on the death of her husband, Peter

Dear Margie,

On the night before the funeral, I lay awake thinking about an event which I would have liked to narrate about Peter at the funeral. Even though I knew there could be no opportunity, I shaped it into this short speech during the night.

Peter was an interesting man with many facets to his personality, interests, and accomplishments. But I want to tell you about one incident which moved me deeply. It occurred in Barbados several years ago. I had said something to Peter that was deeply offensive and obviously painful, after having been provoked. After a sleepless night, I went to his place, accompanied by Annette and Silvie, and apologized. I anticipated a ferocious tongue-lashing and, much more likely and much worse, a curt dismissal. What happened took my breath away. Peter shook my hand warmly, and his words were, "Would you like to hear something that I've just written?" Would I indeed! He read us a touching short story about a distant event in Montreal. I was on cloud nine with relief so intense that I had to struggle to concentrate on his story. I had dreaded a deep and enduring rift, but his magnanimous response had blown the whole thing away in a moment. Few people could have done that, and certainly not I.

Leo
25 March, 1997

xii. Jim Giffen

For Jim Giffen, my close friend and colleague for over fifty years. I spoke the following words at a small gathering on 7 October, 2004, a few days after his death, and again on 26 November, 2004 at a Memorial Service in the Music Room of the University of Toronto's Hart House.

JIM

Our hearts are broken. Nothing prepared us for this loss, and there is a feeling of unreality as I write these words. Jim was always at the height of his intellectual powers — a brilliant razor-sharp mind coupled with a wickedly funny tongue. The combination was truly formidable. He could extract the nub of a discussion with a quip that made further comments superfluous. His humour was nearly always irreverent, often ribald, sometimes biting, at other times just light-hearted, but always wonderfully perceptive. The only times I can recall when that wicked wit was not present was when he talked proudly and affectionately about his children and grandchildren.

I wish I could remember more of these instances. Perhaps if there had been fewer, I might have taken more note of them, but they flowed effortlessly and endlessly like a fresh stream, never missing, and they left us laughing and laughing and laughing. He was the most engaging companion.

I have always cherished one instance, which involved putting-things-in-their-proper-perspective. It occurred in the Borden Building in the early 1960s. The scene was the main hall outside the departmental office. The chairman stood emperor-like, surrounded by the members of his court from whom he was seeking counsel. A serious problem had just arisen. A young new secretary had arrived wearing a tiny miniskirt. What should be done? (Keep in mind that this was in the early 60s, shortly before the world turned upside down, and the miniskirt was still a novelty; this one was so short, it left little to the imagination.) The chairman and his court, all male, chewed on the problem like the proverbial dog on a bone, without resolution until Jim came into sight. The chairman who, when confronted by any serious issue, almost always said, "I wonder what Jim would think" eagerly sought his advice. "Easy," said Jim without hesitation, "Just give her lots of filing on the lower shelves." That was pure Jim.

But you can find examples for yourselves. Just read Jim's account of his chairmanship in the book marking the Sociology Department's 40th anniversary. All the chairmen during that period were asked to write a piece about their tenure. Jim's had been in the worst of times. The department was bitterly divided between the militant radical students and, much worse, their faculty allies, on the one hand, and, on the other, a smaller group of us older troglodytes. (We were in our forties and fifties).

As chairman, Jim had to hold the Department together, but he was both by conviction and association clearly a member of our group, and therefore highly suspect and vulnerable. With shrewdness, diplomacy, and patience he succeeded admirably, but at great cost to himself. So, understandably, he was most reluctant to revisit that scene when asked for his contribution to the book. He said no, but was pressed to reconsider. Out of his revisiting that gut-wrenching ordeal came an account that is a funny, light-hearted, and irreverent masterpiece. Here are three typical sentences — the first and last, and one more. First, the opener: "This brief but turbulent period was notable for its excessively participatory democracy." The closer went: "And when the pot smoke settled, we thought we could see a better road ahead." I can't resist one more — about how Jim became chairman of the department: "A draft movement limped through the corridors of the Borden Building and I, unhinged by the implied flattery, agreed to a three-year term, counting time served." He often referred to committees as "the pooling of ignorance."

With Jim gone, everyone knows that the rent garment gets stitched up again somehow. But no matter how that happens, without Jim there will be a huge void in all of our lives.

Leo Zakuta

Leo Zakuta

A toast for Jim Giffen before the first meeting of our dinner group after his death. The group, which met from time to time, included the Giffens, Bretons, Elkins, Roberta Markus and ourselves. A remembrance of Jim seemed appropriate. Since Annette and I were the hosts, I offered the toast below to Jim. (I cannot resist mentioning that I came to the University of Toronto in 1952 as a one-year substitute for Jim, who was on a research leave.)

JIM

Before we begin, I want to say a few words about Jim. His presence, his wide interests, and his marvelous wit contributed so much to our enjoyment of these occasions. That wit always emanated from his razor-sharp intelligence. As you know, he and I went back more than 50 years. We were friends from the first, and he was always a most engaging companion. Nevertheless, we were less than perfectly comfortable with each other for some time. On my part this was due to envy of his cleverness; I considered it a personal failure that I couldn't begin to match it. But eventually the envy evaporated (how's that for alliteration?) and I was able just to admire and enjoy it, and as the years went by, we became very comfortable with each other. There is something comparable but also different among tennis players. The similarity is that only a few players have fine natural hand-eye coordination; most, like me, do not. The difference is that envy seldom comes into it, because people know that it's inborn. We may wish we had it, but since it can't be learned or acquired, we can only admire it without yearning for what we know is impossible. Like Jim's sense of humour.

In addition, Jim and I were, for ages, the only links to almost half of each other's life at the Sociology Dept. of the U of T — such a multitude of people and events. So his death severed my only living link to all of that, and I miss him all the more. But let us think fondly of him today. Can't you almost see him sitting here with a stream of quips and comments bubbling forth irrepressibly? So let's have a toast to Jim.

Leo Zakuta
7 December, 2005

*Frank Brodie, Bernard Goldstein, Gerry Wise, and Leo
Montreal, 1945*

*Reunion of old friends
Leo, Bernard Goldstein, Frank Brodie, and Buddy Boltuck
Toronto, 1995*

xiii. Bernard Goldstein

For Bernard Goldstein's funeral; read for me by Buddy Boltuck

BERNARD

Bernard entered my life 60 years ago when he and Bernie Perelmuter, "the two Bernies," transferred into my Grade 6 class at Alfred Joyce Public School from Guy Drummond. They made an impact because they were always among the top students. For the next 6 years Bernard and I were classmates rather than friends, though being in the top group produced a certain affinity. In 1942, our first year of college, I suddenly entered Bernard's circle of friends through an invitation to their Current Events Club, which met on Sunday evenings in members' homes to learn something about the world, a clear reflection of that time (yes, the other Bernie was in it too.)

The Club was merely the formal shell or expression of a large and, in my eyes, extraordinarily congenial group of boys and girls, all in our first year of college or last year of high school. Most were, in the words of the sociologist William F. Whyte, "college boys" (and girls), whereas I was a "corner boy," a member of a "gang" (the term was more innocuous then), not one of whom ever went to college, so the group's appeal for me was not surprising. We were all at McGill or Sir George Williams — Bernard was among the latter — but that distinction was inconsequential. Our social life was in the circle of friends, not on the campus. (We were all Jewish, the children of first or sometimes second generation immigrants, something so taken for granted that only the thought of today's audience brought it to the surface.)

Before long, Bernard and a few others persuaded us to transform the Current Events Club into a CCF Youth Club.

(The CCF, for those unfamiliar with Canadian politics, was the predecessor to the New Democratic Party, a social democratic party slightly to the "left" of the New Deal. More accurately, the CCF became the NDP through a name change.) Our less politically involved friends didn't follow us into the CCF, while Hazel Berish and Leonard Levine, among others, less fully convinced, remained on the periphery. Hazel and Leonard came faithfully to the weekly meetings, perhaps because they were the very heart of the larger group. From the outset, both Bernies and I were right in the thick of the Outremont-Woodsworth Unit, as we grandly called it, along with Arthur Rotman, Gerry Wise, and briefly, Frank Brodie. Bernard, probably because of his somewhat regal manner, was usually in the Chair, and I even then was the Secretary. Our mentors were a group of the same vintage and outlook described in the current *New Yorker* article about Irving Kristol and his set at City College's Alcove No. 1.[17] They were determined to wean us away from the "soft sentimentality" of social democracy to the "hard, tough-minded realism" of the Trotskyites. But to no avail; they made not a single convert.

Bernard was among the first to leave our circle of friends when he went to the U.S. for graduate study. He was thus spared the ignominious fate that befell our CCF Youth Group by 1946 after a mere two years of life, when a bridge-playing mania swept everything before it. I doubt Bernard would have approved.

I next met him in the summer of 1949 when he and Rhoda came to the University of Chicago to study sociology. I had been there in the same field since the previous fall. That sweltering summer Bernard and Rhoda and Buddy Boltuck and I lived in adjacent tiny suffocating apartments in a building on ... was it Woodlawn and 43rd

---

[17] Jacob Weisberg, "The Family Way," *New Yorker*, Oct. 21 and 28, 1996.

Streets on the South Side? Buddy and Bernard had met at Sir George Williams, and Bernard had probably brought Buddy into our CCF Youth Group. Buddy stayed and became a core member of the larger circle of friends, and Bernard's lasting friend. He and I used to tease Rhoda with what would now be regarded as dreadful racist jokes. Race was not the deep, scarring issue in Canada that it was in the U.S. Even though Rhoda knew our sentiments were the same as hers, and Bernard, as usual, seemed unperturbed, she couldn't help rising to the bait. Finally Bernard asked us, in terms that brooked no argument, to "cut it out." And that was the end of that. And just as well.

I didn't see Bernard for ages after I left Chicago in 1950. The next meeting that I recall was many years later, with Coralie, at our house in Toronto. After that, we seldom met until the two splendid reunions of our old and enduring group of friends, in Montreal in 1990 and in Toronto a year later. (I think Bernard initiated the first one.) At these later meetings, the change in Bernard that seemed to have begun with his association with Coralie became increasingly evident. What changed was not his convictions — his commitment to the causes of his youth remained — but his temperament. He had always had a sharp mind; in his earlier years, it had been more closely tied to a sharp tongue. He had been reserved and not easy — at least for me — to know well; a slightly acerbic manner helped to maintain an aura of aloofness. In his later years, that guard seemed to drop and he appeared to mellow. He became more genial and companionable, and was obviously happier. It is that image of Bernard which remains with me now.

Leo Zakuta
Toronto October 1996

xiv. Oswald Hall

Oswald Hall and I, Amended Version (11 October, 2007), email note

Late in the night after our gathering at the Faculty Club, I suddenly realized that I had forgotten an episode which told important things about Oswald. I was disconsolate about that omission, because it would have given everyone a better appreciation of him and his place in our Department, and my remarks would have been much better balanced. (Perhaps the afternoon's events had awakened my memory.) To correct that omission, I am sending an Amended Version (separately) of those remarks to everyone in the Dept. who was there last Friday, plus a few other people at the U of T & York. I am doing so now, having just received that list and their e-mail addresses. I will also send it to Oswald's family and the non-Dept. people who were there on Fri. The new part is on the last page.

Leo

Oswald Hall and I: Amended Version

Oswald Hall died on Aug. 31st just short of his 100th birthday. Eulogists often talk as much about themselves as about their subject. I seldom approve, but here I am doing the same thing. Though he and I were colleagues at the U of T since 1956, and his articles on the medical profession were top-notch, I will talk mostly about the one year when he was my teacher at McGill, and his unexpected effect on my teaching career.

As a McGill undergraduate, I took split honours in English and sociology. The English part was splendid, but the sociology was a flop. I had enrolled in sociology because I thought that it was related to socialism, but after the introductory course, I concluded that it was merely the substitution of jargon for simpler language. Later, I was excited by the books of Margaret Mead and Ruth Benedict, but in retrospect it was more enthusiasm, though that was important, than substance. My first vision of what sociology could be came from Herbert Blumer's excellent article on social movements, which Forrest Laviolette had assigned. It turned me instantly from a fervent CCF'er to an almost neutral observer, and it started me on the distant road to my PhD thesis and book on the CCF. (Several years later I was a student of Blumer's at the University of Chicago. He was the most inspiring teacher I ever met, with a highly unorthodox view of sociology, which I share.) The best thing I learned from Carl Dawson, the great pioneer and dean of Canadian sociologists, and for many years department head at McGill, was his emphasis on "a naturalistic approach" to sociology. Since he never explained that phrase, I didn't quite understand it then, but figured it out later. That former Baptist minister had it dead right. All of this was such a long time ago.

I have always felt that the first real sociologist that I met was Oswald Hall. Some years before his arrival at McGill, he had been a student of, and strongly influenced by, Everett Hughes, another great sociologist, at the University of Chicago. He came to McGill in the Fall of 1946, just as I entered the M.A. program, and conducted a graduate seminar. It was a large class; the veterans were returning, among them such people as Rex Lucas, Frank Jones and others, and it included us newly minted B.A.s. In our undergraduate classes, we had usually been able to conduct sociological discussions with a mixture of jargon and cloudy phrases. But not with Oswald. Not at all. He was not cutting or rough. He simply asked questions, such as "What precisely do you *mean?*" or "If we pursue that, where does it take us?" Questions like that. I felt — perhaps it was my imagination — that an undeserved miasma of resentment was building up as Oswald pulled the skids from under our easy sociological existence. But I was impressed. The course had plenty of substance and displayed Oswald's disciplined mind. He was a bit of a forbidding figure — he seemed a trifle remote — but he was a youngish man in full command of his subject and he changed the sociological landscape at McGill.

Near the end of that course, Oswald dictated to us a long and hard list of potential exam questions. One began "Part (a) Write the Table of Contents for a book titled Industry and the Community." Then I heard a loud voice saying "Part (b) Write the book." To my astonishment and dismay, the voice was mine, but Oswald didn't seem to mind.

Next year, he assigned a book for me to present at the Department's staff/graduate seminar, which he ran. Perhaps he was being mischievous, but it was also a logical choice. I was regarded as a protégé of Carl Dawson and a firm adherent of his classical ecology, and the book had the unappetizing title *Land Use in Central Boston*. But it was an exciting book in which, as Oswald probably knew, Walter Firey, its author, had laid waste convincingly to the classical ecology of Mackenzie, Park, and Burgess, Dawson's heroes. In my presentation, I endorsed Firey's viewpoint enthusiastically, doubtless to the dismay of Carl Dawson, who was, of course, present. I always wondered afterwards whether Oswald had been testing me. The answer, I think, is yes. A little later, Bernie Meltzer, who was then teaching at McGill, and would be a fellow student of mine at Chicago, told me that after the seminar Dawson had said to him, "After all these years, Leo still doesn't get it." That was sad; he had done so much for me.

When I left Chicago, Oswald, now Chairman, offered me a teaching job at McGill. I remembered what Everett Hughes, who had taught at McGill before my time, had once said to us in a class at Chicago. "I see that there are some McGill people here. McGill likes to hire its own graduates just as soon as they're through at Chicago. But if you go directly back to McGill without teaching somewhere else first, you will be regarded as less than a full colleague for some time." In any event, the matter was moot. I was already committed to Del Clark and the University of Toronto for one year to pinch hit for Jim Giffen, who was on leave.

There, Vincent Bladen, then Head of the Dept. of Political Economy, of which we were a part, once stopped me in the hall and asked me abruptly, "Who do you think is the better sociologist — Oswald Hall or X (another McGill man)?" I answered unhesitatingly, "Oswald Hall. He's very good." I have no idea how much the opinion of someone so low on the totem pole counted, but I was delighted to hear soon after that Oswald was coming to the University of Toronto.

At the U of T, he indirectly did me one great and lasting service of which I'm sure he was never aware. He was teaching a course called "Small Groups" using George Homans' fine book of the same name, and asked me to conduct the tutorials. I had conducted such groups as a graduate student at McGill; it had been an ordeal. They were dull, stiff, awkward, and unproductive, and getting students to participate was like pulling teeth. I resolved not to repeat that experience. Oswald gave me a completely free hand to do as I wished. I found a way to engage the students and to get many of them to participate willingly. I was able to do this week after week. Later I extended this technique to my own seminars. I did not ask the students to present papers in class, which I had found unproductive, but engaged them in seemingly freewheeling discussions, though, as earlier, I always had an agenda and goal in mind.

Eventually, I used this method in my undergraduate classes, even fairly large ones. I would stand in front of the lectern without notes and conduct an hour-long discussion with many willing participants. Often it involved examining their presuppositions on entering the course. In my courses on the family, sex, and status, this was easy and, I thought, useful. It was also the form of teaching that I really enjoyed, and I would keep it going as long as I could until inevitably students would approach me and say something like, "You know, Professor Zakuta, this course has been going for some weeks and I haven't even got a single note." At that point, I knew the jig was up and it was back to the duller job of lecturing again. All of that emanated from the freedom which Oswald Hall had given me as his tutorial assistant so many years before. But enough — and more than enough — of me. All I want to add is that Oswald was a valued colleague with a first-class head for sociology.

Leo Zakuta
5 October, 2007

Additional Part:

I want to tell you about an episode which I witnessed in 1981, late in Oswald's career, that illustrates so clearly something important about him and his place in our Department. It involved a PhD Oral Defence. This examination, which is held under the auspices of the graduate school, is a very formal and serious event governed by many regulations and stipulations. In this instance, a student was coming from Australia to defend her thesis.

I was present only as her nominal Supervisor. The actual Supervisor had departed to another university some time earlier, and the graduate school requires that a Supervisor be designated. I was named because she knew me better than anyone else — indeed, she had been the best student I ever had — and we could work comfortably together to complete the process and make the many necessary arrangements for the oral examination. She submitted a fine piece of work, and there should have been no problem.

The difficulty was a certain member of her Exam Committee, indeed of her Thesis Committee, which mattered even more, from another department. (The graduate school requires that the Exam Committee have at least one member from an outside department. In this case, he was from OISE.) The normal procedure is that if a member of the Thesis Committee is not satisfied with the thesis, the exam is not scheduled until the candidate has done all she can to meet his or her requirements. But I was unable to get any comprehensible response from our OISE member. I could not even tell whether he had read the thesis. I felt that he was going to make trouble because he had done the same thing in an almost identical instance a short while before. (Dennis Magill knows all those circumstances. He handled that bitter controversy for our department. I read that file with a heavy heart, because our candidate's Thesis Committee had been established long before all of this. We were stuck with him.) My efforts to elicit his response were still getting nowhere. Could that one wayward member upset the apple cart? There was no way of knowing. According to the rules of the graduate school, it takes only two negative votes at the Oral Defence to reject a thesis. Thus, if he could persuade just one member of the Exam Committee to join him in a negative vote, the thesis would founder. That would leave the candidate with only one option — to appear for a final time before exactly the same Exam Committee with a presumably improved piece of work. This time just two negative votes would automatically terminate her PhD candidacy at the U of T. We all know what that means for an academic career.

Should we have tried to remove our silent OISE member from the Exam Committee?

Not really. It was too risky. He might well have resisted, leading to a bitter struggle in the graduate school, with who knows what outcome and what rancour if we failed. Even if we succeeded in removing him, we would have to find another extra-departmental member, give that person the thesis and wait for his or her evaluation, all of which would entail a long delay. It was my duty, as Supervisor, to obtain the evaluations of the thesis from the External Examiner (from an outside university) and from the members of the Thesis Committee, and to get a sense of the reactions of the other members of the Exam Committee, as well as to schedule the Examination. I completed the first task; all were favourable, although one said he might want some additional work. That was extremely worrisome. But no matter what I did, only silence was forthcoming from our OISE member. It seemed ominous, but I felt that I had no choice but to schedule the examination.

Thus the exam was scheduled, the candidate was on her way from Australia, there was still no reply from our elusive member, and perhaps one member of the Exam Committee was not fully satisfied. It was alarming.

The exam seemed to go well, but the critical event would be immediately afterward when the candidate had left the room and the Exam Committee had to determine its verdict. Oswald, who wouldn't have known about our problem — I didn't share it with anyone on the Exam Committee — led off that discussion with these unforgettable words: "This is an occasion when the members of the Exam Committee could profit greatly from reading this thesis and listening to its defence. ..." Such praise is rare at PhD Orals and, given its source, I realized instantly that the outcome of the exam was no longer in doubt. What a glorious relief! Others added their support. But Oswald's high praise and stature had, as I knew, effectively stifled any potentially strong opposition, perhaps even from our mystery member. He was there but said very little. The thesis was accepted easily and unanimously. It was another manifestation of Oswald's generosity, his high standing among his colleagues, and his first-class head for sociology.

Leo Zakuta
6 October, 2007

xv. Tannis Lee

Letter to Richard Lee on the death of his mother, Tannis Lee. Her house was the first place I lived after arriving in Toronto in 1952.

Dear Richard,

I was saddened to read about your mother's death. I can't be sure that you remember me, but we met several times at your house where I rented a room from 1952, days after I arrived in Toronto to teach at the U of T, until it was sold in 1954. Though I did not know your mother well, and it was so long ago, I can picture her as if it were yesterday. She made such a strong impression — elegant, cultivated, intelligent, gracious, and friendly.

We often talked about American politics — I recall that she had spent some years in Washington — and especially about Adlai Stevenson, a mutual favourite, who was then involved in his first campaign against Ike. I thought myself lucky in all respects to have landed, mostly by chance, at 14 Prince Arthur, and to have known your mother.

That address has many pleasant memories for me. When the apartment building was built on that site, I moved in as soon as it was ready. Then when I married, a year later, my wife and I lived there too; our apartment overlooked Herbert Irvine's garden, which was certainly interesting. We stayed there until we moved into our present house in 1961.

If my often unreliable memory hasn't betrayed me, I believe that you went into the book publishing business. In any event, what is rock solid are my many agreeable memories of your mother and her house. I often talk about them to my own family.

Sincerely,

Leo Zakuta
12 May, 1994

xvi. Leonard Levine

Leonard has finally left us. His departure was very gradual. Even when he arrived at Leisure World 5 years ago, he was no longer the Leonard of old. Though he was always cheerful and lively there — Leisure World named him the Resident of the Month shortly after his arrival — I used to tell friends who asked about him, 'The good news is that he likes Leisure World; the bad news is that he likes Leisure World." He undoubtedly welcomed the feeling of safety and of being looked after, but the old, fastidious Leonard would certainly not have liked Leisure World. Perhaps the best thing we can say about these last 5 years is that he was so well looked after. He seemed to experience so little pain and suffering, even to the last moment. His nephew Brahm assumed the main responsibility; living in Florida, that must have been difficult. He was ably assisted by Leonard's late niece Barbara, her friend Flo, and his devoted caregiver, Elsa. Rhoda too remained especially close to him throughout, as did Bernice, Anita, and Mary.

But to tell Leonard's story properly, we must turn to his earlier years, when he was really a presence. Who has not thought, while listening to a eulogy, "If only he could have heard these words while he was still alive!" Leonard had that rare opportunity, as he heard the tributes of his friends at a splendid gathering at the Blackstones' to mark his 60th birthday. That's why I wish to repeat now what I said in his presence on that lighthearted occasion 20 years ago.

~~~~~~~~~

What is it about Leonard that inspires such universal affection? We became friends suddenly in 1942 as part of a large, congenial, and enduring group that had formed at Strathcona Academy. He and I spent much time together at McGill, partly because we were both so enamored of one particular English professor that we took all of his courses together. I was often at Leonard's house and became attached to his parents, who always received me with warmth and hospitality. On one of our first excursions together, in 1942, he and I and Frank Brodie, a charter member of our group, went together to His Majesty's Theatre to see the celebrated Paul Robeson — Jose Ferrer — Uta Hagen production of Othello. Two years later, Leonard and I walked home slowly from the Kent Theatre way out in NDG, mesmerized by the magic of Olivier's Henry V. It was part of Leonard's life-long affinity, which I share, for literature, theatre, movies, and now TV in the British mode. Its latest manifestation — now that advancing age brings with it a single-minded pursuit of pleasure — is our mutual devotion to such confections as Yes, Minister and As Time Goes By.

Our high school group flourished throughout our college years. For many of us, it was at the centre of our lives, and superseded the friendships that originated at college. Despite the many inevitable turnovers, it has continued until the present, and still accounts for many of our closest friendships. What has all this to do with Leonard specifically? It would be easy and true to say that Leonard was always at the heart of that group, but that hardly tells the story. He knew everyone and everything, and he kept the group alive through his extraordinary skills as a recruiter-cum-procurer. At first, I attributed it to his strategic location at the desk in the Y library, but it was soon clear that that was merely a convenience.

At college, for instance, it was Leonard who crossed the Great Divide and led the descent into Baron Byng territory, where he found the pickings abundant and even distinctly human. Some of us here tonight never fully regained those heights, having become tied for life to Baron Byng'ers, a singularly ungrateful lot when you consider. ... But I digress. Where was our boy? Everywhere. He had not only rescaled the heights, but was moving into the distant hills of NDG, and he could even be seen from afar on the dizzying peaks of Westmount. College may have been the great pot which melted these social distinctions, but Leonard was the chief catalyst.

However, we don't want to overlook his special skills as a procurer. (Today the term would doubtless be "social facilitator.") Leonard was always catnip to the ladies — he said enviously — and his taste in women was impeccable. The result was a steady influx of remarkable girls, far more than even Leonard could handle, and so his friends inherited the overflow. Among my most cherished friends today, 40 years later, are some of those "Leonardo girls."

I owe one special debt to his social engineering. Years later, in the summer of 1956, I came back to Montreal for a few weeks holiday. I naturally turned to Leonard to find out which girls that I had known were still in town. He needed only a moment to come up with names. The one that most appealed to me was Annette Segal, and by the time I returned to Toronto some weeks later, we were married. In fact, the only other girl about whom I had ever been serious I also owed to Leonard.

The Levine cavalcade continued throughout the years with a succession of new and sometimes surprising faces. Some of the most unlikely appeared with alarming but predictable frequency at the ski houses which Leonard and his friends rented annually in the Laurentians. Leonard was the kingfisher — or as he somehow came to be known, the Deacon — who brought these assorted trophies back to the nest. The rest of us may not have known what to do with them, but Leonard always did. More Catholic than the Pope, at least in his tastes, he attracted and was attracted to an extraordinary variety of people, and had that rare capacity to enter their lives in whatever way they felt comfortable. His range of interests and knowledge extends all the way from delighting Jonathan Miller,[18] during his stay at McMaster, by referring to an obscure literary work by Miller's mother, to discussing with my son an equally obscure rock group about which no one over the age of 30 could possibly know. He had a unique and warm relation with the children of his friends.

Some years ago, right after his arrival at McMaster, he came with Annette and me to a party hosted by friends of ours whom he had never met. Within minutes, it became clear that the hosts shared more acquaintances with him than they did with us. Were it anyone else, it might have been dismissed as a coincidence, but it only meant that Leonard had now been in Ontario for all of three weeks.

To know and be convivial with so many different people is unusual, but to be so universally esteemed and held in affection is rare indeed. It requires an indefinable

---

[18] The British polymath: physician, author, television presenter, medical researcher and historian, theatre and opera director, comedian, public intellectual, sculptor. [AZ]

magnetism, an interest in others, and a kind of social daring or adventurousness that someone like me, who is petrified of stumbling outside of his own narrow grooves, can only admire. So, it is with admiration and affection that I propose a toast to Leonard.

5 April, 1986

I will add only the toast which I proposed to Leonard nine years later (on May 27, 1995) at a party celebrating McMaster University's awarding him an Honorary Doctorate of Laws: "This signal honour which we are celebrating speaks so eloquently by itself that no words of mine can embellish it. It remains only to mark the occasion by raising a glass to Leonard."

And now he is gone.

Leo Zakuta
5 March, 2006

xvii. Rex Lucas

Rex Lucas: Eulogy for a friend and colleague. He was a tall, handsome ex-RCAF officer when we first met as graduate students at McGill.

REX LUCAS

Rex was a dear friend. It was a friendship that grew through a long association as colleagues, often through difficult times that brought a group of us together. It was not easy to get to know Rex; he had a reserve and natural dignity that kept one at arm's length, thereby permitting him to establish the degree of intimacy with which he was comfortable. He valued composure and self-control, and usually saw the display of strong feelings as a sign that these qualities were wanting. He had a strong aversion to confrontation. I cannot recall how often he reproved me with a "Now, now" or an "Oh dear," or a weary sigh, for what he clearly regarded as yet another intemperate outburst. Eventually he would say good-humouredly, "I'm not going to sit anywhere near you" as we entered departmental meetings. It took me a long time to learn to respond, "That's what you think."

However, behind his reserve and reluctance to show his feelings, one soon discovered how deeply he did care — about his students, friends and colleagues, his department and university, about everything he undertook. His loyalty and devotion inspired affection and loyalty in turn. One also responded to the superb sense of style manifested in so many aspects of his life — from his manners to his house. It was an insistence that things be done well — not simply correctly, but also elegantly.

I recall especially vividly a display of feelings that for Rex was uncharacteristically strong, open, and relentless. He was outraged by the shabby way in which our department once entertained colleagues from another university. It wasn't merely his sense of style that was offended. What he couldn't get over was our discourtesy and lack of hospitality to those who, on their part, had received us with lavish hospitality.

My strongest memory of Rex, however, is not of a specific occasion, but of our leisurely walks home together from the Borden Building on many a late afternoon. We had developed a fixed route, mostly of Rex's devising but which suited us both, that avoided the city streets in favour of the greenery. It took us past the flower beds at the Women's Union, across Queen's Park and through the grounds of Victoria College, to the corner of Bloor and Bay, where we stopped to conclude our conversation and went our separate ways. There was time on these walks to hear and tell all the stories in detail. The unhurried pace, the agreeable surroundings, and the pleasure of Rex's company make these walks a poignant memory.

Rex delighted in the absurdities, incongruities, and ironies which abound in the university as in any organization, and it was always a special pleasure to share these with him. At the same time, he had an unusual sensitivity for the vulnerability of others, which led him to make special efforts to see that their feelings were respected and that unnecessary pain was avoided. We mourn the loss of a splendid colleague and a genuine gentleman, and we miss him as a friend.

Leo Zakuta
1 October, 1978

xviii. Peter Lustgarten

Eulogy for Peter Lustgarten, my brother-in-law

PETER

A long time ago, when we were all quite young, Peter, Sylvia, and Jacob visited Annette and me in the Laurentians. Neither Abba nor our children had yet made their appearance, and Jacob was just learning to talk. His most memorable phrase was "tea milk," a concoction which he often requested — I won't say demanded — in the middle of the night. Peter always got it for him, no matter how often nor how inopportune the time. Annette and I were amused and somewhat scornful of such indulgence.

How wrong we were! The "tea milk" syndrome was simply an expression of Peter's singular, remarkable, and enduring devotion to his family. Nothing was ever too hard for him when it involved helping his wife and children, but it was more than that. He got so much pleasure from his involvement in their lives, and his pride in his sons and grandchildren was writ large for all to see. But what was so gratifying was that Sylvia, Jacob, and Abba responded to that devotion by reciprocating it fully. And his sons carried their father's example into their own families.

His family's devotion to Peter was lifelong, although it became most apparent during his last difficult period. Because he lived far away, it fell to Jacob to make especially heroic efforts to be with Peter, Sylvia, and Abba throughout their ordeal. His medical expertise was not only a strong support for all, but combined with a fierce passion for preserving quality of life. And, as you all know, Peter responded astonishingly. I first wrote these remarks in mid-April, when I thought I would need them immediately. But Jacob performed a resurrection, and Peter remained in the midst of life for an additional four and a half months. In mid-July we celebrated Jacob's birthday at a family dinner on the Lustgartens' deck on a perfect summer evening. The atmosphere was serene and easy, and Peter was an active participant from his place at the head of the table. Sharing this happy occasion with him was moving and unforgettable.

As for Abba, Sylvia described him as being "solid as a rock" throughout, words which certainly apply to her. Her patience was endless, and her help immeasurable. She was truly heroic. On a recent occasion, Peter called loudly, as usual, "Sylvia" and then added simply, "You're ok." The great gatherings of friends and relatives at Peter's bedside in the hospital and at his home showed how many lives he and Sylvia have touched. All of this was an expression of the powerful impact which Peter's warmth, friendliness, interest, and cheerful good nature had on so many people. How sad it is that this kind and caring man is now not one of us.

Leo Zakuta
9 September, 2004

xix. Diego Marin

Letter to Rick Marin, Jamie's friend, on the death of his father, a professor of Spanish at the University of Toronto

Dear Rick,

Your tribute to your father in today's *Globe* (in Lives Lived) was beautiful.

I hardly knew him, unfortunately. Ours was essentially a "Good morning" acquaintance as neighbours, and our conversations centered on exchanges of information about you and Jamie. (His pride in your achievements was manifest without ever being flaunted.) I knew almost nothing about his varied and interesting career(s). Your brief biography was therefore informative as well as moving. I wish that I had known about his participation in the Spanish Civil War,[19] which my family cared about deeply and followed closely though we lived in Montreal and knew no one who was involved in it. Although I was just a boy, these memories are still vivid, and I would have liked to talk to him about it. We all send our condolences to you and your mother on the loss of so fine a father and husband.

Leo Zakuta
2 October, 1997

---

[19] As a Republican officer.

xx. Lou Sherman

*Letter to the children of **Lou Sherman**, my long-time friend*

Dear Nicky, Joseph, and Minda,

Thank you for your note, Nicky. I am writing to all of you to let you know how one of his friends felt about your father. (Your mother knows how much I cared for him.)

After his death, I realized that even though one's best friends are sometimes irritating or difficult, I never had such feelings about Lou. It must have been because of his rare combination of qualities, both those present and absent.

Those present were his warmth and good humour, while the missing ones were pretence, guile, and malice. There was something gentle about Lou, which was all the more appealing because it was accompanied by a sharp sense of humour and a special eye for and enjoyment of the ridiculous in people's behaviour. Together, all of this made him a splendid companion and an excellent friend. I have a lasting memory of his uncanny knack for capturing accents and phrases — Jewish, West Indian, (east) Indian and others. They were so exact that it was hilarious, and we talk about it still. It was also done good-naturedly and affectionately rather than derisively, and the amusement was especially infectious because it used to break Lou up too.

For many years, we — and perhaps your parents too — fell into a domestic routine which resulted in our seeing much less of each other than we would have liked. But during the forty years in which I knew your father, I can't recall or imagine an occasion when I did not look forward to seeing him or enjoy his company. When my mother died a little over a year ago, none of the cards and letters which we received moved me as much as Lou's. It was that warmth and affection in him which inspired reciprocal feelings in his friends, and I will always think of Lou with such a mixture of sadness and pleasure.

Leo Zakuta
14 February, 1984

xxi. Stefan Stykolt

Stefan Stykolt, Jim Giffen, and Harry and Sheila Eastman became friends as undergraduates in the Department of Political Economy at the University of Toronto. They all became colleagues in that department for life, and remained close friends until the end. Stefan and Jim were co-editors of the Canadian Forum from 1954 to 1959. Jim and I, as sociologists, were also members of that department until 1963, when a Department of Sociology was established. Stefan was also the first of my U of T friends whom Annette met. They hit it off instantly. He died in 1962 at the age of 38.

My essay in *The Living Name* (University of Toronto Press, 1964) follows. There were 22 contributions in all.

STEFAN STYKOLT

On a day in mid-September, 1961, I picked my way through the building materials, furniture, and cartons that lay strewn about the corridors of the nearly completed Arts Building (later Sidney Smith Hall) in search of Stefan's office. I had just returned to Toronto after a month's absence and wanted to say hello to Stefan before getting to work. On the door of his office, however, was a typed card stating that Prof. Stykolt was unable to see students and referring them to one of his colleagues. These notices are not in themselves a cause for concern. They usually betoken a minor ailment, an out of town meeting, and the like. The one slightly discordant note was that student registration was in full swing, an activity in which Stefan, as Supervisor of Studies in Political Science and Economics, would normally be deeply involved. When I phoned him at home, he reported that he had been ill, that it was apparently nothing serious, but that he was going into the hospital for a more thorough diagnosis. We arranged that my wife and I would visit him there two days later, on the 24th.

When we arrived, Stefan looked, as usual, vigorous and exuberant. The conversation was light-hearted. After we expressed surprise at finding him in hospital, he related the sequence of events which had brought him there, said that he had undergone very disagreeable "tests" since his arrival, and then inquired about our summer. From there we drifted inevitably to "the new (Arts) building," and especially to some peculiar aspects (mainly the small windowless inner offices). This discussion was interrupted by the arrival of the doctor. We retreated to the corridor for about fifteen minutes and returned immediately after his departure. "Did he hurt you?" Annette asked Stefan playfully as we entered. "Yes," he replied in a strained voice, "not by what he did but by what he said. He said that it may be cancer." An operation was scheduled for the next week. Before we left, he asked us not to tell anyone about it, "because if the news gets around, they'll take my courses away from me," which I thought totally improbable.

Our next visit began with Stefan's jokes about his "baby dolls," as he termed them, a pair of light weight, short-legged pyjamas which we had given him because of the late-summer heat wave. He was wearing them and seemed amused and delighted by his appearance. The conversation on this occasion — and subsequently — was, except for the references to his illness, just the same as it had been on so many previous ones — largely about mutual friends, colleagues, and acquaintances, some talk about politics, and much talk about departmental politics. Stefan neither dwelt on his condition, nor did he ignore it; he talked about it with a freedom and directness that enabled his visitors to reply in kind and to leave with the feeling that they too had been courageous.

He was immediately beset by the worry that, to protect him, he might not be told about his condition. He secured a pledge that he would not be spared, from which he derived obvious comfort. Thus, right after the operation, he was told that it was inoperable cancer, and he took the news calmly. On our next visit, before hearing that diagnosis, we asked him how he was. He shook his head slowly and sadly from side to side and told us that he had been given from one to five years to live.

Within minutes, he was discussing his immediate plans and hopes. These centered on leaving the hospital — he enjoyed joking with the nurses but loathed being hospitalized — and resuming his teaching. He carefully calculated both of these dates, and reported proudly the extent of his daily walks, because he saw them as a gauge for his readiness to be discharged. He hoped to begin his fourth-year seminar on October 23rd — he thought it a piece of good luck that his seminar had coincided with Thanksgiving Day, because that meant that he would have missed only two sessions — and planned to take over his second-year course immediately after Christmas.

In the meantime, he began to tackle matters that had been accumulating, dictating letters and making arrangements from his hospital bed. He asked friends to close Burnegie, his summer place in Muskoka, for the winter and wrote them a long list of instructions. He had always been extremely attached to Burnegie and must now have wondered if he would ever see it again. The most important arrangement was the careful scheduling of visits, over which he maintained complete control until the end, even after he could no longer speak on the phone himself. Visits were by arrangement.

Visitors were essential, but Stefan wanted them to come when he had the inclination to see them and, above all, the strength to talk to them. (After Christmas, when he became weaker, he often asked visitors to check again before coming or else either he or a friend would phone to request that the visit be put off to another day. If that day was not specified, Stefan said that he would phone in a day or two to arrange it. To my knowledge, he never failed to do so.)

When he was confined to hospital or home, visitors were his chief source of interest and entertainment. Once, while still in hospital, he described with his usual attention to detail the recent visit of a colleague. "His manner," Stefan reported, "was suitably grave and funereal and he had obviously come to verify the rumours of an impending vacancy in the department." Stefan brushed aside good-humouredly my remonstrance that there might have been other motives. He was enjoying his own explanation and his rather ludicrous picture of the event. "Promotions and other things are at stake" he explained, raising his hand and tilting his head toward it in the gesture that means that's-all-very-well-but-let's-be-realistic. "Under the circumstances, what could be more natural than an inspection to clarify matters?" he concluded, thoroughly amused.

By the end of October he was back at the university, stooped, frail, his clothes hanging loosely, walking slowly and with evident difficulty, but the cut and thrust of his conversation was not one whit altered. I think that what startled and haunted others most was not that Stefan carried on so many of his usual activities, but the growing contrast between his physical appearance and the complete absence of change in the clarity and penetration of his mind, in his interests and reactions, and in his total absorption in whatever subject was under discussion.

He took over his seminar early in November; I met him in the hall immediately after, as he was about to walk home. He was tired, he said, but he was obviously very pleased. He had lectured for two whole hours, he said, and, in reply to my question, explained that he had to begin the course this way and that he had always done so. The room, he continued, was conveniently located, and when I said I would like to get it for my classes, he replied that it was not available. To acquire it, he concluded with a broad grin, it was first necessary to have cancer. Stefan's wit had always contained a streak of gallows humour. Once, after some minor reversals, before his illness, he likened himself to a "lamp post on which every passing dog stops to pee." "Life," he used to say, "is a constant downward revision of standards." He liked to cite his father's saying, "With the rich and famous, always a little patience."

He now came to the university regularly, but had begun to work even harder at home. Before his illness, he had accepted an invitation to present a paper and participate in the Colloque Franco-Canadien de l'Institut de Science Économique Appliquée in Paris in mid-December. The great appeal which France and Paris always held for him was now considerably heightened. He began preparing his paper and was making satisfactory progress despite his incessant worry about having it ready on time. But he was not recovering his strength as he had hoped, and was gradually becoming aware that he had much less time to live than he had initially thought.

Throughout this period he questioned the doctors and others who were expert in the field systematically and exhaustively about his condition. He wanted to know about every aspect of the disease. What precisely was his condition? Exactly how would the disease affect him in every subsequent stage? How would he die? What was the nature of cancer, in general? He wanted all of these questions answered frankly and in full detail; vagueness angered but did not deter him, and he probed relentlessly until they were answered and until the answers were completely consistent. It was far from a morbid curiosity; he was obsessed with the desire to know and understand. "The more he was told," one of his doctors related, "the better he accepted it." After one of these detailed clinical discussions, Stefan explained his composure in the face of death: "All my life I have been trained to accept what cannot be changed. I have checked my condition and I am satisfied that there is nothing further I can do about it."

Out of his questioning had come the full realization of how completely hopeless his illness was, and the short time that might remain. He had been weighing three main alternatives, he reported. The first was to write a book on which he had worked for a considerable time; another was to continue teaching, while the third was the trip to Paris, which would mean much hard work on his paper beforehand. He ruled out the first because he would not have the year required to complete it. The same thought applied to teaching; he realized that he would be unable to take over his second-year class, as he had hoped.

He therefore set his sights on Paris. The more fully aware he became of his condition, the more did his hopes and plans focus on the three weeks abroad — and not beyond. His chief concern now was for his strength to hold out until the trip was over. He planned the trip in three parts. The first week was to be spent seeing old friends and enjoying the city; the second would be taken up with the economics meetings, while the last week would be spent visiting an old friend in Malaga, where he would rest and relax.

With this objective uppermost, he worked hard and steadily on his paper, though he continued to meet his seminar, took friends to lunch, attended dinner parties, and visited his family and friends, once driving his car to

Kingston. He completed the paper, bought properly fitting clothes for the occasion and flew off to Paris.

Paris was a total success. For the first week and a half he enjoyed the best health of his entire illness. He went everywhere, ate everything, and enjoyed himself immensely. He began the second week in the same fashion. He presented and defended his paper ably and vigorously, and participated in the discussions and social affairs. Many of the meetings and days were very long. He described later to his friends, with a mixture of amusement and admiration, "how the French love to talk," and thus the seeming endlessness of the ceremonials. However, during the last few days of the meetings, he began to wilt visibly, and he arrived in Malaga so weak that he thought he might never get home. He therefore returned to Toronto immediately, and arrived on Christmas Day, a week earlier than planned.

From that point on, he weakened steadily and perceptibly, and remained at home, spending his time increasingly in bed. On our first visit after his return, he described his trip and especially the meetings, in detail, and went on to discuss his impressions, while in France, of the current crisis in Algeria and the position of de Gaulle. On a subsequent visit — he allotted turns to friends and relatives to prepare dinner for him — he got out of bed and dressed to have dinner with us, although he was now virtually confined to bed.

My last visit with him occurred in the latter half of January. The semi-annual meeting of the department, several days earlier, had been totally different from the cut and dried ones to which we were accustomed, although even in the latter the play of personalities and the odd preoccupations of some of his colleagues had furnished Stefan with much amusement. As Supervisor of Studies, he would have played a leading part in the recent meeting and, even from bed, he had had a hand in the preparations for it. His colleagues had come to consult him about various proposals, and phone calls were exchanged. For those with any familiarity with the department's inner politics, in which Stefan was thoroughly versed, the meeting was fascinating and, at least to some, wonderfully funny. Stefan, I knew, would have relished and savoured it immensely, and I resolved to tell him about it as fully as possible.

He was in bed when I arrived, as he was almost constantly these days. He looked terribly frail, and began by asking me to talk to him because he found it difficult to do much talking. I began to describe the meeting, about which he had heard very little. From the start, he was completely absorbed, and soon he was questioning me closely and commenting — frequently, caustically, and often at length — on the events and people. The roles which his friends had played delighted him, while he found the conduct of some others extremely funny and almost unbelievably incompetent. Time and again, referring to their "fecklessness," he shook his head, eyes half-closed in his characteristic gestures indicating stupidity almost too funny to be borne. He had predicted to a friend, he said, that this (the general outcome of the meeting) was exactly what would happen.

Frequently, the narration of these events and the remarks of the participants left him doubled up with laughter, often at his own quips and observations. Each time he indicated with his hand that the laughter was unbearably painful, his features meanwhile convulsed with amusement.

I had come to see him intending to stay no more than half to three-quarters of an hour. It was much later when I left. The entire discussion centered on the meeting and the department, and, after the first few minutes when I did nearly all the talking, there was little, apart from the physical circumstances, that differentiated it from many others in preceding years.

I saw him for the last time a week later when I arrived to pick up Annette, who had been visiting. I went in to greet him for a moment and, as I was leaving, he concluded characteristically, "Thanks for lending me Annette."

He continued to weaken steadily. He had learned to administer the injections of morphine himself, to control the pain, but was careful to balance that with the aim of keeping his mind clear. His doctor reported that his handling of the drug was thoroughly self-disciplined. What he wanted most, since his fate was beyond his control, was to have the fullest possible control over what remained of his life. Two days before he died, his doctor decreed, over Stefan's objections, that he must now have a nurse to look after him during the nights. Until then he had been cared for by friends, although he alone determined their coming and going, and he got out of bed for every meal.

On the evening before his death, upon his insistence and exerting an immense effort, he was helped out of bed and into the next room. There, with a pleased expression — he was no longer able to talk — he sat down and joined two friends. On Tuesday, February 13th, shortly after noon, Stefan died peacefully at his home. On a late spring day, in accordance with his wish, his ashes were scattered at Burnegie.

Leo Zakuta
1963

Stefan was closely attached to his family. He had no children, but was outspokenly proud of his nieces, and enjoyed narrating their exploits. He and Harry Eastman collaborated for years on important economic research that was instrumental, among other things, in the formulation of the Canada–U. S. Auto Pact. In his eulogy for Harry in 1999, George E. Connell, former President of the University of Toronto, talked about that collaboration. Shortly afterwards, I wrote him the following.

You told me that you had never known Stefan. ... He and Harry had much in common besides economics and their friendship as students. Both were "European" gentlemen in the finest sense; their tastes and many of their non-professional interests were remarkably similar. Intellectually, they were a match for each other. Since you knew Harry so well, you will understand what that says about Stefan. Where they differed most was in temperament. Where Harry was cool, reserved, and unflappable, at least outwardly, Stefan was the very opposite — outgoing, instantly convivial, and passionate. Like Harry, he had an extraordinary sense of humour, but Stefan was the "tiger burning bright." To his friends, he was an enormously entertaining companion — I never met his equal — but woe betide those who incurred his displeasure or who undertook to cross swords with him.

LZ
July, 2006

I am also including remarks spoken by Harry Eastman at Stefan's funeral, because of what they tell about Stefan and Harry. Harry began by reading a paragraph that had been written by Stephan himself.

We are here to pay our last respects to Stefan Stykolt. He was born in Zgierz, Poland on October 12, 1923. He came to Canada in January 1941 and soon became fond of his adopted country. After studies at the University of Toronto and elsewhere, he returned to Toronto in 1951 to become a member of the Faculty of the University [of Toronto]. He remained here until his death. The chief interests of his life were the companionship of his friends, and his work. May his name live among us.[20]

The words above were those of **Stefan Stykolt**. As one of his friends, I will add a few of my own. He was born in Poland, a fact we have tended to forget, so fully did he participate in life in Canada. This reminds us of how greatly Canadian life has been enriched by the war-induced arrivals of European intellectuals. His own life was enriched by his consciousness of his Polish origins and the memories of his childhood that have been maintained by his deep bonds with his parents and his love for them, his sister, and her family.

His life and work reflected his concern with truth, his powerful and elegant intellect, his loyal and affectionate nature, and his strong will. He had a very wide knowledge within his chosen field of study: economics. His specialty was the study of industrial organization, but he was also interested in pure theory and in international economics, and had contributed articles to learned journals in all these fields. He had a thorough acquaintance with the literature in most other areas of economics. His clear intelligence and felicity of expression illuminated the questions to which he turned; his quick mind aided those privileged to engage in discussions with him.

He was an able teacher. He had great natural talents. He had a spontaneous clarity of expression that was based on an intimate knowledge of the material he was presenting and on a remarkable command of language.[21] He had a sympathetic

---

[20] From *W.J. Stankiewicz* (ed.), *The Living Name: A Tribute to Stefan Stykolt from Some of his Friends* (Toronto: University of Toronto Press, 1964).

[21] Even more remarkable, perhaps, for one who didn't encounter the English language until age 17, was his

concern for students as individuals. They felt this and responded to it. He was profoundly convinced of the usefulness of knowledge and of logical thought, and imparted to his students a sense of urgency to learn and a recognition of the significance of the subjects. He supplemented these qualities by painstaking care in the preparation of his lectures and in all his many contacts with his students.

He found satisfaction in his work, for he knew that discovering and imparting knowledge is the function of a professor, and his success, the sole real and permanent reward. His search for truth had another aspect, which was his care for exactitude. He was called upon to perform many administrative tasks. Whether it was as co-editor of the *Canadian Forum*, or in the administration of university or his personal affairs, his logical mind required a precise and systematic approach. He was conscientious because he had always in his mind a conception of the general framework in which he was working, and was conscious therefore of the long-run consequences of overly-casual conclusions. His ability to create a model of the universe appropriate to the task at hand and his toughness of mind made him decisive as well as conscientious.

His attempts to grasp reality were not limited to the relatively easy sphere of economic analysis and the administration of ordinary affairs, for he was a man of wide culture. He sought to understand all human behaviour. To some extent also, he sought the meaning of man's existence, of his own existence and destiny. He had a wide and growing

---

> thorough and deft command of its impolite vocabulary. He learned to mix it with the polite one with startling effectiveness. I also recall a different matter. In the 1950s we went to a performance of black, female, African dancers, all topless; it still strains credulity 50 years later. When we emerged from the theatre not knowing what to say, Stefan was the first to speak: "My, those girls have straight backs." [LZ]

knowledge of English and French literature and excellent critical judgement. He admired Proust above other authors and was a member of the society: Les Amis de Marcel Proust.

Stefan Stykolt had a very wide circle of acquaintants and friends. He enjoyed social occasions, and his liveliness of spirit and incisive wit made him widely known. His friends cherished him for his warm and loyal nature, for his unfailing courtesy and consideration for them, for his intelligence, his erudition, his wise judgment, his good taste, his resolution of spirit, and his courage. The combination of traits that were his, and the strength of his personality, bound them so strongly to him that we are faced now in our lives with an immense gap, very imperfectly filled by memory. He showed his high qualities during his last days. He sought to understand his fate. He controlled the conditions in which he lived until the very end. His courage never failed him. He died nobly, an undefeated spirit. May his name live among us.

Harry Eastman
February 1962

xxii. Gerry Wise

Letter to Dorothy Wise, on the death of her husband.

GERRY WISE

We heard about your terrible loss yesterday from Chana Paleyew. Gerry and I were good friends from 1942 to about 1948. I have such fond memories of him — cheerful, very funny and good humoured. We didn't meet again for almost 50 years, when he recognized me (or heard my name) on the tennis courts in N.D.G. I had to do a double-take, because the familiar large shock of hair was all gone, but when we established our identities, we embraced and hugged like long-lost brothers. It went on and on, oblivious to the curious stares of the people around us. Our last meeting, you may recall, was at our house, where, as is usual with good friends from the distant past, the intervening years melted away immediately as if they had never existed. He was such a lovely man.

Annette and Leo Zakuta
31 January, 2003

xxiii. Keile and Hershel Zakuta (my parents)

MA

In accordance with my mother's wish, there will be no ceremony. She wanted this event to be as simple as possible. You all know what an extraordinary person she was. You will understand why I feel that no words of mine can do justice to her memory. The light has gone out of our lives.

Leo Zakuta
14 October, 1982

(After my remarks, my uncle, **Joe Ain***, spoke extemporaneously and very movingly about his sister, my mother.)*

PA

Pa's feelings about this occasion were the same as Ma's, so we will proceed just as we did then. His great physical stamina enabled Pa to survive Ma for three and a half years, but his life really ended with hers.

There is only one thing to say now — to Ken. I would like you to know, Ken, just in case you don't, how fully both Ma and Pa appreciated your extraordinary care and solicitude for them, not only in their last illnesses, but for so many years before. Ma talked about it always — she was, of course, the spokesman for both — about your constant concern for their comfort, anticipating their every wish and requirement. "He doesn't know what to do for us! Nothing is ever too hard for him," she used to say. That was always such a comfort for me too, because there was so little I could do. I'm grateful for the excellent care which you and Bea arranged and managed for both of them when they became increasingly helpless. In this way both of them were able to end their days in their own home in peace and comfort. Your devotion was obviously on Pa's mind when he told Ma something she repeated to me: "I had a hard youth but a very good old age."

Leo Zakuta
31 March, 1986

Hershel, Keile, Leo, Sarah, and Joe
Montreal, 1975

Leo Zakuta

Annette, Leo, Arnie, Bea, Michael, Jamie, Sharon, and Kenny
Zakuta (standing)
Hershel, Silvie, and Keile Zakuta (seated)
Keile's 80th birthday, 1978

Leo in the Procession at Silvie's graduation
University of Toronto, 1987

II WRITINGS

i. Membership in a Becalmed Protest Movement[*]

"In politics the thing to do is build yourself an army." The remark is attributed to the late Jimmy Hines, a successful Tammany Hall politician of the 1930's. In June, 1945, half way between the Regina Manifesto and the Winnipeg Declaration, the Co-operative Commonwealth Federation, at the head of the largest army in its history, prepared for the reward of virtue and patience — power in Ottawa and Ontario. The problems of building that army and then maintaining it under the adverse conditions following June, 1945, constitutes the theme of this paper.

In its first decade the C.C.F. had successfully welded a united, national organization out of a federation of parties and groups along a social-democrat and agrarian-protest spectrum. The absence of a New Deal party gave the "movement," as its members still call it, its opportunity. Its central bond was a common hatred of capitalism, allegedly responsible for the depression and its accompanying hardships. It was, however, less than unanimous about the remedy. The Regina Manifesto of 1933, the party's initial declaration of faith and intentions, was framed in the social democratic tradition. "No C.C.F government," it concluded, "will rest content until it has eradicated capitalism." But no statement of policy could ever avert the inevitable debate on "how far" and "how fast" socialism should be implemented.

The topography of C.C.F. beliefs can be roughly charted by identifying its closest friends and mentors and its

---

[*] "Membership in a Becalmed Protest Movement," paper presented at the annual meeting of the Canadian Political Science Association, Ottawa, June 14, 1957; published in *Canadian Journal of Economics and Political Science* 24:2 (1958), 190-202.

ideological boundaries on the "right" and "left." Its chief, though not unanimous, favourites have always been the Labour and Social Democratic parties of the Commonwealth, Scandinavia and especially Great Britain. Its supporters ranged all the way from people who were made uneasy by talk of socialism despite endless assurances, to those drawn enviously to the glamour of revolutionary intrigue and virile, uncompromising militancy which they associated with Communism and Trotskyism. While these "left wingers" pressed the leaders constantly to declare themselves on the questions of "how far" and "how fast," the great majority entrusted these matters to the leaders and concentrated instead on building the organization.

Besides constructing a national organization, the C.C.F. showed signs of strength in most of the west in the 1930's. But after almost a decade, the debt side of the ledger was more impressive. In the 1940 federal election the C.C.F. made no gains over the election of 1935 (despite the disappearance of its chief 1935 rival, the Reconstruction party), electing only three members outside Saskatchewan and only one east of Manitoba. The party's ranks were split and its leadership uncertain about a war policy as its pre-war pacifism died a lingering death. East of Ontario, C.C.F. strength was virtually non-existent, and in that key province it was extremely weak.

The party's hopes of national success have always hinged on extensive support in Ontario. But from 1935 to 1942, through one provincial and two national elections, not a single C.C.F. candidate was elected in Ontario. The initial crusading impetus was spent by the mid-thirties, as a sharp decline in membership indicated. The Communists had weakened the party's left flank and disturbed the rest of the organization by a persistent, coaxing United Front appeal. There was no money, and organization was rudimentary and ineffectual. In short, although it was never very radical, the C.C.F., at least in Ontario, had come to resemble the classic image of the radical sect. It was small, poor, ineffectively organized, and isolated from the larger society. Much of its energy was directed at internal targets in a grinding series of accusations, hearings, and expulsions designed to maintain ideological purity, especially against the threat from the "left," and to find scapegoats for its failures. After almost a decade of existence, the C.C.F. was, to all appearances, no more than another western protest movement.

In view of Ontario's critical importance to the C.C.F., it is probably significant that the reversal of the party's national fortunes began in that province in 1942, with the dramatic victory in the South York by-election. The C.C.F. had begun to build its army late in 1941. It marshalled an unprecedented force of volunteers and money for the South York campaign and for those that were to follow. In the next few years the party won one dazzling victory after another, often surpassing even its own expectations. Like many organizations, the C.C.F. often faces the tricky problem of generating sufficient optimism at elections to mobilize the ranks and infect the sympathetic and of simultaneously avoiding the pitfalls of exaggerated hope. Unrealistic expectations tend to dishearten the faithful and mislead the public into maximizing the party's defeats and minimizing its victories. But suddenly the C.C.F.'s "optimists" became its "realists" and the rest the fainthearted. When it faced the "double election" of June, 1945, the party held office in Saskatchewan and was the official Opposition in Ontario, Manitoba, and British Columbia. It had some reason, therefore, to believe that power nationally and in Ontario was not far off.

That sight, however faint, of the Celestial City played an important part in the C.C.F.'s reaction to subsequent defeat and adversity. Recalling that time of brimming confidence, one should be aware that it was not so much the prospect of fulfillment as its suddenness that took the party by surprise. Belief in inevitable triumph has always been a fundamental article of socialist, and sectarian, faith. The 1936 report of the Ontario C.C.F. executive concluded with the affirmation that "The stars in their courses are fighting for the cause of socialism." Socialist doctrine had forecast both the wandering in the wilderness and the eventual arrival in the promised land. What it had not provided was a timetable of these events.

On June 4, 1945, however, the voters of Ontario cut the C.C.F. representation in Queen's Park from thirty-four to eight, and one week later, of the 245 members elected to the House of Commons, only twenty-eight represented the C.C.F., all but one of them from the west. Ever since, despite several temporary upsurges, the party has been fighting a retreat — gradual, orderly, but relentless. Its perspective has shifted from expanding to holding steady although it can still generate considerable energy for that task.

When the C.C.F. faced its followers after these two disastrous defeats, it could no longer rally them against adversity in the same way as it had after earlier setbacks. Not only had the condition of the country altered; the C.C.F had become a very different kind of party during its years of success and, in the process, lost much of its protective insulation against defeat. The changes in the C.C.F. — ideological, structural, and emotional — and the party's adaptation to them, are the subject of the larger study of which this paper is a part. They are discussed briefly here under the headings: Beliefs, Organization, and Morale.[1]

---

[1] The study concentrates on the Ontario section of the C.C.F. although at times it embraces the national organization and at others it focuses on metropolitan Toronto, from which the C.C.F. draws more votes, members, dollars, and leaders than from any other community. The information is based on observations as a participant in a riding association and

Beliefs

William Kornhauser's impressive study of American liberals and radicals[2] illuminates the hazards that beset these political groups. The chief threat to a radical organization is that its uncompromising rejection of the social order may isolate it from its audience through derision, unpopularity, fear, and even repression. Liberal groups, on the other hand, may lose their distinctive identity and sense of purpose if they fail to differentiate themselves clearly from the traditional parties. This danger has been particularly acute for American liberal organizations because the Democratic party has been so potent a rallying force for liberals and even socialists since 1932.

The absence of such a force in Canada during this period permitted the C.C.F. to attract a much greater range of support than any American equivalent. Except for the Communists and some insignificant Trotskyite splinter groups, the C.C.F. has virtually monopolized "left of centre" politics, a position which relegated to secondary importance the question of whether it was primarily liberal or radical at any point. The C.C.F.'s product required few minor differentiations in the absence of serious competition for the potential market. Despite these advantages, the party has not found it easy to steer a safe course between the twin

---

numerous other C.C.F. groups over a five-year period, and on some formal interviews and many informal conversations with a wide variety of C.C.F.ers. Recently the Ontario leadership very generously gave me access to its records, including the minutes of the meetings of its top councils since they began, membership records, financial data, and the like.

[2] William Kornhauser, "Organizational Loyalty: A Study of Liberal and Radical Political Careers," unpublished Ph.D. thesis, University of Chicago, 1953.

shoals of isolation and loss of identity. Its consistent lack of success before 1942 indicates its earlier isolation from the main stream of Canadian politics, while its most pressing recent danger appears to be the absence of sharp distinctions from the other political parties. Some documentation of these points is in order.

If the C.C.F. of today is compared with the party before the war, the missing qualities are the most striking. Along with so many socialist parties, the C.C.F. has lost much of its indignation and, with it, most of its hope of the socialist utopia. The "capitalist boss" has almost vanished as a symbolic, rallying enemy, and with his disappearance the sectarian spirit fled. Mitchell Hepburn and George Drew, convenient short-run ogres, have departed, and the C.C.F. has had to make do with C. D. Howe and share him with the Conservatives at that.

The nature of the C.C.F.'s thinking in the 1930's is evident not only in the concluding passage of the Regina Manifesto, quoted previously, but in passages such as the following, taken from the report of the Ontario executive to the provincial convention in 1936:

> ... every C.C.F. member should insist and understand that in no sense is the socialism of the C.C.F. mere reformism, mere gradualism, or compromise with capitalism of any kind. A C.C.F. government attaining power must proceed promptly, drastically, thoroughly to liquidate the power of capitalist forces and secure for the socialist party in control of the organs of the state the most ample assurance that capitalist interests could not sabotage, weaken or overthrow socialism. The C.C.F. must recognize and prepare for the most ruthless opposition ... must be fully conscious of the opposition that will seek to destroy our efforts and the danger of the final stages of the struggle. Anyone who does not understand the nature of the struggle has no place in the

C.C.F. ... The C.C.F. is on the uttermost left in objective and understanding, or it is nowhere.

In the 1956 Winnipeg Declaration, a major statement of policy by the national convention, the C.C.F.'s supreme authority, the party finally abandoned the vision of the classless utopia. The Declaration's tolerance of private enterprise was by no means a new policy for the C.C.F. What made the document so significant was that it represented the party's decision to enunciate its revised beliefs in the most open, official, and binding way possible.

Finally, the brief conversation below, which occurred at a C.C.F. educational conference to discuss the Winnipeg Declaration, illuminates the change in the party's outlook. The participants were divided into small discussion groups. The group of four, whose remarks are recorded here, consisted of a top Ontario leader, two veteran local "leaders," i.e., executive members of riding associations, and one rank and file member. The last fortunately was a member of the left wing minority or the following conversation would never have ensued:

> Group chairman (local leader): "Now we come to the question of whether we can get rid of inequalities. Can differences in income be eliminated?"
> Rank and file member: "We should eliminate these differences. They're getting greater all the time."
> Chairman: "I don't think that's necessary or desirable."
> Top leader: "What we need is not equality of income. We have to raise the floor of wages."
> Rank and file member: "We should have a ceiling on wages. Factory workers make just as great a contribution as any others and they're just as valuable."
> Chairman: "No, they're not as valuable and important. It's easy to replace them."
> Top leader: "Some people are content on $3,000 a year for example. Others want more and are willing to pay for it in work, education and responsibility."

Rank and file member: "But the factory workers have to have dignity as well, and socialism has to provide it."

Top leader: "Certainly. That's why we're so in favour of unions. The problem is to get people to take responsibility. Most people don't want more. The more ambitious ones want more and look for it. I can't be horrified by ambition, by people who want to get ahead and become president of the union or of the company."

Rank and file member: "Isn't it our job to protect people from the more powerful?"

Top leader: "Yes, that's what we have to do ... but we can't prevent leadership, or do without it."

Chairman: "Yes, and don't forget the sacrifices the leaders have to make. The responsibility and worry doesn't end at 5 o'clock. For instance, the president of a company may be phoned late at night because something's gone wrong."

Top leader: "What gives me a pain are those people who don't work but who go to meetings of directors .... But we can get at those deadheads through taxation."

Second local leader (speaking for the first time): "There can't be complete planning without interfering with personal liberty. The mesh would be too small."

Rank and file member: "Prices are always getting higher. Every time that you go to the store everything is a few cents up."

Perhaps some of these people were pushed a little beyond their beliefs in this discussion. Nevertheless, their remarks require no further elaboration or interpretation. An interesting sidelight to this episode is the fact that the *New Commonwealth,* the Ontario C.C.F.'s newspaper in the 1930's, contains far harsher indictments of capitalism than a series of articles by the chairman of this discussion group.

The C.C.F.'s altered attitude to private enterprise and its appearance of differing from other parties on immediate rather than long-range objectives led a Toronto paper to warn it of " ... the danger ... [of] ... losing its distinctive identity in the public mind. CCFers will now come closer to fitting Prime Minister St. Laurent's definition of them: 'Liberals in a hurry.'"[3] However, who would venture to

---

[3]   *Toronto Daily Star*, Aug. 2, 1956.

predict whether the C.C.F. would gain or lose from such a public image as long as there is no Canadian equivalent of the Democratic party to swallow it up when it gets too close? While the Liberals were in office, the C.C.F. continued to enjoy a near monopoly of the "left of centre" position. If the Conservatives continue to hold office and push the Liberals "leftward," the C.C.F.'s problems of maintaining a distinctive identity may be just beginning.

Organization

The main stages in the C.C.F.'s career constitute the framework of this section. Although precise dividing points in such matters are always rather arbitrary and some overlapping is inevitable, these phases divide the C.C.F.'s 24-year history neatly and effectively into three 8-year periods. The first period, 1933-41, corresponds precisely to the years of isolation described earlier. The second period, 1942-9, begins with the C.C.F.'s upsurge and ends with the resounding defeat in the 1949 federal election, which clearly terminated its tenuous claim to be a major party. Throughout the third period, 1950-7, despite its continuing strength in Saskatchewan and British Columbia, the C.C.F. was again a minor party nationally, though far different in character than it had been in its first phase.

Official Structure

Before the changes in the C.C.F.'s organization are examined, the party's basic constitutional structure must be looked at briefly because it provides the more permanent framework within which these changes have taken place. The official organization is on three main levels. The riding associations are the basic units. Their delegates, the delegates of the affiliated organizations, and the outgoing provincial council constitute the C.C.F.'s annual provincial convention, the final authority in provincial affairs. The convention and the larger ridings elect the provincial council, the governing body in the province between conventions. The provincial council, in turn, elects the executive, which meets much more frequently to plan and oversee the party's daily operations. It does so largely through standing committees which report to it regularly. Nationally, the ridings, the national convention, the national council and executive, and the affiliated organizations are linked together in the same way as the corresponding provincial bodies.

The provincial organizations have considerable autonomy, and the national office usually deals with the ridings through the provincial body. The ridings too have some independence. As may be expected in any organization with such a division of powers, jurisdictional issues may at times be troublesome. Finally, the party's administrative personnel are mainly voluntary; only a small portion of the group is paid.

From Sect to Party

Discussing the C.C.F.'s history and changes, a veteran top leader expressed the common view of his colleagues: "We had no organization worth talking about until around '42 or '43. That's when we began building a real organization." He was referring to the lengthy process of expansion, "centralization," as he put it, and consolidation in which the structure of the party and the participation of its members were altered beyond anyone's anticipation. Reorganization went on throughout the second period. Expansion and centralization highlighted its first half, and the second half, following the setbacks of 1945, was primarily a time of consolidation. When the third period began, around 1950, the Ontario C.C.F. had dug in, as will be seen later.

Organizationally, the party was poorly prepared for the success which began to overtake or perhaps overwhelm it in 1942 and 1943. It lacked the money, personnel, and experience to capitalize fully on these developments by building a solid, durable structure, especially outside Toronto and a few other urban, industrial centres. As the quest for power became more real and urgent during these years, the C.C.F. leaders in Ontario felt hampered by what they regarded as serious weaknesses in organization, which they set out to correct.

They first attacked the enduring problem of the C.C.F. clubs, which, until the early 1940's, were the basic units of the party in Ontario. They were somewhat more autonomous than the later riding associations, and the recurrent problems caused by their structure stimulated the C.C.F. to build a political party out of its rather diffuse and spontaneous movement. While every club had a territorial base, many ridings contained more than one club with no co-ordinating body. Many of the resulting jurisdictional and ideological battles within ridings were recorded in the minutes throughout the 1930's. When the provincial council and executive attempted to arbitrate, they exposed themselves to angry charges of dictatorial interference. In addition there was considerable friction and irritation which never reached the official record.

The frequent lack of harmony and close contact among the clubs in a riding made them very unwieldy election organizations and eventually contributed to their replacement, wherever possible, by riding associations. In creating these latter bodies, the party's leaders were also concerned about the problem of discipline. By reducing the autonomy of the individual clubs or by merging their members in a larger riding association, the C.C.F. also hoped to reduce the embarrassing menace of Communist overtures. But mounting membership and electoral success provided the chief impetus to the party's efforts to build an organization suited to fight elections and to accommodate the thousands of new members. Their rapid influx — the Ontario C.C.F. multiplied its membership almost ten times between 1942 and 1945 — made the change from clubs to riding associations all the more imperative in the eyes of party officials.

The flood of new members apparently alarmed many "old timers" who sadly saw "their movement" slipping out of their hands and worried about the motives and beliefs of the newcomers, whose arrival they regarded as a mixed blessing. Many new members were thus made to feel less welcome than they had anticipated. A top leader, in an unexcelled position to know this situation, described many of the clubs as "very ingrown little groups," an indication that the administration regarded them as ill-suited both for electoral purposes and for incorporating the tide of new members. It hoped that the riding associations would be much better suited to the requirements of a vigorous and rapidly expanding organization, because they would be larger and somewhat more impersonal than the clubs and would therefore be freer of the impenetrable barriers of cliquishness that had arisen from the long and intimate association of small groups. But above all, it regarded the "old timers" as primarily "talkers" and the newcomers as potential "doers."

Among the other structural changes which accompanied growing success were the selection of the first provincial leader in Ontario in 1942 and an effort to develop a larger, more professional staff with a clearer division of work. The C.C.F.'s election procedures in Ontario were standardized and brought under greater central control. In 1944 the first C.C.F. Government took office in Saskatchewan after a landslide victory. That triumph was regarded as further proof, if any were needed, of the value of riding and poll organization. Ever since, the C.C.F. has sought to emulate the business-like organization of the Saskatchewan section and, incidentally, of the other political parties, which it resembles in that respect.

The reorganization that accompanied the successes of the early 1940's was not accomplished without cost. The pre-war clubs possessed some characteristic sectarian features. They were usually smaller and more sociable than the less spontaneous riding associations, since any small group of friends could form its own C.C.F. club. (Thus the cliquishness which later was such a handicap to an expanding organization was, in the earlier period, an important asset to one which clung precariously to existence.) The members of these dubs were often united by a common view of themselves as a small core of rebels and visionaries in a hostile and apathetic society, dedicated to fulfilling the prophecy of a new and just social order. The relative isolation of the clubs from the community around them and their orientation towards the more distant future combined with their easy sociability to produce in them intense activity and interest. Many of the clubs were able to involve a limited number of members quite deeply, though the involvement was at times as short lived as it was intense. In the depression era of low earnings, widespread unemployment, and surfeit of leisure, the party membership card was for many C.C.F.ers a low-cost ticket to politics, social life, and entertainment. In the words of a former leader, "For us the CCF was mother, father and the church."

Of course, the war and full employment had an incalculably large hand in changing all that. But, in addition, the C.C.F.'s success had turned the party's interest to organization. Meetings were held monthly instead of weekly; abstract and more remote political discussion was replaced by devotion to organizational matters which, in the words of one leader, "are of interest only to those already involved." As the clubs gave way to riding associations and abstract political discussion to interest in organizing, the earlier social and intellectual bases of involvement became seriously jeopardized. For a while the enthusiasm that swept the party in its triumphant period infused the riding associations. Significantly, membership soared throughout the C.C.F. from 1942 to 1945, but plummeted immediately after the twin defeats of 1945. When the party's fortunes and prospects declined, many of the earlier sectarian conditions that had been conducive to involvement were irretrievably gone. In the intervening years, both Canada and the C.C.F. had changed considerably. The former had experienced several years of prosperity and the latter was becoming a genuine political party, primarily concerned with elections and organization. Such a party has a different source of cohesion than the radical sect. It depends much more on the prospect of immediate success than the sect, which thrives on hope long deferred.

During its second phase, too, the C.C.F. began to enlist strong support from the trade unions. Its membership had always contained many individual trade unionists, but sharp divisions existed in both the party and the unions on the question of establishing official relations, as the British and American trade union traditions about political action vied for supremacy. The C.C.F.'s decision to welcome union affiliations and the rise of the C.I.O. in Canada broke the impasse and brought organized support to the party in the form of affiliations and endorsements by union bodies.

The main reinforcements came from several of the new, mushrooming C.I.O. unions, many of whose officers were C.C.F. leaders or sympathizers. This system of interlocking directorates opened to the party far-reaching connections, first in the C.C.L. and recently in the merged union body [CLC, AZ]. Most of the officials who bridged the gap between the C.C.F. and the unions entered the unions through the C.C.F. rather than the other way about. The leaders who formed the nuclei of several of these unions were recruited from the C.C.F. on the basis, among other things, of personal and ideological affinities.

The careers of these men have followed a somewhat similar pattern. Before their unions were established, they were ardent C.C.F.ers. In the C.C.F.'s second period, 1942-9, they were deeply involved in the unions and in the party, rising in both these growing organizations. But since then, their union work has clearly come first, although their attachment to the party has continued, as is attested by their continued membership, the fact that they themselves and, in some cases, their organizations, have made sizable financial contributions, and by their efforts on its behalf in the labour congresses and federations. The Political Action Committee has been a very tangible and important expression of their continued support. The reason why they recently have left the leadership and administration of the C.C.F. to others is, however, a subject for later discussion.

Consolidation: Finances, Membership, and Administration

With the help of the unions, the party eventually established a relatively solid financial base. It took time for the idea of supporting the C.C.F. to move down and across union hierarchies. The decline and fall of the Labour Progressive party, the C.C.F.'s chief enemy in the unions, undoubtedly eased the way to official support. However, continued C.C.F. weakness at the polls may lead to an "agonizing reappraisal" regarding the maintenance of that support; such talk has been in the air in the last few years.

The party's unprecedented current financial stability is by no means attributable to the unions alone. Most of its funds still come from its own members. The sharp and protracted decline in membership after 1945 precipitated an acute financial crisis which the C.C.F. countered by initiating a highly successful system of graduated membership fees, resulting in increased per capita contributions. The decline in membership was arrested by the beginning of the third period and, since then, the membership figures have displayed unprecedented stability.[4]

Stable membership, greater per capita contributions, and the financial assistance of the unions made the party more solvent, and it was therefore able to obtain a larger, more professional, and more economically secure administrative staff than ever before. The efforts of this staff, particularly in conducting regular financial and membership drives, have contributed significantly to the party's consolidation. But a more adequate interpretation of its recent stability must await the next section of this paper.

Morale

This difficult term must be defined briefly here as a blend of the shared desire for and confidence in organizational success. The sources and indices of C.C.F. morale form the theme of this section; the discussion proceeds from the external and tangible aspects to the more internal and intangible. It begins with the C.C.F.'s record in attracting votes, members, and money and then discusses the more elusive relation between participation and expectations of success. Finally, beyond these other aspects of involvement and motivation, lie the twin, though not completely identical, questions of the individual's commitment to the party and its claims on him. These will be considered in turn.

---

[4] Immigrants. especially British trade unionists and Labour party supporters, appear to have been an important source of C.C.F. recruits in the latest period.

Membership and finance have been discussed previously. With respect to votes and public support, the C.C.F. has lost ground gradually but seriously. In October, 1943, the Gallup Poll showed the party leading the field nationally, with the backing of 29 per cent of the electorate. In the election of June, 1957, it received 11 per cent of the vote. In Ontario provincial elections, the C.C.F. vote has receded from a high of 32 per cent in 1943 to 17 per cent in 1955. In the federal campaign of June, 1957, the party's primary objective was to retain third place against the challenge of Social Credit.

Participation and Expectations of Success

Despite official reassurances, some leaders take a pessimistic view of the C.C.F.'s prospects. An example is the following assessment made at a meeting of the national council early in 1956 by one of the very top leaders, whose position perhaps facilitated a measure of detachment:

> ... We have to look very realistically over the period of the last 10 or 15 years and recognize that we have lost ground. The best indication of our weakness is that the old-line parties are no longer afraid of us. The average person on the street doesn't keep backing a fighter who has been knocked out five or six times in a row and has no prospects of ever becoming champion. You have to have a party that looks as though it is going somewhere, a party that is increasing its prestige and its strength, and frankly I don't think we are.[5]

The following assessment of the members was made by someone who has been close to many top leaders for a long

---

[5] Minutes of the C.C.F. National Council, Jan. 13-15, 1956.

time, and is still fairly active, despite the tenor of his remarks: "Well, you know it's getting more and more hopeless, and they're older, tired and disillusioned. They put their efforts into other organizations, unions, churches and so on. ... It's just that we're dying from lack of oomph. The reason is simply that our cause has disappeared." Another very prominent leader commented to a colleague in private conversation: "Even if the CCF doesn't survive in its present form, it will survive in some other form."

The number, types, and social position of the party's candidates have changed noticeably, especially in the last period. The total number of candidates has declined steadily since 1945, the peak year, both nationally and in Ontario. In the two earlier periods, at least 90 per cent of the C.C.F. candidates in Toronto were from the middle class; in the recent period that figure dropped to 73 per cent. For the first time many of these candidates were women and industrial workers.[6] These two groups accounted for two-thirds of the party's candidates in Toronto in the 1957 federal election. The number of "sacrifice" candidates, as they are privately called, has grown and some have appeared in former C.C.F. strongholds.

As hopes gradually diminished after 1945, many C.C.F. voluntary leaders drifted away from administrative involvement. Personal achievements and ambitions, growing family obligations, and the heavier demands of their careers, including increased union responsibilities, gnawed steadily at the time and energy available for the party. The senior

---

[6] This development does not reflect a change in the composition of the party's general membership or of its local leaders in Toronto. No corresponding change in the ratio of middle-class to working-class members has occurred in either of these groups in the recent period. In both the second and latest periods, middle-class members constituted half the leadership of the riding associations and just over one-quarter of the total membership.

salaried officers were involved in a somewhat different tug of war. Money and careers were usually the critical considerations for them, as time and energy were for the voluntary leaders, and discouragement was the common factor in both equations. Although party salaries increased substantially over the pre-war pittances, the salaried officers were still unable to enjoy the mode of life available to most of their middle-class associates both inside and outside the C.C.F., most of whom were in more lucrative careers in the professions, business, and trade unions. The struggle for a middle-class standard of living on a party salary drove some deeply into debt. As the party's prospects waned, these officials weighed increasing family responsibilities and attractive opportunities outside the party against their heavy investment of years, efforts, hopes, and ambition in the C.C.F. Family obligations were the doorway through which they usually made their exit, fortified by the feeling that the long years of "sacrifice" merited a respite and relief. With varying degrees of involvement, both the salaried and voluntary leaders usually remained in the party. More significant is the paucity of young, vigorous, and ambitious aspirants to replace the original nucleus, now older, more tired, and involved elsewhere.

Some C.C.F. representatives have followed more individualistic political careers, notably in municipal politics, and have usually been drawn away from the party. The C.C.F. seeks their active participation in the organization, but compliance with these claims tends to limit their opportunities to establish contact and support in the other associations of the community, the life-blood of a conventional political career. But in evading the party's claims, they may expose themselves to the suspicion of seeking too personal a following and the accusation of expediently turning their backs on the party that gave them their start. Though scarcely audible now, the old sectarian alarm that the leaders may become too deeply involved in the outside world is still sounded, occasionally by the left-wing "purists," as they are scornfully called.

Although most C.C.F.ers, including the leaders, endorse and encourage these individualistic careers, the resentment and suspicions of the hard-shelled minority act as an irritant and repellent. In addition, during the course of building a career, especially in "non-partisan" municipal politics, these representatives tend to become involved in many other groups besides the C.C.F and become concerned with their problems and perspectives. Finally, the decline in the C.C.F.'s political power lessens the value of a connection with it for leaders with other sources of support. The party's weakness also discourages them from seeking or even accepting provincial or federal nomination.

Consequently, C.C.F. candidates, at least in Toronto, are less likely to be graduates of municipal politics than their Liberal and Conservative opponents. The relative obscurity of its candidates tends to reduce the C.C.F. vote and with it the party's future expectations, thereby making it even harder to obtain a strong candidate next time and prolonging the spiral of defeat and discouragement. All these signs of demoralization tempt one to conclude that "nothing fails like failure," as the following editorial in the *Ottawa Journal* floridly explains:

> ... any party kept too long in opposition falls a prey to frustration and despair; its ablest captains tempted to abandon it and younger men discouraged from joining it. Politicians no matter how determined, weary of "following suns that flame and fade in a day that has no morrow." And young men of ability shrink from joining a party which offers no reward for ambition. Thus in such circumstances an opposition becomes

feebler and feebler, drained of the drive it must have if it is to perform its functions adequately.

The Party and the Member

An investigation of how C.C.F.ers view their party's prospects leads to the questions of their participation and involvement. You may recall Lenin's scornful comparison of the parties that merely "sign up" members with those whose recruits are expected to dedicate "not merely their spare evenings but the whole of their lives" to the movement. Among the mixed traditions inherited by the C.C.F. was a much milder socialist variation of Lenin's standard. But that ideal became increasingly unattainable and ineffectual. The party has long been anxious to obtain these spare evenings, although, as in every organization, any willingness to participate inevitably leads to greater demands.

But the C.C.F.'s claims on its members for time and effort have elicited a feebler response in the last decade. In riding after riding, the great majority of the members are "inactive." They renew their membership faithfully each year, if asked. But they are rarely, if ever, seen at meetings or during election campaigns. Other evidence points to the same pattern of unexcited loyalty. Of 200 members of Toronto riding executives in 1945, 77 per cent of the middle-class and 52 per cent of the working-class individuals were still C.C.F. members ten years later. Furthermore, the average financial contribution of both active and inactive members has risen considerably in the past decade.

The inference from these facts appears to be that the C.C.F.'s limited claim on its members and their memory of a deeper commitment are the primary source both of the party's strength and weakness. Unlike more radical groups, which secure a stronger hold on the lives and emotions of their members, the C.C.F. makes more limited claims and has a weaker hold, and thus the types of highly emotional breaks with church and party now so familiar tend to be avoided. Apparently in the C.C.F. one can avoid serious involvement more easily or else one can drift steadily away from it and still maintain an official connection and a measure of attachment to the party. On the other hand, these claims and commitments are still sufficiently strong to obtain candidates and campaign workers (though both appear to be decreasing), greater financial contributions, and "sacrifice" candidates, and to wring from the less active majority renewals of membership, money, and occasional participation.

Perhaps the people who gave time, energy, and enthusiasm more freely in the days when money was scarce now find money more plentiful while time, energy, and interest have run low. Possibly they honour the obligations they still feel and ease their conscience by contributing in cash what they can no longer give in active participation. By doing so, they keep the party's finances and membership stable, at least for the time being. Whether the party's claims and the members' commitments can be revitalized by renewed prospects of success at the polls is a question that only time can answer.

~~~~~~~~~~~~

The C.C.F. is one of many groups that have travelled some distance along the familiar road from sect to church. Its sectarian characteristics faded rather than disappeared with prosperity and political success. The worldly achievements of many of its leaders and members helped to soothe the party's anger and obscured its vision of the "new commonwealth." It could no longer impart to its members the comforting and stimulating images of themselves as rebels against society and prophets of a new social order. Nor have such roles been in great demand in recent years and certainly not through the medium of radical politics.

The C.C.F. became a much more conventional party in belief, organization, and participation. The morale of such a party hinges on its prospects of imminent success. The continued decline of these prospects discouraged many of the leaders and followers from active participation. The result was a still further lessening of involvement, morale, and, consequently, future prospects of success. The core of the "faithful" and the memory of a deeper involvement remain, however, as important sources of continued loyalty and stability. Whether they can arrest the downward spiral of defeat, discouragement, and diminishing interest is the question on which the C.C.F.'s survival as a national party hinges.

ii. The Radical Political Movement in Canada[*]

"WHATEVER HAS HAPPENED to the C.C.F.?" The regularity with which the writer has been asked that question epitomizes its current problems. What the questioners have in mind — often indicated by the words which they accent — are the C.C.F.'s disappearance from the limelight and, less frequently, its sluggish manner and conventional viewpoint as compared with an earlier period. (The Cooperative Commonwealth Federation, a political party with a social democratic ideology, has been the dominant force in Canada's "left of centre" politics since its formation in 1933.)

---

[*] "The Radical Political Movement in Canada," in S.D. Clark (ed.), *Urbanism and the Changing Canadian Society* (Toronto: University of Toronto Press, 1961), 135-50.

The simplest answer to this question is to refer to the changes which have occurred in both the country and the party since 1933, suggesting that the public lost interest in the C.C.F. because of prosperity and welfare legislation, and that the party became conservative and apathetic because as its members grew older and more prosperous they acquired other interests and responsibilities. Although that answer has some validity, it is much too simple.

It fails to explain why, of the many socialist parties which encountered these kinds of conditions, some grew large and serene and others remained inconsequential and fiercely at odds with "the world," while the C.C.F. took neither of these paths but became "worldly" despite its "failure." It is this unusual course of development by the C.C.F. that the present article undertakes to examine.

The C.C.F.'s worldliness is sufficiently visible in every aspect of its character[1] to suggest, at first glance, another answer to the original question. As one steps away from the party and looks about at other organizations, one might well reply, "Nothing very remarkable has happened. The C.C.F. has simply gone the way of all, or at least of most, organizations."

---

[1] A party's "character" is used here to refer to its prevailing type of ideology, structure, and membership involvement. The process in which that character becomes more worldly is called by the familiar, if awkward, term "institutionalization." It refers to the sequence of changes in which a new crusading group tends to lose its original character as it becomes involved in "the world," and to become increasingly like the established worldly bodies against whose very nature it initially arose in protest.

The institutionalization of the C.C.F. constitutes the main theme of the study of which this article is a part. See Leo Zakuta, "A Becalmed Protest Movement," unpublished Ph.D. thesis, University of Chicago, 1961.

Both the party and "the world" have indeed come a long way towards meeting each other since the birth of the C.C.F. The party's urge to "shatter to bits this sorry scheme of things entire" has grown feeble and its vision of the co-operative commonwealth into which the world would be remoulded become dim. The public and the "old parties" have come to accept many of its ideas which they had once rejected as unthinkable. The viewpoints of the party and "the world" are still some distance apart, but they have ceased to outrage one another. Indeed, that very convergence has become the most serious threat to the C.C.F.'s existence, though only because the party is so weak.

As the C.C.F.'s initial struggle for acceptance drew to an end, the usual changes occurred. The excitement subsided and the host of enthusiastic amateurs turned its main attention elsewhere (although most retained some allegiance), leaving the party's direction increasingly to the much smaller groups of professionals, attached to the central offices, which had begun to grow in the meantime. The latter have, however, gained influence not simply by default but because they are more deeply and fully involved. As professionals, their livelihood and entire careers are, of course, at stake, but, like their counterparts anywhere, they regard themselves as more competent than any amateur, however zealous, can be. They have developed techniques for the management of the organization that are geared to its more settled and less personal character. These methods include those which any professional group employs to cope with the fact that it is the amateurs who possess ultimate control of the organization.

Some of the amateurs continue to hold meetings, as they do in most voluntary organizations; but, as elsewhere, these meetings are less frequent, more sparsely attended, and almost exclusively devoted to conducting the "business" of the local branch. In fact, though not in form, they tend to treat fundamental policy as established and received rather than as "issues" which require local determination.[2] This description might apply, however roughly, to most groups which begin with a new and unacceptable idea — religious denominations, welfare bodies, and perhaps even business organizations — as they and their members secure comfortable places in the world. It was just this process in radical political movements that Michels described so well and illustrated so profusely, though perhaps with an excessive flavour of disenchantment and of exposé.[3]

What makes the C.C.F. distinctive, however, is that it has been acquiring the qualities described above without having achieved a comparable place in society and, indeed, while it has been losing the modest position which it had attained.[4] In brief, its character has grown more worldly while its position has been becoming more precarious. This combination of character and position departs not only from the pattern of socialist and other parties, but also from the conventional institutionalization cycle suggested by Dawson and Gettys,[5] which presumably applies much more widely. However, to explain this departure it is first necessary to show how political parties differ from other organizations and then, how minor parties differ from both political movements and major parties. In the light of that analysis, the distinctive place of the C.C.F. in the socialist world becomes more apparent and more comprehensible.

---

[2] For a description of the corresponding groups in the British Labour party, see R.T. MacKenzie, *British Political Parties* (London: 1955), 539-58.

[3] Robert Michels, *Political Parties: A Sociological Study of the Oligarchical Tendencies of Modern Democracy* (Glencoe IL: 1949).

[4] "Position" is used throughout to refer to the group's strength, as determined by popular support, rather than to an ideological stand.

[5] C.A. Dawson, and Warner E. Gettys, *An Introduction to Sociology* (3rd ed.; New York: 1948), 689-709.

Political Parties[6] and Other Organizations

All organizations whose membership is predominantly voluntary, including political parties, share certain hazards and conditions of existence which differentiate them from non-voluntary bodies. The chief one is harnessing their membership in the absence of some of the main devices that are available to other types of organizations. Because voluntary members are not subject to the usual bread-and-butter incentives, these groups must do without this central mechanism of human control. Instead, they depend all the more heavily on their members' inner convictions and concern about the approval of their fellows so that a weakening of either is particularly damaging to voluntary groups. At best, regular routines of work and participation are difficult to establish in organizations of this type and are, therefore, often sources of anxious preoccupation. (Frequently the group devotes much effort and money to mobilizing its voluntary members as a necessary preliminary, with the public as ultimate target.)

Although political parties share these problems with all voluntary organizations, they nevertheless encounter special ones of their own in attempting to secure and hold a clientele and membership. Every group faces uncertainties when its clientele is free to choose whom it will patronize, and competition for a clientele is, of course, the common lot, extending far beyond voluntary organizations. In politics, however, the conditions of that competition are unique in ways that create a special relation between the party and its clientele, the electorate. The distinctive feature is that, of all organizations which provide goods and services, only political parties cannot (legally) offer these in direct return for patronage (votes). The reason is, of

---

[6] It should be understood that the entire discussion of political groups applies only where elections are free.

course, not only that the ballot is secret, but that only the winner(s), by controlling the government, is in a position to fulfill any obligations. (One can argue, however, that any party which makes a significant show of strength may indirectly provide a return to its patrons.)

Because winning is so important, the services of a political party are, unlike those of other organizations, widely sought only if the party is already very popular or is apparently becoming so. (This accounts for most of the difficulties encountered by new parties and for the special importance of the "bandwagon" in politics.) In more familiar terms, many a voter concludes that his ballot would be "wasted" if it is cast for a party which he feels has "no chance." Consequently, if he votes at all, he is likely to do so for a party which he likes less but whose seemingly superior prospects make him feel that his vote is not meaningless. This tendency obviously contributes significantly to the stability of the political system by helping to keep the major parties strong and the minor ones weak. Therefore, unless a political party appears to be "going somewhere," it is unlikely to maintain even a steady level of existence. Because other kinds of organizations can prosper or at least maintain a stable clientele without having any prospect of overtaking their larger rivals, they can lead more settled and less hazardous lives than can political parties.

In a major party, however, these uncertainties are counterbalanced by the numerous ballots which it obtains from people who do not regard it as their first preference but vote for it nevertheless, because they wish either to remove its main rival from office or else to prevent it from getting there. This tendency is sufficiently extensive to make most major parties seem virtually indestructible.

Minor Parties and Other Political Organizations

The position of minor parties, however, deprives them of this form of built-in insurance, and, except where they are protected by the proportional representation system,[7] they have a much higher mortality rate than do major parties or radical political movements. Several conditions make minor parties far more susceptible to the rule of "up or out" than are other political as well as non-political organizations.

The first is that the special relation, described above, between a political party and the electorate also exists, although the details differ, between the party and its own members. The members invest far more in the party than do the voters, giving it some combination of their energy, time, devotion, money, or possibly career. To realize a return on that investment, they must regard the party as a potential winner. If not, they are likely to question the value of their investment and to transfer it elsewhere. Though the time span which they employ may be longer than the public's, and they usually obtain other rewards, the fundamental similarity of the relation remains. Thus the

---

[7] The proportional representation system, which is so prevalent in Europe, is much kinder to minor parties and less helpful to major ones than is the system which prevails in the English-speaking world. (Indeed, it tends to make the distinctions between "major" and "minor" less clear than they usually are under the latter system.) These facts account both for the multiplicity of parties where proportional representation is used and for the high correlation between the strength of parties and their attitudes towards these two types of electoral systems.

The remainder of this discussion deals with minor parties in the simple-plurality, single-ballot system. (For a detailed discussion of how that system affects political parties and especially the minor ones, see Maurice Duverger, *Political Parties,* translated by Barbara and Robert North [London: 1954]).

decisions of the members and officers of a political party resemble those of investors. The study of any particular party reveals how greatly the contribution or withdrawal of the investments of members and officers (and not only the support of voters) can affect the party's fortunes, and how much such action depends on the hope of *winning* the contest of popularity.

The preceding discussion has suggested that minor parties owe their high mortality rate to the readiness with which the public loses interest in them and their own members lose heart. This link between a party's survival chances, on the one hand, and its character and position, on the other, becomes clearer when the minor parties are compared in these respects to major parties and to political protest movements which have not yet taken on a party character.

Ideologically, the minor parties are in a difficult position. Political protest movements usually possess a clearer *raison d'être* in their highly distinctive viewpoint. The major parties, though rather alike in viewpoint because their strength and proximity to power make them representative of and sensitive to many shades of public opinion, nevertheless, also possess a more obvious self-justification than do the minor parties — the possession or imminent prospect of power.

Each of these positions provides an effective basis for claiming support from the public as well as from party ranks. Political protest movements demand support on the grounds of a transcendental moral justification rather than on the grounds of impending victory. Major parties are less outraged by the state of things and less utopian in their promises, but they seek support on the grounds of their immediate prospect of holding office. Both of these positions provide obvious, if very different, justifications for existence in the struggle for political survival.

The position of the minor parties is uneasy, by contrast, because they cannot press either of these claims for support very effectively. When "the world" has ceased to outrage them and their visions of utopia have grown faint, they can do little more than intone the rituals of crusade. For example, much of the fear and anger which the depression aroused in the C.C.F. was mellowed or perhaps anaesthetized by the continued post-war prosperity; simultaneously, the immediate rather than the distant future became the party's main concern. In addition, their remoteness from power renders the other claim for support virtually unusable.

Establishing a *raison d'être* which is both comprehensible and compelling seems to be an inherent problem of minor parties. The difficulty becomes compounded in times of blurred doctrinal differences, such as the present, and when, like the C.C.F., the minor party must search for a place within a cherished two-party system.

Structurally, minor parties occupy an intermediate position between the proselytizing movements which are more personal and tightly knit and the major parties which are held together more loosely and formally. Although the minor parties are more firmly planted in "the world" than are the proselytizing movements, they are less deeply and intricately rooted in it than are the major parties.

If the C.C.F.'s case is typical, the minor party's membership may be greater than it was in the earlier, more sectarian period. But a larger proportion of it is less involved, maintaining little more than a formal connection with the party and refusing to be stirred into active participation, despite all of the party's efforts.[8] (The importance of the large, inactive membership should not be

---

[8] For a study of the difficulties experienced by some minor American parties in maintaining membership loyalty and participation, see W. Kornhauser. "Organizational Loyalty: A Study of Liberal and Radical Political Careers," unpublished Ph.D. thesis, University of Chicago, 1953.

underestimated. It provides the party with much of its money and perseverance, the latter because of the constant hope that this "sleeping giant" can be awakened.) The efforts to do so, however, like most of the organization's activities, come increasingly under the direction of a hierarchy of paid officers who develop more formal ways of carrying on the party's affairs.

The kind of structure described above is, of course, even more characteristic of the major parties. But the latter can be stirred with greater ease and, once aroused, they reach farther. The stimulant is the anticipation of holding office; while their organizations are more effective because of their greater size and range of connections in the community, proximity to power enables them to marshal leaders and followers, candidates and funds, both from their own ranks and from other groups.

Emotionally, the minor party cannot draw heavily on either the motive power which drives a crusading movement or that which feeds a major party. Fear and indignation are the chief ingredients of the former, and utopian hopes are the sparks which ignite them. These elements cannot exist without a menacing set of villains (for example, capitalism's inherent depressions and a tendency towards fascism) and a stirring vision of the future (an abundant and classless society, for instance). But as the minor party's villain and vision recede, so does the energy which they generate.

Despite their growing resemblance to their major rivals, the minor parties cannot harness the latter's main source of energy either. Its chief ingredient is the anticipation of worldly achievements, both personal and otherwise, and the igniting agent is the prospect of impending victory. The feebleness of that prospect naturally deprives the minor parties of most of this motive power.

In summary, minor parties differ from political movements and major parties in the following ways: their *raison d'être* is less distinct than the former's, but less workable than the latter's, their organizations are more formal and firmly rooted in "the world" than the former's but less so than the latter's; and their members are less involved than the former's but less easily activated than the latter's. Minor parties are thus closer in position to political movements and closer in character to major parties. But the former owe their survival chiefly to their character and the latter to their position. In other words, minor parties resemble each of these other groups most in that aspect which contributes least to these other groups' survival.

It would be misleading to conclude that minor parties live in the worst of all possible worlds; the C.C.F., for example, still draws more support than it did in its initial phase. But these parties have lost the protest movement's sustaining faith in the inevitability of ultimate triumph without being in a position to acquire the major party's assurance of taking office as soon as the public tires of its main rival.

These conditions account for the special susceptibility to the rule of "up or out" of those lesser political groups whose character comes to resemble that of the old and secure members of the establishment. They further indicate how difficult it is for these groups to achieve a secure place in society, compared to most non-political organizations of similar size and worldliness. This difference, in turn, leads to differences in character. The C.C.F.'s viewpoint, for example, is plagued by doubt and uncertainty as the party searches for a new *raison d'être*, and its organization has been steadily enfeebled by the extensive demoralization which, in manifold forms, has spread throughout it.

The C.C.F. and Other Socialist Parties

We can now return to the question of why the C.C.F., although unsuccessful, nonetheless acquired a worldly character. That combination, although rare in the socialist world, is not uncommon among minor parties. However, the question remains: Why did the C.C.F. not become either a major, worldly party or an inconsequential, other-worldly sect?

One might argue that only those socialist parties which achieved a minimal degree of momentum fairly early in their careers were able to achieve major party status by the democratic process. The evidence for this argument is that every one of the social democratic parties which did attain that momentum climbed steadily to power or to its threshold, and remained a major party. The failure of the United States Socialist party, on the other hand, might be attributed to its inability to achieve that minimal degree of propulsion.[9]

Whatever the plausibility of this argument, it obviously does not apply to the C.C.F. The latter acquired as much momentum, in the early 1940's (Table I), as any socialist party ever had, but its progress was quite uncharacteristically arrested and abruptly reversed, and it failed to establish itself as a major party. In view of its departure from so ubiquitous a pattern, that failure gives a final twist to the query of "whatever happened to the C.C.F.?" Why was the pattern reversed so sharply in Canada, and only there, once it had got so well under way?

---

[9] At the height of its popularity, in 1912, the Socialist party won only 6 per cent of the presidential vote and only one seat in Congress. Since then it has been sidelined in all but name from the main political arena.

TABLE I

C.C.F. POPULAR SUPPORT IN CANADA, 1940-45*

Date		\ Party Percentages				
		C.C.F.	Liberal	Conservative	Bloc Populaire	Other
1940	Mar. (election)	9	55	31		5
1942	Jan.	10	55	30		5
	Sept.	21	39	23		17
1943	Feb.	23	32	27	7	11
	Sept.	29	28	28	9	6
1944	Jan.	24	30	29	9	8
	Sept.	24	36	27	5	8
1945	Jan.	22	36	28	6	8
	June (election)	16	41	28	3	12

*Gallup Poll, reported in Dean E. McHenry, *The Third Force in Canada* (Berkeley and Los Angeles: 1950), 136.

The most obvious explanation of this failure seems to lie in the general political system which Canada shares with most of the English-speaking world. That system, we have observed, does not provide comfortable accommodation for more than two parties at a time. New parties, because of their regional bases, have challenged its established tenants more successfully in the provincial field than in the federal. (At present, 1960, Canada's three most westerly provinces are in Social Credit or C.C.F. hands.) But the dominance of the Liberals and Conservatives nationally has remained unbroken since Confederation.

Despite several attempts, no other party has ever won federal power. The C.C.F. and Social Credit have been the most recent and, in an important sense, the most unusual aspirants to that goal. Other new parties have been either popular or persistent, but never both. Some, like the Progressive party of the early 1920's or the Reconstruction party of the mid-1930's, blossomed suddenly and even spectacularly, but faded almost as rapidly — the common fate of most new parties that originate by splitting off from the established major ones.[10] Other political groups, such as the Communists, the Trotskyites (despite several splinterings), and the followers of Daniel de Leon, have survived for decades on the dark outer fringes of the political scene. Only the C.C.F. and Social Credit were able to combine popularity with durability, and even the latter was virtually obliterated as a national party in the 1958 federal election. Nevertheless, the success of other social democratic parties, and particularly of the British Labour party, is decisive evidence that small, third parties are not inevitably doomed to that status, and such success suggests that the formal political system does not in itself account adequately for the C.C.F.'s weak position.

There are, of course, substantial differences between the history and character of Canada and other countries which are reflected in the differences between the C.C.F. and socialist parties elsewhere. For example, unlike most of its European counterparts, the C.C.F. arrived on the scene too late to participate in the main battles for political liberty,

---

[10] In origin and type of life cycle these parties have less in common with the C.C.F. than with such third parties in the United States as the Bull Moose, the two Progressives, and the Dixiecrat. These also began by springing full-bodied from the major parties, following unsuccessful efforts to win control of them, disintegrated after only one genuine trial of strength, and were largely reabsorbed by their original parties.

The Canadian Progressive Party had a somewhat more independent origin and, after disintegrating, its radical minority was instrumental in founding the C.C.F. See W.L. Morton, *The Progressive Party in Canada* (Toronto: 1950).

the franchise and trade union legitimacy. The fact that these goals had been achieved, as a consequence of North America's special conditions, was undoubtedly responsible for the C.C.F.'s late start and for its lack of a massive trade union base, both of which have handicapped it severely, although neither seems to have been an insurmountable obstacle in itself.

Although all of the major socialist parties, those in the new nations excepted, were formed by the beginning of the twentieth century, age by itself has not guaranteed success, as the United States Socialist party[11] and others demonstrate. Nor have formal alliances (collective affiliations) with trade unions been essential to the success of socialist parties, as the evidence from continental Europe indicates.[12] But the socialist parties which did succeed seem to have obtained the votes of the great majority of industrial workers. The C.C.F.'s failure to obtain these votes and match these successes has been attributed by F.H. Underhill and others to the distinctive conditions of political life in North America.

---

[11] The Socialist party, although formed in 1902, only two years after the British Labour party, is very much weaker than even the C.C.F.

[12] Formal collective affiliation exists only in the Swedish and Norwegian parties and in both cases, only on the local level, in contrast to the practice in the British Labour party. In Norway, these affiliations constitute only about 35 per cent of the present Labour party membership. (For a more detailed discussion of these arrangements and of the main types of relations between the trade unions and the socialist parties of the democratic nations of continental Europe, see "Structural Relationships between Trade Unions and Labour Parties," a series of three articles by Paul Malles, Assistant to the Director, I.C.F.T.U., in *Canadian Labour*, Oct., Nov., and Dec. 1959.)

... socialism [in Canada] ... was obviously an importation, partly from Marxians in continental Europe, and partly from the more moderate parliamentary socialists, the Fabian socialists, of England. It obviously didn't originate in Canada; the C.C.F. was an attempt to adapt these European ideas, primarily the Fabian ideas, to Canadian conditions.

... I feel the C.C.F. was an attempt to set up a British type of party system, a division between left and right. We [the C.C.F.] were defeated by Mr. King because he was a good North American and he saw that our politics wasn't likely to work that way.[13]

The efforts to explain the C.C.F.'s failure call attention to its "environment," the examination of which is a task beyond the scope of the present paper and one which obviously requires a different type of investigation. But, however much the special North American or Canadian environment may explain the party's weakness, it cannot account adequately for the C.C.F.'s departure from the usual paths taken by political movements which have felt decisively rejected. Its fate was especially unusual for North America, where reform parties, if unsuccessful, tend to collapse and blow away or shrink into purely regional

---

[13] F.H. Underhill, "The Radical Tradition: A Second View of Canadian History," published transcript of two broadcasts on the CBC Television Series 'Explorations,' June 8 and 15, 1960 (CBC Publications, Toronto). See Morton, *The Progressive Party in Canada*, 270, for a similar explanation of the Progressive Party's failure. These views leave unexplained, however, the fact that the C.C.F. did come very close to power or to becoming Canada's second party. The timing of its upsurge, several years before the next election was due to be held, undoubtedly played a large part in its failure to achieve either of these objectives.

groups, and where radical movements, if the climate is uninviting, seem to shrivel and crawl back into a hard, sectarian shell.

Any of these developments would have been more typical of an unsuccessful political movement than the one that did take place. The C.C.F. did not collapse; neither did it dwindle into a spent sect or a purely regional party. Instead, as a minor national party[14] it has retained and developed the worldly character which had blossomed during its period of great expansion.

If nurture alone fails to account for this distinctive combination, then nature must be added. An examination of the members of the C.C.F.'s general ideological family reveals their "natural" processes of change and clarifies how and why the C.C.F. has departed from these patterns. To illuminate that departure more fully both the established and the unworldly socialist parties must be considered.

The C.C.F. and the Major Socialist Parties

A comparison of the growth of the C.C.F. and of its major relatives reveals one significant difference.[15] Once the latter had attained the level of popularity reached by the C.C.F. in the early 1940's, none suffered a serious reversal before becoming safely established as the first or second party in the land.[16] Thus when they eventually met defeat, they still

---

[14] Although the C.C.F.'s strength in the five most easterly provinces is negligible, it has retained sufficient support in the rest of the country to qualify as a national party.

[15] For a record of the popular support of these parties, see Leo Zakuta, "A Becalmed Protest Movement," Appendix B.

[16] To appreciate the magnitude of the C.C.F.'s double defeat (in Ontario and federally) in June 1945, one should not compare these results with those of pre-1942 elections. One should contrast them instead with the 1943 returns in

remained the chief alternatives to the parties in power. (Many of them had already held or shared office.)

How significant this difference was becomes apparent if one compares the process of change within the C.C.F. and these other parties. Although the character of the C.C.F. changed remarkably during the party's brief interlude of success,[17] the main changes to more conventional forms occurred after June 1945, while the party was still reeling from defeat, with its popular support, membership, and revenues shrinking steadily.

In contrast, the major socialist parties had developed their more conventional viewpoints, incentives, and organizations during long periods of steady growth which frequently included tenure of office. When their progress was finally reversed, they had already secured a new *modus vivendi* — as established alternatives to the parties in power, a position which insured them heavily against the hazards of defeat and change. When defeat forced the members of these parties to recognize that they were participating in the conventional political process rather than in an irreversible crusade, the prospect of forming the next government continued to arouse them to action. That same prospect provided an effective and easily understood *raison d'être* when their socialism became less clear and ardent. And it enabled these parties to hold together in defeat the organizations and the alliances which they had built during their long and steady rise.

Ontario, with the 1944 victory in Saskatchewan, with the sequence of by-election victories, with the Gallup Poll reports and, above all, with the soaring hopes and imaginations of C.C.F. supporters upon the eve of these 1945 contests.

[17] The period of rising popular support lasted less than two years, achieving its high-water mark by September, 1943, while that of organizational expansion endured little more than three years, ending abruptly in June, 1945.

The C.C.F., in contrast, was badly hurt by the combination of defeat and change (Tables II and III).[18] Defeat led to hopelessness which sapped the energies of many members and deflated the interest of the public. And when the early faith in utopian socialism withered, no stimulating *raison d'être* was available to replace it.

Consequently, these twin losses — of hope in present victory and of certainty in ultimate triumph — inflicted fatal or critical injuries on much of the party's organization. They left the C.C.F. neither a major party nor a political movement, defeat demolishing the former and change the latter role.

TABLE II

NATIONAL ELECTIONS 1935-1958: SEATS WON BY PARTIES*

Party	1935	1940	1945	1949	1953	1957	1958
Liberal	171	178	125	190	170	105	49
Conservative	39	39	67	41	51	111	208
C.C.F.	7	8	28	13	23	25	8
Social Credit	17	10	13	10	15	19	0
Others	11	10	12	8	6	5	0
TOTALS	245	245	245	262	265	265	265

*Canadian Parliamentary Guide.

---

[18] The reversals of 1945 had left it Canada's third party, much weaker than its two main rivals and very remote from power.

TABLE III

NATIONAL ELECTIONS 1935-1958: PERCENTAGE OF POPULAR VOTE, BY PARTY

Party	1935	1940	1945	1949	1953	1957	1958
Liberal	44	55	41	50	49	40	33
Conservative	30	31	28	30	31	40	54
C.C.F.	9	9	16	13	12	11	10
Social Credit	4	3	4	2	5	6	2
Others	13	2	10	5	4	3	1
TOTALS	100	100	99	100	101	100	100

It is in these respects that the "natural" processes of institutionalization have taken so unusual a course in the C.C.F. Instead of following the typical protest movement — minor party — major party sequence of its stronger socialist confreres, the C.C.F's career more nearly approximates a sequence of protest movement — major party — minor party. This unusual sequence of rise and decline appears to have twisted the C.C.F. out of the more familiar socialist forms. The essential difference was not that the C.C.F. was catapulted into "the world" and became deeply involved in it — this happened to many socialist parties. Instead, it was that, although the party experienced a profound change of character during its middle (major party) phase,[19] it failed to establish a secure place in that world. Had it done so, as it fully expected to, it would have resembled its major relatives in position as well as in character.

---

[19] The C.C.F. regarded itself as almost a major party and was so regarded by the public and the other parties until the federal election of 1949 made its minor party status unmistakable. The changes in its character during this phase are described in detail in Leo Zakuta, "A Becalmed Protest Movement," chs. VI-IX.

The C.C.F. and the Minor Socialist Groups

If its position distinguishes the C.C.F. from the major socialist parties, its character separates it from the lesser groups of the "left." These groups are much less involved in the struggle for power and have retained much more of their sectarian character, adding to it only the qualities common to those political groups which the public has never taken seriously.

Even the United States Socialist party might be placed in this category. Its distinctive features in the past two decades have been its other-worldliness and insignificance in the struggle for power, both of which it shares with numerous other "left wing" groups. Many of these other groups have either repudiated or not been concerned with the more conventional forms of the struggle for power. Instead, much more than the C.C.F. ever did, they have rejected the world and looked towards an entirely new and utopian social order, awaiting the cataclysm which would usher it in and provide the opportunity and the necessity for their leadership.

There are still other socialist (and non-socialist) groups which are essentially parties-in-exile but which have little hope or desire to return to the scene of their original endeavors. They maintain their ideology and some aspects of their structure with surprisingly little change. But their stability also stems from the absence of a deep involvement in the issues of here and now. However, instead of dwelling in the remote future, their hearts live in the past and in another place. The Communist party also looks elsewhere, a fact which governs most of its behaviour, including its time perspective.

The C.C.F.'S Distinctive Place in the Socialist World

Their perspectives of time and place seem to divide the socialist and other "left wing" parties in the democratic countries into two broad categories which correspond closely to their strength (position). The first consists of the parties whose main concern is with the present and with their immediate surroundings; most of these are large and powerful. The other category contains the parties whose primary orientation is to another time or place or both and, except for the Communist party in Italy, France, and pre-Nazi Germany, they have been small and weak.

In which category does the C.C.F. belong? Its character has become close to that of the major socialist parties, but it increasingly lacks their secure status. Its position, on the contrary, has been nearing that of the minor socialist groups (although it is very much stronger than any of them), but it increasingly lacks their sectarian character. Thus the C.C.F.'s main distinction appears to be that it has been developing the character of a major party while moving towards the position of a minor sect. In the terms used previously, the C.C.F.'s strength and its perspectives of time and place seem to be heading in opposite directions. It is this unusual relation between them, for which the party's peculiar pattern of success and failure is chiefly responsible, that creates the impression of a disparity between the C.C.F.'s position and character.

One may ask why the C.C.F. did not return to its original character after its reversals. The answer lies in the depth of its (and its members') involvement in the conventional world as well as in the state of the latter since the war. Although the world has been hard on the party, it has been much kinder to its individual members and to the public at large. A drastic change on the broader Canadian scene might have led either the existing leaders and members to reject the social order once again and to recapture the character of a militant political movement or to a wholesale turnover of personnel with the same result.[20] Since that change in the environment did not occur, the C.C.F. retained its worldly character despite a weakening position.

The C.C.F.'s Prospects

One cannot help wondering how long the C.C.F. can keep riding these two horses, character and position, if they keep travelling in opposite directions, without being torn asunder. The answer seems to hinge on two main possibilities, the arrival of strong trade union reinforcements and a drastic change in the political climate from that of the past decade and a half. These possibilities constitute the party's chief sources of continued hope.

But if neither of these events materializes, or perhaps if only the latter does, the C.C.F. may follow the path taken by the United States Socialist party after the peaks of strength it rose to in 1912 and 1932. If a leader emerges with the magnetic appeal of a Woodrow Wilson or a Franklin Roosevelt or, as seems more likely in the Canadian political system, if a sufficiently decisive issue arises, one of the major parties may draw off a substantial segment of the C.C.F., those whose views have moved farthest into "the world." The distance that these people would have to travel is no longer very great, and they might

---

[20] For a description of just such a change in the United States Socialist party in the early 1930's, see Daniel Bell, "Marxian Socialism [in the United States]," in D.D. Egbert and S. Persons (eds.), *Socialism and American Life* (Princeton: 1952).

The formation of the C.C.F. in 1932-3 resulted from the same kind of influx in personnel and change in character of the Canadian socialist movement at exactly the same period.

find themselves in the same position as the Socialist party stalwarts who became supporters of the New Deal.

The other horse could then ride off unfettered in the opposite direction, carrying a handful of the more militant and utopian of the C.C.F.'s followers. Thus, by reducing the party to a fraction of its present strength and returning its time perspective to the more remote future, such a development would restore the "natural" order of the socialist world. It is partly to ward off just such an eventuality that the leaders of the C.C.F. are now striving so desperately to build a "new party."

iii. Equality in North American Marriages*

During the past several generations there have been important changes in North American family relationships. While this essay emphasizes the husband-wife relation, its main perspectives also apply to the relations between parents and children. The "data" presented here come from the casual observations of family life that are made by everyone, rather than from a formal empirical study of the family. Accordingly, I am assuming that these observations of the North American, urban. middle-class family — the only one that I know at first hand — are sufficiently well known that they can be discussed here without that careful documentation of actual behavior that eventually will be necessary.

My central point is that certain changes in the behavior of family members toward each other stem from alterations in their mutual sentiments — feelings toward one another; these feelings, in turn, are closely linked to shifts in their standards and forms of family organization. For the sake of economy, these standards and forms will be taken as given, as will be the general conditions out of which they arise: namely, the growth of democratic ideology, cities, and industry; the mobility and mixture of people; and the development of an essentially new society. I will not try to explain why the values and forms have changed, but will simply describe the new ones briefly and concentrate on how they have affected family sentiments and thereby behavior.

---

* "Equality in North American Marriages," *Social Research* 30:2 (1963), 157-70. Leo entitled the paper "Till death do us part? Shifts in Family Structure and Sentiments"; the title was changed by the journal's editor.

Ideological Changes and Romantic Marriage

I have been trying in vain to recall from whom I first heard the suggestion that our fiction — popular as well as "serious" — provides an intriguing symptom of how significantly the married relation has changed in our society. The argument, which is perhaps familiar, goes as follows: In the past, love stories were ordinarily about courtship, and they usually concluded with marriage. The emotional relations of the married were of much less consuming interest, presumably on the assumption that they contained little of comparable fascination. In contrast, today's fiction, drama, and movies frequently center on the emotional relation between husband and wife; typically, they are already married when the story begins. The inference obviously is that those intense feelings which we think of as romance now occur much more often within marriage than they once did. If this inference is valid, why does contemporary marriage produce feelings of romantic involvement or such distress at their departure that the couple may dissolve or seriously consider dissolving their marriage? To pursue this question one must find the structural and ideological conditions which seem most closely associated with romance in general first, then those with its growing importance in contemporary marriage.

In general, romance seems to occur where the partners feel that they choose each other freely rather than where others, usually the parents, do the choosing. (Whether the choice is really "free" is not only beyond proof but, from the perspective of the social scientist, as totally irrelevant as whether man's will is really "free." It is the actor's sense or feeling of being free to choose that matters, just as a man's view of whether another's will is free or not governs his feelings and behavior towards him.)

The suggestion that romantic feelings are linked to a sense of free choice raises a parenthetical quarrel and question. The quarrel is with those exhortatory treatises on marriage and the family, unfortunately so numerous in the social sciences, that almost invariably warn the reader about the "romantic fallacy" and the dangers of "building" a marriage on so feeble a foundation as romance instead of on presumably more solid stuff, such as similar views about money, in-laws, child-rearing, and religion. One wonders how many of these writers have been sufficiently inspired by their own preaching to put it into practice.

The quarrel aside, the question is: If the "romantic fallacy" refers to expectations that are quite unlikely to be realized, why select these as if they were somehow unique? Are people not constantly launching new enterprises, activities, and organizations with the highest (one could almost say the "wildest") of hopes, some of which we label "utopian"? And don't many of these bodies, like most marriages, survive despite the subsequent abatement of their members' initial hopes? But who in our fraternity is ready to counsel against this general human tendency? Perhaps romance or falling in love may occur whenever people commit themselves, with a sense of free choice, to any undertaking about which they have great expectations. If so, the numerous parallels which have been drawn between "conversion" and "falling in love" should not be surprising.

Returning to the main question, how does the sense of free choice affect romance in marriage? Many obvious circumstances make divorce or separation seem much more feasible to a contemporary couple than to their grandparents and thus give them a greater feeling of choice than was once the case. The argument, however, that ideological and structural changes are responsible for the development of, or concern about, romance in marriage must rest on some distinctive grounds. These are more easily seen if we compare those two familiar models — the "patriarchal" and "contemporary" family types.

Three structural changes from the first type to the second seem to be closely linked to the growing importance of romantic feelings within marriage. They are, in ascending order of importance: the family's smaller size, the greater mobility of the family, and the equality of the married couple. These features have been termed structural solely as a matter of economy; properly, they should be called "ideological-structural," since each one of the changes in family form has occurred because the people concerned felt that they should.

The family's contraction results from fewer children and fewer relatives in the household. As a result, the child may become more deeply involved with the fewer remaining adults so that in his subsequent marriage he seeks the intensity of emotional involvement which he has already experienced. Framed in this way — the more adults in the family, the greater the dispersal of emotional involvement — this argument does not seem very convincing. The reduction in family size may not be important in itself. But it has been accompanied by another, though somewhat unrelated, change, which has made it important — the growing equality between parents and children, which tends to intensify their mutual involvement by lowering the barriers that authority usually creates. Once the generations can become closer, numbers become important because the typical family contains fewer adults to serve as the focus for the children's involvement.

The family's greater mobility also tends to intensify the mutual involvement of its members by throwing them together more than would a more stable existence. If the unit which moves is usually the nuclear family, then it cuts itself off from its closest relatives as well as from its whole network of friends and acquaintances. Weakened ties with outsiders increase the members' mutual dependence and reduce their avenues of escape from one another. Although many families may not move, the growth of so many large organizations, including government, with their numerous branches, probably means that increasing numbers regard relocation as a distinct possibility. If so, it need not be actually moving, but merely the prospect that heightens the married couple's feeling of how much their happiness hinges on the "success" of this one tie which not only endures when all others are severed but which, by the very breaking of other ties, becomes all the more important. Under these circumstances, would they not count somewhat more heavily on the congeniality of this relation?

It is the third condition of equality that merits the most serious consideration. Its general effect is similar to that of the other two — it brings people together more often and more intimately. Status differences everywhere seem to inhibit free and easy association, and the more pronounced they are, the more separate are the parties, except where their association is formally specified. This principle is built into the official military structure in the form of separate messes that limit extracurricular association and therefore, presumably, personal involvement across hierarchical levels. We see it arise somewhat more spontaneously in the cafeterias of work organizations and in relations between racial and ethnic groups — in the latter cases, it is called segregation.

Consequences of inequality: In an apparent paradox, the barriers to ease and intimacy are often less where the status differences are very great, so that a man may have a much freer and easier relation with his slave or servant than he does with his employee or even with his children, or, in some family systems, with his mistress than with his wife. These considerations, incidentally, should warn us against dismissing too lightly the statements of those white Southerners who claim that they love their Negroes. Before condemning the unspoken qualification, "in their place," as hypocrisy, we should ask if this is really very different from the parent who loves his children but who would be furious if they began to do certain things conventionally reserved for adults. P.G. Wodehouse has persistently rung one change on this theme in the delicately balanced relations between Jeeves, the manservant who is equal to every occasion, and his master, Bertie Wooster, who is equal to none of them. Jeeves' invariable way of demonstrating his displeasure with his master — of punishing him, as we say in our flat sociological speech — is by a cool but courteous refusal to exceed his station by offering the advice and suggestions that Bertie requires to cope with his current crisis. Thus, as in many accounts of the Negro in the old South and of others in servitude, Jeeves owes not only his intimacy with his master but also his considerable influence over him to the fact that he not only knows his place, but likes it.

What permits ease and intimacy in these various instances is, of course, that status differences are so large and clear that a more relaxed relation brings no suggestion of fundamental equality between the parties. Furthermore, the relaxation of formalities in relations of this type is ostensibly subject to the pleasure of the superior, and the parties do not associate as equals in any of the situations in which friends ordinarily meet. These considerations indicate that the links between friendship, sociability, and equality deserve a comprehensive examination.

The main point, however, is that if separate activities and restrained relations arise out of status differences, then separation and restraint should be much more prominent in the "patriarchal" than in the "contemporary" family. A casual glance at Toronto's large, post-war, Italian immigrant district shows how obviously they are more prominent. True to the traditions of their Italian patriarchal rural society, males congregate sociably in exclusively masculine groups in the streets and restaurants, and the women presumably stay home. If the customers in the restaurants are couples, it is fairly certain that they are not first-generation Italians. That the present Toronto pattern is not unusual is clear from William F. Whyte's portrait of comparable Italian groups in Boston in the 1930s.[1] His account, by the way, suggests another parallel between the gang and family. In both cases, the lower status members stay close to home, while the others feel free to roam. The Italian segregation of the sexes has innumerable counterparts the world over, including the British working man's pub and the exclusively male clubs of his "betters." (It is tempting to observe how neatly the proverbial closeness between the British wife and her "mum" and the alleged fondness of Englishmen for their dogs both fit into the general pattern. But this may be merely circulating the stereotype.)

If status differences lead to segregation because people usually seek the companionship of their "equals," then the marital relation in the patriarchal family should display the same kind of separation in matters of sex and companionship as it does in most other activities. And, by all accounts, it does. Allowing for whatever exaggeration is introduced to achieve humor or drama, the stories, movies, and literature of continental Europe in the Victorian age or of contemporary rural society in France, Italy, and elsewhere indicate both the prevalence and the relative openness — the two are obviously interdependent — of extra-marital affairs for men. The relatively-open acceptance of prostitution and of having a mistress on the grounds that "boys will be boys" or, less indulgently perhaps, "men are like that," coupled with the clear understanding that girls should be "lady-like," suggests once more the link with status differences. Again, it is the higher status category that is permitted freedom; who can roam, perhaps symbolically;

---

[1] *Street Comer Society* (Chicago: University of Chicago, 1945).

and who at least feel that they have a choice that is less readily available to the lower status group.

One test of this general argument would involve looking at family systems with varying degrees of status difference between the spouses in order to examine the accompanying patterns of sexual fidelity. Thus, in the traditional Chinese family, in which the husband's standing was especially lofty, concubinage was apparently much more acceptable than was its counterpart in Europe, and the concubine's position was correspondingly higher. In the Chinese family, though below the level of a wife, the concubine was often brought into the household and, significantly, her children were considered legitimate. Wifely infidelity, as one would expect, was regarded as more outrageous and disastrous than it was in the European family. The elevated status of the Japanese *geisha* is another case in point. (It would be interesting to know how the occupation of the *geisha* has been affected by the reported rapid "Westernization" of the Japanese family.) Whether polygyny is a further point along this same continuum should be relatively easy to determine by determining whether it is always associated with even greater male dominance.

The contemporary "American" pattern, in which husband and wife are much closer in standing, fits neatly into this scheme on the other side of this argument. Whether extra-marital affairs are less frequent in this system is impossible to say because of their more clandestine nature, but the secrecy itself is the best evidence of its greater unacceptability to all concerned. Were it possible to know, one would expect that infidelity is also more evenly distributed between the sexes in this system than in the patriarchal.

I have pursued this theme in order to show both the extent of separation between wives and husbands in the patriarchal system as well as the link between separateness and relative rank. Relations between the sexes, married or unmarried, between the old and young, and between countless other groups all display essentially the same pattern. Our assumptions about what it is natural for people to do together obviously involve assumptions about their relative status. In most parts of the world, as introductory sociology students soon learn, men and women do not ordinarily dance, walk, or spend their leisure time together. Frequently, they do not even eat together — that seemingly universal expression of equality — and, in the more patriarchal homes in the North American society, parents and children eat separately much more regularly. Finally, our conventional assumption that sex relations, at least in marriage, are highly personal hardly corresponds to that of many males in the more patriarchal societies who make the distinction between duty and pleasure or between work and play that so often differentiates the formal from the informal.

Consequences of equality: The extended remarks about the consequences of inequality are a background against which we can see more clearly the consequences, in sentiment and behavior, of greater equality. For various reasons, the status of women and wives in Western and Westernized societies has increased considerably while that of men and husbands has dropped somewhat, so that a woman's relationship to them in marriage has become much closer to equal. By reducing the distance which inequality imposes, both the range of association and of reciprocal emotional involvement increase. By emotional involvement, I refer not only to feelings of affection but also to their opposite. Both are likely to grow within the same relation. The central argument is that since mutual involvement increases and becomes more complex, feelings of antagonism and hatred are also likely to become intensified. (The reciprocity of involvement requires emphasis to distinguish these instances from those enduring relations characterized by intense involvement on one side and a much more casual attitude on the other. These asymmetrical feelings are common in authority relations, in which the superior ordinarily looms much larger in the mind of his subordinate than vice versa. Employee and boss, child and parent, and wife and husband in the older family system of the Orient are all instances of this type of unequal emotional involvement.)

As their positions become more equal, the prospect of informal or sociable association seems more natural and appealing to husbands and wives. In effect, they now view their prospective relation in terms of something like friendship, the main requisite of which is, of course, status equality. As a result, wives and husbands tend to leave their sexually compartmentalized worlds and to do many things together which their grandparents did not. Ideologically, this change is expressed in such phrases as "partnership," "companionship," and even "togetherness." Their companionship, we have seen, is fostered not only by their greater equality, but also by being more cut off from relatives and friends, including the adult kin who have disappeared from the household. The possibilities of friendship — perhaps it had better be called companionship — are further augmented by some blurring of their former distinctive roles and activities. Not only is the wife freer to venture from the home to work for pay, or on behalf of "worthy causes," or simply to play — all, incidentally, formerly reserved for higher status groups, either men or women of the wealthy leisure class — but her husband is also more likely to participate in the formerly exclusively wifely tasks — in the kitchen, nursery, or even in public by sharing the shopping. Thus, like friends and equals, they do numerous similar things, many of them together.

The combination of these conditions — a smaller, more mobile, and more equalitarian family — leads not only to a more informal, intimate, and complex marital relation; it also leads to a new conception of what that relation ought to be, that is, to new standards of what constitutes a successful marriage. Both partners are likely to expect and to want the more intense mutual involvement that the altered structure of the marriage relation facilitates and to judge the success of their marriage in terms of the extent and the character of that involvement. Under these circumstances, the sense of personal congeniality or, in the more usual phrase, "compatibility," becomes a, or perhaps the, central criterion on which the partners assess the success of their marriage and decide on its future.

Those who regard these developments with dismay or distaste usually conclude that marriage has come to mean less to the contemporary couple, since so many do decide to terminate it. The advocates of the new often argue, on the other hand, that these decisions indicate the very opposite; namely, that people now expect more from their marriage and are unwilling to settle for the unhappy relations that previous generations endured. But this argument, like any evaluative one, is insoluble and beside the point. It is not a matter of greater or lesser expectations but of different ones. And the heavy emphasis placed on personal congeniality means that many of the relations that do not measure up to the expectations of at least one of the partners will be terminated.

Furthermore, the new marital structure and expectations create additional hazards to the permanence of the relation. By facilitating very strong involvement, they are likely to lead, at least on occasion, to more intense antagonism and bitter clashes. Feelings of equality contribute to this possibility by removing or threatening to remove ultimate authority from the husband and thereby open the way to struggle for power, since the right to decide is no longer vested in a position but in each individual's conviction of what should be done. Finally, if their relation "goes sour" chronically, both partners are likely to feel the consequences as more devastating than did their grandparents. Unlike the latter, they have fewer avenues of escape from each other, they face the agonies of decision about the formal status of their marriage, and their deeper mutual involvement tends to produce stronger friction and animosity. It is therefore hardly surprising that, under these conditions, so many contemporary couples find their marriages too intolerable to endure. (In addition, if equality tends to reduce or conceal the incidence of husbands' infidelity, it simultaneously increases its seriousness as an offence and thus its threat to the continuation of the marriage.)

Thus instead of regarding a "high" rate of divorce and separation as a somewhat alien virus which has managed to infect the North American marriage system, we may, perhaps more profitably, view it as an inevitable outcome of the distinctive ideology, structure, and sentiments of that system.

I have suggested previously that the sense of free choice seems a necessary condition for romance — whether before or within marriage. Several obvious conditions provide this sense to the contemporary married couple. Among them are, of course, the greater prevalence and acceptability of divorce, one further instance of how an effect is also a cause, as well as the greater earning power of women, that facilitates the step for both partners. If I seem to have under-emphasized this last condition, it was mainly out of reluctance to overemphasize it. While it seems extremely important, its exact significance is very difficult to determine since divorce and women's earning power have both risen considerably over the long run. Unless one can somehow separate these variables, precise statements about their relation seem impossible. These considerations naturally lead to speculation about Hollywood, where both divorce and the earning power of women seem to have reached unprecedented heights. Here is the community in which the status and income of women is least dependent on their husbands and where equality between the married partners and the sense of free choice about continuing the marriage are at a peak. It is under these circumstances, I would guess, that the concern about romance in marriage is most intense since the feeling of great freedom makes the continuity of the marriage contingent on little else. And despite all of the tongue-clucking about Hollywood, it seems clear that marriage still rates very highly there. How else can we account for Hollywood's apparently endless optimism about marriage in the face of such seemingly overwhelming odds?

The shifts in the standards and structure within the family, and more generally between the sexes, and between adults and children, have several other effects on sentiments and behavior that seem worthy of note. As a result of the diminishing status distance between the sexes, in general, and between the various age levels, males and females seem increasingly at ease with each other and so do the young with their elders, though the reverse is not necessarily as true.

More specifically, greater equality seems to reduce the fear, deference, and perhaps even awe that children once had toward their parents, and possibly wives toward their husbands. The contemporary father who lectures his son, "I would never have dared speak to *my* father as you do to me," may be doing something more than repeating a universal and timeless lament of fathers; he may, for a change in this endless litany, be uttering a simple truth. Correspondingly, husbands are more likely to be attentive and sensitive to the wishes, tastes, and viewpoints of their wives and children than they have been in the past, one example of which is the new ideology of sex relations in the twentieth century.[2] Status equality seems to be the

---

[2] Significantly, that ideology emphasizes "sensitivity" for the male, "freedom" for the woman, and reduction of the traditional or stereotyped differences in their sexual roles

central condition for reciprocal sensitivity to the wishes and feelings of others. And this is a point that warrants fuller examination than is possible in this short essay.

How these shifts in structure and sentiment affect the cohesion of the family merits some special consideration. In this matter I take as my whipping boy George Homans, as a perverse repayment for the considerable debt that this paper obviously owes him. In *The Human Group* he refers to the contemporary family as one of "low integration" and to its more patriarchal predecessor as one of "high integration."[3]

But is "integration," or whatever we call the binding ties, all of a piece and thus simply a matter of more or less? In the older family type, cohesion or integration depended more heavily on specialized and physically interdependent roles with a fairly clear, if elaborate, chain of command, as well as, of course, considerable emotional involvement and interdependence. In the contemporary family, specialized roles, physical interdependence, and authority are all still of central importance, but the balance has been shifting away from these aspects towards the emotional involvement on which the cohesion of more informal groups depends. In brief, the family has been moving away from the elaborate, formal, and involuntary structure characteristic of large and stable organizations toward the smaller, more intense, and more volatile association of freely consenting equals which is characteristic of more informal groups.

---

and responses. And, as might be expected, the evidence of Alfred Kinsey and his associates strongly suggests that these modes of behavior are much more prevalent in the middle class, especially among the more highly educated.

[3] *The Human Group* (New York: Harcourt, Brace, 1950), 280. The essay's general indebtedness to the writings of Ernest Burgess and Talcott Parsons on the family and marriage will be sufficiently obvious to most readers so that specific references have seemed unnecessary.

Conclusion

I will conclude with a venture into the more fanciful, where the sociologist can tread more easily than he can test. If changes in the relations between the sexes can affect their conscious sentiments toward each other, then why can they not similarly affect those feelings that are more buried and which are manifested only indirectly in overt behavior? If males have experienced a loss of status relative to females, then one should expect that at least some — like any group which has suffered a loss of status — would exhibit various forms of compensation for the loss and resentment toward the usurpers, and that these forms would be perhaps partly in the realm of fantasy.

Possibly the popularity of magazines of the *Playboy* type represents such a reaction. After all, the central themes of these magazines can be interpreted easily enough in terms of both compensation and resentment. There is self-enhancement through the vicarious association with the habits and objects of the rich and lofty. But the outstanding "plaything" of the "playboy" is women. His sure and easy "way with women" is perhaps his chief qualification for solid standing as a "playboy." The growing discrepancy between the fantasy — the smooth, self-assured, sophisticated, and uninvolved male mastery of uniformly devoted and eager women — and the increasingly free and equal relations between the sexes may be the source of the apparent popularity of these periodicals. Another branch of this type of periodical — a "lower" one by popular repute — expresses the male's resentment much more directly, sexual "sadism" permitting him to participate vicariously in a more vigorous revenge on those who have robbed him of his glorious patrimony.

iv. "We Distinguish — They Discriminate": Observations on Race Relations[*]

"Only so (by making comparisons) will we get that relative freedom from time, place, and particular circumstance that is required of those who would analyze processes."[1]

One picture always comes to mind when thinking of Everett Hughes as a teacher. He is standing at the lectern in front of the class, his glasses, which he had just removed, in his hand, and, with unconcealed relish, he is putting the finishing touches on some illustration. To his students, those finishing touches were the mark of a singular master craftsman. The craftsmanship lay in the precision and seeming effortlessness with which he would dissect the most commonplace situation and, with a deft and unexpected comparison, lay bare its core. The sense of discovery which resulted from this expert weaving together of the particular case and general principle made us feel that this was what sociology was all about and opened an exciting view of its possibilities.

His written work also demonstrates how effectively this skill lifts the restrictions of "time, place and particular circumstance." When students ask, in obvious disbelief, "Can sociologists ever be objective?", I usually suggest they read French Canada in Transition. *Here they can find a thoroughly dispassionate treatment of a most delicate, passionate and "socially relevant" subject; remarkable perception, which exploits an unusual variety of research techniques; and, as always in Hughes's writing, a gracefulness of style*

---

[*] In Howard S. Becker et al. (eds.), *Institutions and the Person: Essays Presented to Everett C. Hughes* (Chicago: Aldine, 1968), 69-79. Contributors were asked to preface their essays with a personal reminiscence of Professor Hughes.

[1] E.C. Hughes, Introduction to *American Journal of Sociology* issue on work (March 1952), 57:424.

unmatched, to my knowledge, in sociology. Perhaps the strongest testimonial to its merit is that, 25 years after its publication and despite unabated interest in its subject matter, French Canada in Transition *remains without challenge the definitive work in its field and a fresh source of pleasure and illumination every time it is re-read.*

One morning, after an introductory sociology class (in which race relations had never been discussed), a student approached me and initiated the following conversation:

Student: I'm from South Africa and feel bad about the way things are there. Can you tell me if the whites in South Africa are acting as they are mainly to hold on to their power and then rationalizing to justify it?

Author: Well, you probably know more about the situation than I do. But I want to ask you about the word rationalization. Do you think that the whites feel that it's not right that they should rule and the natives should be ruled?

Student: No, I think in their hearts they feel they're wrong.

Author: Do you think they feel they're superior to the natives?

Student: Yes.

Author: Don't they feel that their rule produces order and prosperity and that native rule would mean chaos, another Congo? That's what one keeps hearing from Rhodesia these days. If the whites see themselves as the source of order and prosperity and native rule as the source of bloodshed and chaos, wouldn't you expect them to feel much superior and to feel that they should rule and that both groups are better off with this arrangement?

Such discussions have doubtless become commonplace in recent years, but the student's point of view echoes one that is still popular among social scientists. Many of them, studying race relations in such places as South Africa, Rhodesia and Mississippi, work from the twin assumptions that the whites in these places treat the Negroes badly and that, "in their hearts," they know it is wrong. Few sociologists[2] perhaps would admit to so simple a characterization of their viewpoint, which makes its prevalence beneath all sorts of elaborate theories all the more intriguing.[3] Both assumptions obviously bar a sociological understanding of the relations in question. The first, as the observer's value judgment, is irrelevant, while the second seems inaccurate. Indeed, what evidence there is suggests the opposite: these whites act as they do because they believe it just and proper.

Before examining that evidence, let us consider why the opposite assumption — of guilt masked by rationalization — is so common. Its popularity illuminates some of sociology's special difficulties. First, few sociologists systematically try to see things through their subjects' eyes. Many refer occasionally to Thomas' "definition of the situation" in order to explain a particular point, but the brief walk-on role which they assign to this principle shows how little it counts in their scheme of things.

However, by overlooking the views of others, the investigator tends to commit an elementary and serious error, one which he often warns his students about: he

---

[2] For the sake of economy, the term "sociologists" will include social psychologists throughout this paper. The latter have devoted a remarkable proportion of their attention to race relations.

[3] See, for example, Gordon W. Allport's definition of prejudice: "thinking ill of others without sufficient warrant," in *The Nature of Prejudice* (Cambridge [MA]: Addison-Wesley, 1954), 7.

assumes that these others hold values similar to his own. Therefore, if their behavior seems contrary to these values, he attributes it to fears and desires beneath the conscious level which overcome the actors' conscious values. As a result, he often emerges with the following type of explanation: the "good guys" (that is, those with values essentially like his) act on the basis of conscious, ethical considerations, such as the so-called American Creed, while the "bad guys" act on the basis of "lower" motives more or less hidden from the conscious self by a screen of rationalizations which make peace with the conscious self by alleging that the other race deserves or desires no other treatment.

Within this general scheme for explaining the "bad guys'" behavior, there seem, in the area of race and ethnic relations, to be two main subtypes. The first, exemplified by John Dollard's *Caste and Class in a Southern Town*,[4] states that the real motives of the whites in denying the Negroes equal status are the "gains" which the whites make financially, sexually, and in prestige at the latter's expense. These motives are clearly "low" in the conventional scheme of things, and so the white man conceals them from himself by rationalizations about the mental and moral inferiority of the Negro. The second type of explanation, of which perhaps the best-known example is *The Authoritarian Personality*,[5] is now more common. Its main assumption is that race prejudice is a pathological form of behavior which emanates from "damaged" personalities, compelled by their own "injuries" to hurt others "weaker" than themselves.

These types of explanation, I have suggested, stem from a failure either to perceive or to lend credence to the "bad guys'" explanations or justifications of their behavior. How

---

[4] New York: Harper, 1937.
[5] Theodore Adorno et al. (New York: Harper, 1950).

that failure distorts the sociologist's perception of race relations is illustrated by the familiar and naively optimistic talk about the American Creed. The American Creed, with its emphasis on equality, sociologists often argue, provides the Negro with powerful support in his struggle for equality. The white Southerner, however attached he may be to the old and familiar order, nevertheless allegedly subscribes to that creed and accordingly experiences some inner conflict about denying the Negro equality, a conflict which ultimately weakens his determination to resist the Negro's quest for his "rights."

> The conservative Southerner is not so certain as he sometimes sounds. He is a split personality. Part of his heart belongs to the American Creed. The Southern conservative white man's faith in American democracy and the Constitution, *which he is not living up to,* is a living force of great importance for the future.[6]

In this quite characteristic approach, the American Creed is what *the sociologist* thinks it is — it has an objective, clearly identifiable character. It cannot be whatever its adherents think it is. All of this in the face of overwhelming evidence to the contrary. The following imaginary conversation is designed to show how misleading a picture of Negro–white relations may emerge from this oversimplified conception of the American Creed. It takes place between an interviewer of the Rose-Myrdal persuasion and a white Southerner.

Interviewer: Do you agree that racial and religious discrimination are contrary to the fundamental principles of American life?
White Southerner: Yes, I agree.
Int.: And you therefore disapprove of racial discrimination?

---

[6] Arnold Rose, *The Negro in America* (New York: Harper, 1964), 150 (italics added).

S. W.: Of course, I do.

Int.: Then are you in favor of integrating our schools and making it easier for Negroes to vote?

S. W.: Certainly not.

Int.: Why not? How can you justify this treatment of the Negroes when you say that you oppose racial discrimination?

S. W.: I do oppose racial discrimination. I am also against having Negro children in our schools and hordes of Negroes at the polls, not because of their color but because they lack the necessary qualifications. The right to vote should not be handed out indiscriminately — no country does, and mixing two groups with such different educational standards and accomplishments in the same classrooms would do both groups more harm than good.

Int.: Since you consider the Negroes less qualified, what has made them that way?

S. W.: What difference does that make? We're only talking about whether now is the time to integrate schools and abolish literacy tests.

Int.: Still, as a believer in the principle of equality, doesn't your conscience bother you about denying so many Americans full equality?

S. W.: No. Why should it? Take my grandfather, for example, and perhaps yours too. Mine was firmly opposed to giving women the vote. He claimed that it would be the worst thing that could happen to them and to the country. They weren't interested in politics, he argued, which was just as it should be. And whether he was right or wrong about women voting, I doubt that he ever felt guilty about opposing it.

Let's take another example. Do you think that everyone who now opposes lowering the voting age to 18 feels guilty about violating the American principle of equality? Are the reasons they give just a camouflage for the real ones which they are ashamed to mention?

Int.: But the 18-year-olds will get the vote in only three years.

S. W.: Exactly! When they're qualified.

Int.: Well, in that case, how can you justify denying the vote to those Negroes whom *you* consider better qualified than most whites?

S. W.: My grandfather used to say that he knew women who had forgotten more about politics than most men would ever know. Still, he never thought that was any reason for giving every woman the vote. Would you give it to every kid of 13 just because some of them know more than most adults?

The merits and representativeness of the Southern white's argument are irrelevant here. I have put these rather improbable words in his mouth for three other reasons. First, they show how, by failing to perceive others' views, the sociologist may distort their motives. For example, in assuming that the American Creed or even the Fifteenth Amendment has a fixed, objective meaning, the interviewer misses two vital truisms. The first is that, as the imaginary dialogue indicates, everybody is an egalitarian and nobody is. Everyone believes in equality for those whom he considers his equals and in inequality for those whom he regards as either his superiors or inferiors. The other point is just as simple — how anyone determines the worth of another group depends entirely on the criteria which *he,* not the investigator, considers relevant. That, of course, is why the interviewer's efforts to show the Southern white the "inconsistency" of his views seem doomed to futility. Since these two base their positions on different criteria, each is able to sustain a sense of consistency in the face of the other's attacks. Thus, consistency, at least in matters of this sort, is not a question of fact but of faith and, like all such matters, lies only in the eyes of the beholders. If this argument seems to belabor the obvious, one need only recall that not only the Rose-Myrdal view, cited earlier, but many other popular theories, including that of "cognitive dissonance," are based on the opposite assumption.[7]

Second, if we look at the interviewer's choice of criteria, the imaginary conversation demonstrates how the sociologist's place in his society may color his perception of it. Most sociology texts open with a warning to the student to this effect. They admit that the sociologist

---

[7] Leon Festinger, *A Theory of Cognitive Dissonance* (New York: Harper, 1957).

suffers from the handicap of having grown up in a particular society, which shapes his views and values. The emphasis on race and ethnic relations in North American sociology, for example, naturally reflects the historical dominance of this issue in both the United States and Canada. However, as the textbooks seldom continue, the ideological atmosphere in which the investigator lives may affect not only the questions he asks but also the answers he "finds." The immediate milieu of most American social scientists who study race relations is distinctly "liberal," and many are ardent advocates of racial equality. This fact coupled with the belief, as illogical as it is invariable, that one's moral position is scientifically sound results in the perspective illustrated in the preceding discussion of the American Creed.

Commitment to a cause is always a barrier to objectivity where that cause is involved. And since many social scientists feel so deeply about racial and ethnic equality, they find it hard to understand the viewpoint of those who deny it in particular instances. An astonishing number of investigators in this field are more concerned with whether their subjects' statements about other groups are valid and, if not, with why they hold invalid beliefs, than with whether the people who made them consider them valid, though only the last is relevant in explaining their behavior. Thus, instead of detachment, their subjects arouse the investigators' anger, contempt, or pity, and, not surprisingly, their professional literature is often a tiresome mixture of praise and denunciation.[8]

---

[8] For a summary of the findings and a critical evaluation of research on race relations in the United States between 1948-1958, see Herbert Blumer, "United States of America," *International Social Science Bulletin* (1958), 10(3):403-47; reprinted in the UNESCO publication, *Research on Race Relations* (New York: UNESCO, 1966), 87-133.

Finally, the Southern white's comparisons of Negroes with women and children were inserted because they offer a clue, I believe, to a more discerning approach to race and ethnic relations. The previous paragraphs have argued that objectivity is essential for useful research. But how can it be attained? Biases are not shed by acts of will nor by being written down for the reader's enlightenment. The only ways of reducing them that I know are either by absorbing the views of one's subjects through extensive contact with them or by somehow forcing one's way imaginatively into their minds. The latter, obviously a poor second choice, is often the only one available. How many of us know intimately many white Southerners, let alone Rhodesians or South Africans? And what is meant by the vague phrase about trying to enter their minds? The comparative method, as usual, provides an answer. If one sees race relations not as a unique phenomenon, as sociologists so often do, but as status relations, new paths to objectivity and understanding open readily.

Thus, instead of trying to discern the alien and perhaps repugnant views of white supremacists, we might substitute those of two other groups once sharply divided by status in our society, men and women. This battle, if not over, is not in the excited state that it was in some time ago and that American race relations are in now. It is therefore relatively easy to look at the views and feelings of the antifeminist men (and women) of several generations ago and see what they have in common with those of today's white supremacists (and acquiescent Negroes). While this idea is hardly new, its full value remains to be exploited.[9]

---

[9] All of this is neatly encompassed in the words, if not the intention, of R.E. Park's statement that the Negro is "the lady among the races." "Everywhere and always it [the Negro's "racial temperament"] has been interested rather in expression than in action: interested in life itself rather than in its reconstruction or reformation. The Negro is, by

However, detachment of this kind is not the only avenue to objectivity and fresh perception. Another path is paradoxically through comparisons which permit a vicarious sharing of the prejudices involved. This does not mean acquiring those of the white supremacists, a manifest impossibility. But how would we feel about children voting? If we answer that that would be ridiculous or if we feel reluctant to let them vote, are we not, as members of a "higher" status group, denying equality to a "lower" one? Would we not explain that denial on the familiar grounds that children are unqualified for these rights and that by withholding them we protect not only the country but children as well? In this case, by sharing their *type* of prejudice, rather than the particular one, are we not better able to discern the perspective of some Southern whites? Do we or those we know well feel guilty about living apart from people whom we fear or whose ways we consider inferior or with whom we feel less comfortable?

---

natural disposition, neither an intellectual nor an idealist, like the Jew; nor a brooding introspective, like the East African; nor a pioneer and frontiersman, like the Anglo-Saxon. He is primarily an artist, loving life for its own sake. His *metier* is expression rather than action. He is, so to speak, the lady among the races" (*Race and Culture* [Glencoe IL: Free Press, 1950], 280).

If Park's observations about the behavior of Negroes and women were essentially correct and if they also apply to children, then either all of these groups possess common biological traits, as Park implied, or else the connections between status and behavior are more subtle than even he perceived.

The best-known of these comparisons between the positions of Negroes and women is G. Myrdal's "A Parallel to the Negro Problem" in *An American Dilemma* (New York: Harper, 1944), Appendix 5. See also C. Kirkpatrick, *The Family* (New York: Ronald Press, 1963), 163-66.

These are all instances of the universal tendency to act toward other groups on the basis of a general or collective evaluation of them or, as it is usually called in race relations, a stereotype. This term too suffers from the common assumption that it describes a phenomenon unique to race relations. We hear constantly about the tendency (which the authors predictably deplore) to stereotype Jews, Negroes or Orientals. But what group or person does not stereotype most other groups, including his own? The larger and more complex the society, the more stereotypes there are bound to be and the more they will be based on second-hand and fragmentary information rather than on extensive direct contact. Each one of us can supply an endless list of personal examples. Stereotyping is universal and inescapable, and always seems to involve judgments about the social position and moral worth of the other group, on the basis of which we act toward it.[10]

If we compare some current stereotypes about other races with those which existed or now exist between the sexes and generations, some basic similarities in the perspectives of all three "higher" status groups emerge. Let us begin with the common stereotype, widely shared in this naive form by sociologists, that Southern whites are prejudiced against Negroes. Careful consideration plus one comparison shows how meaningless such common phrases are. In 1869 the United States Supreme Court explained its ruling denying women admission to the bar: "the natural and proper timidity which belongs to the female sex evidently unfits it for many of the occupations of civil life."

---

[10] For an incisive discussion of this theme, see H. Blumer, "Race Prejudice as a Sense of Group Position," in J. Masuoka and P. Valien (eds.), *Race Relations: Problems and Theory* (Chapel Hill NC: University of North Carolina Press, 1961) and "The Nature of Race Prejudice" in E.T. Thompson and E.C. Hughes (eds.), *Race: Individual and Collective Behavior* (Glencoe IL: Free Press, 1958).

Were the judges prejudiced against women? The question is obviously meaningless. How would the judges have reacted to that accusation? Would they not have been either indignant or amused, perhaps thinking that the accuser was out of his mind, but certainly incapable of understanding theirs? They would have alleged (how honestly we can never know) that their motives were to protect both women and the country, and that, far from being prejudiced against women, they felt just the opposite, which was why they were so prejudiced against women practicing law.

Similarly, do not adults who love their children become indignant if the latter begin to act as their parents' equals in certain situations? If their children were to claim equal rights about sex, drinking, and freedom to come and go as they please, would not many parents punish them severely in order to "keep them in their place"? Upon observing all of this, would we say, "They claim to love their children, but they really only love them" — and add knowingly — "in their place. What hypocrisy!" Would we not place some credence in the parents' claim that the punishment was motivated by a concern for their children's welfare? Would we imply instead that their "real" motives were the desire to conserve their liquor supply or sense of superiority?

Without pushing this analogy too far, might it not throw a somewhat different light on the traditional claim of white Southerners that they love *their* Negroes ("in their place" being taken for granted)? Do not the fear and indignation aroused by the mass desire of Negroes to leave their place have some parallels to the feelings of not so long ago that women might have similar ambitions which would be calamitous for everybody? The basic similarity in all of these situations is perhaps best summarized in that superb saying attributed to Negroes of some years ago: "In the North, the white says, 'Negro, go as high as you can but don't come close,' and in the South the white man says, 'Negro. come as close as you can but don't go up.'"

The idea of "place" is part of every social relation. Our sense of "place" (that is, "who or what I am" and "who or what the other is") always determines our beliefs about how we ought to act toward each other. Stepping out of that place — whether "above" or "below" — is therefore apt to antagonize others or arouse their contempt, especially where the "places" are clearly established by tradition.

If the "lower" status group finds the "higher's" place difficult to enter, the opposite movement, from "higher" to "lower," encounters even more formidable barriers. Girls boastfully "confess" to having been "tomboys," but "sissy" or any hint of effeminacy is a scathing insult to a boy. The "upward" aspirations of children, Negroes, and colonial peoples have often aroused scorn and indignation, but the European who "goes native" and the adult who "regresses" are apt to be viewed in terms of moral decay or psychiatric problems. Who is more suspect and baffling — the male nurse or stenographer, or the female doctor or executive? (This suggests that men condemn male homosexuals so vehemently not simply, or even necessarily, out of fear of latent homosexuality. Perhaps it is only another instance of the outrage and bewilderment that the "voluntary" déclassés seem to generate among their former fellows.)

Thus, although the "upward" bound are the chief objects of discrimination, the "higher" status group is perhaps even more confined to its place than is the "lower." The real difference between them is not freedom from restriction but the different value put on these places, which causes nearly all the traffic to move in one direction.

The efforts of "higher" status groups to keep restive lower ones "in their place," therefore, in one sense, require no special explanation: they are simply part of the general pattern of social control. It takes a strong ideological or theoretical commitment to go searching in the hidden recesses of people's minds for explanations of their behavior while ignoring or discounting the explanations which come spontaneously, emphatically, and clearly from their mouths. This view was expressed elegantly in a recent editorial which, in another context, suggested that "there is little to be gained from examining others' consciences instead of their arguments."[11]

The importance of "examining the arguments" becomes clearer when we see exactly what "rights" and "privileges" both groups in a paternalistic relation tend to deny to the "lower" one. Several generations ago wide differences existed not only in the educational, occupational, and legal positions of the sexes in our society but also in the latitude accorded to them in such matters as smoking, drinking, swearing, sex, and freedom of movement. The so-called double standard pervaded most areas of their lives. That this was a matter of status rather than of sex is evident both from the great changes that have since occurred in all of these areas as well as from the fact that they all were and, on the whole, still are denied to children.[12] When put together, the entire package of "discrimination" is revealing. It suggests that the "higher" status group does not simply and guiltily try to monopolize what it thinks is good — wealth and power, for example — but that both categories, "higher" and "lower," agree on what is unsuitable for the latter and therefore must, for everybody's good, be withheld from it.[13] What, other than a firm

---

[11] From *National Catholic Reporter*, reprinted in *Globe and Mail* (Toronto), Jan. 6, 1967, 7.

[12] That aspiration to "higher" (adult) status may be an important motive in many juvenile offences is suggested by the number of cases involving the illegal use of liquor and cars (boys especially) and illegal sex relations (particularly girls).

[13] The wrath and ridicule to which both sexes subjected the feminists illustrate once again how much a paternalistic system depends on its acceptance by both groups, "subordinate" as well as "superior." They also demonstrate

conviction of the strong and capable protecting the weak and vulnerable, could explain the varied assortment of items in the preceding package? Thus, an examination of their "arguments instead of their consciences" indicates something about the latter as well, which suggests that, in the instances discussed here, we can learn more about race relations by studying the structure, sentiments, and ideology of paternalism than from so-called individual psychopathology.

The well-known and centuries-old controversies about who should be entitled to vote are probably the most conspicuous illustrations of these timeless and universal aspects of paternalism. The historical struggle to extend the franchise down the social scale, first along the lines of wealth and class and then along those of age and sex, and, in our time, to the "colonial" peoples of other colors, has, as everyone knows, always encountered essentially similar arguments — about the dangers of entrusting power to those who were not qualified to use it properly. At the moment the same kind of controversy seems to be arising in our very midst — in the relation of students to the universities' academic and administrative bodies. A paternalistic relation between groups is hardly limited to any place, time, or "personality type," and most of those involved view its passing, like that of any established practice, with either great hopes or great misgivings.

I have not been arguing that the statements of the "higher" status group are in themselves an adequate

---

the implausibility of the guilt-leading-to-rationalizations theories. If men rationalized about denying women "equal rights," did women, whose views were essentially similar to men's, rationalize too? On the other hand, why would women feel guilty, since, unlike men, they were not preserving a monopoly of "privileges" for themselves? Thus, the suggestions that only one or that both groups were rationalizing seem equally implausible.

explanation of the relations between the two groups. Nor are the relations between such groups always paternalistic; most forms of anti-Semitism seem to lie outside that framework, and the relations between whites and Negroes in the United States have moved largely beyond it. I have only been suggesting that the sociologist must neither ignore nor discount the views of those who discriminate and that the kinds of comparisons suggested here may help him to understand these viewpoints should he find them remote and perhaps repugnant. Nor am I implying that all who discriminate or participate in such a system necessarily share the prevailing view that the other group deserves or desires an inferior position.[14] Nevertheless, they do not disagree with it sufficiently to risk the consequences of their fellows' disapproval.

Nor, finally, have I been denying the importance of money and the desire for prestige and power as motives which contribute to the maintenance of the racial *status quo*. Indeed, this kind of explanation is not an alternative to the one discussed throughout this paper but is complementary to it. Thus, if someone were to ask, "Have you ever heard of an elite or higher status group which willingly surrendered its advantages?" could one not reply equally validly, "Never. But have you ever heard of one which didn't believe that those advantages were thoroughly deserved and, what's more, that they were in the best interests of all?"

---

[14] Equally elaborate systems of discrimination arise spontaneously on the other side of the status barrier, when one group sees the other as superior, not merely in position but in merit. Since this is not a favorite theme of sociologists, our knowledge about it comes mainly from the literature about aristocracies, colonialism and the times when the status distinctions between the classes, sexes, and generations were greater than they are now.

Leo Zakuta

I came across a letter Leo had received from **Herbert Blumer**, *one of his teachers during his graduate studies at the University of Chicago, whom Leo greatly admired. The article Leo contributed to the festschrift for Blumer is entitled "On 'Filthy Lucre.'"* [AZ]

UNIVERSITY OF CALIFORNIA, BERKELEY

BERKELEY • DAVIS • IRVINE • LOS ANGELES • RIVERSIDE • SAN DIEGO • SAN FRANCISCO   SANTA BARBARA • SANTA CRUZ

DEPARTMENT OF SOCIOLOGY
BERKELEY, CALIFORNIA 94720

Dec. 8, 1970

Professor Leo Zakuta
Department of Sociology
University of Toronto
Toronto, Ontario
CANADA

Dear Leo:

I have just received my copy of HUMAN NATURE AND COLLECTIVE BEHAVIOR in which you were kind enough to contribute an article. I am writing to thank you warmly for this expression of good will and esteem. I always recall you as one of the best students among the many hundreds of doctoral candidates with whom I had close association. Thus, I am gratified that you are among those who saw fit to honor me with the above festschrift.

I have read your article with a great deal of interest and profit. You have done a very fine and sensitive job in teasing out very important points of distinction that are overlooked by scholars in our field. I like the article very much. I hope that you will continue with you interest in this matter and bring forth other publications on it.

I trust that everything is going along well with you. It has been some time since I have heard from you or about you. Am I wrong in my impression that you are still at the University of Toronto? I hope that in some way our paths may cross so that we could have a decently long chat. Warmest regards.

Cordially,

Herbert Blumer

Herbert Blumer

v. On 'Filthy Lucre'*

lucre: gain or money as the object of sordid desire (from the Latin: *lucrum*, gain)[1]

NO CLERKS OR SELLING IN RICH BOND STREET

London (AP)-Bond Street's very name is the trademark of quality.

Extending from Piccadilly to Oxford Street, its quarter-mile of glassed and gilded windows, doorways, and showcases constitute a tight little enclave of richness without ostentation that exudes luxury, craftsmanship, good taste — and altitudinous prices.

Bond Street is, in fact, so high class that to refer to its establishments as stores or shops seems almost an affront.

Within deep-carpeted interiors are fastidious but highly knowledgeable men and women dealing with the public (some of them would probably faint if you called them clerks) who won't even use the word "sell."

They avoid that crass, commercial verb with such circumlocutions as:

"We recently supplied one of our clients with ..."
"One of our patrons obtained from us ..."
"We were able to provide Her Royal Highness with. ..."[2]

Bond Street's many counterparts have made its distaste for "commerce" thoroughly familiar. Equally well-known is

---

* "On 'Filthy Lucre,'" in T. Shibutani (ed.), *Human Nature and Collective Behavior" -- Papers in Honour of Herbert Blumer* (Englewood Cliffs NJ: Prentice-Hall, 1970), 260-69.

[1] *The American College Dictionary* (New York: Random House, 1947).

[2] *Globe and Mail* (Toronto), October 12, 1964, p. 10.

the charge that it is carefully cultivated, that mercenary and snobbish motives combine to extract the money of the rich by creating the pretense that its establishments are something more than businesses. The newspaper story shows how vulnerable Bond Street's claim is. For all of its sympathy, the story's point is that a shop by any other name is newsworthy, meaning that these are really stores in which hired clerks sell.

But why are these terms "almost an affront"? And what makes the word *sell* so "crass" and "commercial" that it is carefully avoided? Why, in brief, is commerce "crass," not only on the world's Bond Streets but almost everywhere?

The answer is plain when we note who else, according to the convention, does not "sell." Among the models which come immediately to mind are the arts, which are supposedly dedicated to beauty and self-expression, and even more, the professions, which ideally are more concerned with "service" than with "profit."

Are business, the professions, and the arts fundamentally different activities? And do their practitioners approach their work with different pecuniary motives? Sociologists have been inclined, like people at large, either to accept such distinctions at face value or else to deny their validity, but, in either case, to regard these as important and answerable questions. For our purposes, however, they are neither answerable nor relevant. This paper will treat these claims and beliefs as data to be analyzed rather than as questions to be answered, on the grounds that it is the general assumptions about these matters, and not their "real" nature, that determine how people view these pursuits and therefore treat their practitioners. To explain people's behavior, we must find the "reality" which they think exists.

For us, accordingly, a pursuit will be whatever people, including its own, think it is. And our terms — business (man), profession (al), selling, service, profit, and many others — will represent the popular classifications rather than an endorsement of them.

The relatively low standing of commerce seems to be both ancient and general. The Bible, if not inveighing against trade directly, is a storehouse of injunctions against the pursuit of money, which, in the popular mind, is closely connected with commerce, an association largely responsible for trade's low standing.

In his first epistle to Timothy, Saint Paul warns that "the love of money is the root of all evil" and that therefore to enter God's service one must be "not greedy of filthy lucre." Even if one succeeds in amassing it, Jesus serves notice that "It is easier for a camel to go through the eye of a needle, than for a rich man to enter into the kingdom of God." Money is also central in such symbolic events as Jesus' "cleansing of the temple" — "(he) cast out them that sold and bought in the temple, and overthrew the tables of the money changers" — and his eventual betrayal "for thirty pieces of silver."

Many centuries later a similar aversion to trade, money-handling, and usury among Christians and Moslems facilitated the concentration of Jews in these activities, thereby confirming their pariah status. As might be expected, where animosity towards them waned, many Jews turned from their fathers' occupations in trade towards those of higher standing, especially the professions and the arts. (Perhaps because it is the chief weapon with which Jewish "success" is attacked, the sociological explanations of their rapid rise in America have made relatively little of their base in trade as a source of literacy, wealth, and familiarity with the world around them.)

The medieval contempt for the money handler in the West had its parallel in the East, especially in China and Japan, where the merchant often ranked beneath the artisans and even the peasants. In Europe, despite industrialism, being in trade continued to represent a social comedown in most "elevated" circles.

Commercial and industrial society changed rather than destroyed these ancient attitudes. Business careers became more acceptable, but reservations about commerce remained. The traditional Jewish and Christian belief that it desecrates the Sabbath may be dying, but is not yet dead. Dramatic events, as usual, reveal these familiar feelings most clearly. Immediately following the two Kennedy assassinations, for example, television commercials were banned, doubtless out of the feeling that they would — or would be thought to — profane the sacred nature of these occasions. Similar rules are attached to sacred personages, as Canada's Governor General, the Queen's representative, recently joked:

> I'm glad I wasn't fined for some misdemeanor tonight, because I couldn't have paid. Ever since I became Governor-General, I haven't had a dollar in my pocket. Royalty and its representatives just don't carry money. That's what aides-de-camp are for.[3]

What accounts for these qualms and reservations about money, an object supposedly of such universal desire? The rich and varied vocabulary of everyday life provides part of the answer. The terms which disparage an "inappropriate" or "excessive" interest in, or talk about, money range all the way from "indelicate" through "materialistic" and "vulgar" to "crude," "boorish," and "gross." But it takes the unusual to lay bare the heart of the usual, in this case someone daring to speak what many others thought or feared. Some years ago a leading Canadian businessman told a parliamentary committee on prices that his company's policy was "to buy as cheaply as possible and to sell as dearly as possible." The hue and cry among his

---

[3] *Ibid.,* March 25, 1969, p. 2.

interrogators and the public at large expressed the belief that underlies all of these other instances — that pursuit of money, especially of "profit" or "gain," is a clear manifestation of self-interest.

Although self-interest and altruism are obviously value judgments passed on behavior and therefore cannot be regarded as motives by the social scientist, they are seen as among the most powerful and persistent of motives by people at large. And it is to this social, rather than sociological, classification of motives that we must direct our attention.

In general, "self-interest" takes a low place in the human classification of motives; and "selflessness" or "altruism," a high one. The reasons for this distinction seem unfathomable, but its consequences constitute our basic data. For example, it is the belief that the professions offer or ideally should offer a "service which goes beyond self-interest" that contributes to their higher standing.[4]

This does not suggest that people classify individuals so simply. Whether they see particular businessmen as "idealistic" or certain professionals as "money-grubbers" is beside the point. What matters is that they feel that, in business, the pursuit of wealth is so natural and inevitable that only outsiders can control it but that, in the professions, the practitioner himself must restrain it to avoid conflict with the ideal of service. Accordingly, the public protests "excess" business profits on the grounds that "the government shouldn't let them get away with it" but resents the doctors' "preoccupation with money" because "they shouldn't be like that."

---

[4] Accuracy suggests that terms such as self-interest, altruism, pursuit of money, and provision of service be preceded by such phrases as "what is defined as" or "what is believed to be" or, at least, that they be set in quotes. Simplicity of style requires, however, that this idea should henceforth be assumed.

Why people make these distinctions is intriguing. Why do they demand a service ideal from some occupations and not from others? Once they expect it, they consider that work to be a profession or to be worthy of that "honor." Some occupations designate their work as a professional service but encounter strong resistance to that claim.

All of this suggests that the sociological penchant for using external (objective) criteria to distinguish between occupations and professions is essentially barren. It does not mean, however, as some conclude, that classification is unimportant. What does matter is the classification that people — including the incumbents — make, the reasons they make it, and the consequences that follow. Our aim will be to answer these questions.

In general, people distinguish between "higher" and "lower" wants, and they label activities and pursuits accordingly. One example is the stereotype of the *nouveau riche*. He not only pursues the higher wants "insincerely" or indulges the lower ("tasteless") ones "conspicuously," but he allegedly does so for social self-aggrandizement, that is, self-interest. This combination makes his spending "ostentatious, vulgar, and unrefined," a common way in which money is thought to lose its luster.

In contrast, those activities that supposedly cater to the higher wants are labeled professions. Traditionally they have concentrated on such matters as health and life (physical as well as moral and spiritual); legal protection against the loss of freedom, reputation, and wealth; knowledge; and, perhaps stretching a point, the safety of the country.

Because these wants are more highly valued, people are unwilling to entrust them to just anyone. For example, the higher wants are thought to require rare and hard-to-acquire skills, which the consumer (here, a patient or client) therefore feels unqualified to judge. Because of this sense of inadequacy and because he places so much stock on these matters, he turns to those whose skills and motives he feels he can trust.

Thus, if a man believes that his life is in his doctor's hands or that his salvation is in those of his priest and that he cannot judge the services they provide, he draws considerable comfort from the faith or trust that their ultimate concern is his well-being rather than their own. (The same reason may lead him to resent as "impersonal" a show of "brisk efficiency" by the doctor which he would welcome in the department store.)

Out of the ideals of service and trust a distinctive set of rules and expectations arises governing the relations between practitioner and patient, one that can be seen more clearly by comparing it with its counterpart in business. If the professional's skill is thought to require trust, his motivation is supposed to justify it. In trade, however, the time honored maxim is *caveat emptor*. Furthermore, the ideal of service is supposed to restrain the ways in which patients and clients may be sought, thereby ruling out the "blatant" advertising and self-promotion open to business.

Other patterns of control in the two areas are even clearer manifestations of these rules. The store and the medical office will serve as our illustrations. The customer is expected, and, in any case, is considered free, to shop around for goods and services. To shop in a comparable way for a doctor, especially on the basis of price, is "unthinkable" (even if some people do so). The seller is not ordinarily thought to have the right to refuse to sell goods and services which he has available. While the doctor also has no right to refuse his services if he judges them necessary, that judgment is his, as is the form which they should take.

The word that is used in both cases is revealing. It is the customer and the doctor, not the patient, who "order." Three types of people normally give orders: superiors in a hierarchy of authority, doctors, and customers. The last, it is true, order goods and services rather than command people. Nevertheless, there is some parallel in the patient's placing himself under doctor's orders and the businessman or seller taking orders from customers.

The rules define the seller as subordinate to the buyer in additional ways. He "waits on," "helps," and "serves" customers. (In this context, "serves" carries a meaning far different than the presumably voluntary and lofty service referred to previously. Its general sense is closer to servitude and subservient.) His "May I help you?" is expected to show at least a suggestion of deference. He is, after all, thought to be playing this role primarily to earn a living, that is, for money.

The rules about dominance — about who is thought to have the greater right to control the relation — in business are neatly summarized in the oft-stated ideal, however attenuated it may be in practice, "The customer is always right." By contrast, even the cynical phrase that "Doctors bury their mistakes" implies that they are never known to be wrong.

The patterns of control in the two areas differ in still other ways. The customer may buy at any time during store hours; indeed, he usually finds delays in service extraordinarily irritating. The doctor, on the other hand, fixes the time at which he is available to the patient, and the latter usually feels not only a compulsion to appear on time but little resentment and less surprise if he spends some time in a "waiting room" before the doctor "takes" him. (Many business enterprises also have waiting rooms where, however, it is the sellers who usually wait for the buyers to "see" them.) Unlike patients, doctors are seldom "late." They often keep patients waiting, but it is because they are "very busy" and therefore running behind schedule. (The concept "late" is but one more example that the subject matter of sociology is not physical events, but states of mind.)

The phrase which is expected to conclude both transactions is perhaps the most revealing of all. The offering and acknowledgment of thanks is a sensitive index of social structure. The seller is usually expected to thank the buyer, but it is the patient who generally thanks the doctor even if the latter has just pronounced a sentence of death. This particular pattern indicates which party formally defines himself to have been in greater need of the other and therefore the greater beneficiary of the exchange.

TABLE 1

PERCEPTION OF OCCUPATIONS

Profane occupations	Sacred occupations
Impersonal relations	Personal relations
Lower wants	Higher wants
Lesser skills	Greater skills
Responds to the wishes or orders of others	Control of the relation
Open payment	Indirect payment
Strong pecuniary motives	Financial motives secondary
Self-interest appropriate and/or inevitable	Self-interest secondary to the service of others

The medical office and the store represent two of the further points on a continuum representing that cluster of ideas on the basis of which people make moral distinctions among occupations.

The polarities shown in Table 1 represent ideas or images which people attach to particular occupations in a general way. Even if they do not expect to find them in a crystalline form in any particular instance, they nevertheless rate occupations and organizations on the basis of the degree to which they think they either do or should approximate these models. That the models themselves exist in people's minds becomes quite clear from the sentiments aroused when elements of both are thought to be intertwined. Bond Street, as we have seen, is a case in point, although its great prestige almost permits it "to get away with it." Before analyzing this type of establishment we must return briefly to the doctor's office.

Money, we have noted, is widely regarded as a symbol of almost naked self-interest, in contrast to the sacred services and ideal of disinterest of the medical profession. The feeling that money contaminates this image seems to be strongly built into the devices for handling it. One is generally not expected to ask the doctor about his fees, nor, except perhaps in the poorer districts, to pay him directly. Instead, one either pays his nurse — outside of his presence — or, more often, upon receipt of his (un-itemized) "statement," mails a check, which his nurse presumably receives, credits, and deposits, thereby sparing him from any direct contact with it. (A similar gingerly approach to money appears in universities and other circles which speak of stipends, honoraria, emoluments, and increments.)

This suggests one more reason for the medical profession's resistance to medical insurance plans, including its coolness to arguments that such schemes would bolster the doctor's income by guaranteeing payment. They would also thereby end his practice of seeing patients without charge in hospital clinics, thus depriving him of a personal sense of *noblesse oblige* and the profession of a major symbol of the ideal of disinterested service.

What lies at the two ends of the continuum can also be detected by examining the cases in the middle. Instead of Bond Street our example here will be its close relative, the "first class" restaurant, since their patterns of control are fairly similar.

The greater its prestige, the more the restaurant seems to exert, or try to exert, control over the customer or "patron." The time is often arranged by appointment (a reservation), though here the "guest," unlike the medical patient, has the greater say. The establishment imposes rules of dress which lesser restaurants could not hope to get away with, although the recent controversy about pantsuits has demonstrated the problems of enforcement.

Similar difficulties may arise in the seating of its clientele, which this kind of place also attempts to control. However, here too it finds itself uncertain and uneasy when these efforts meet with resistance.

Thus, the authority that these restaurants try to assert is usually discreet and gentle. Lacking much force, it relies on the decorum of the guests for its main support. When challenged, it tends to yield, with signs of discomfort, or to be reasserted in a form which makes a show of deference.

Some establishments of the highest prestige offer the "diner" little if any choice of foods. Food, indeed, is an unacceptable term for dishes which emanate from "culinary art." (One comes here not to eat but to dine.) Where choice is available, the waiters often feel free or are expected to make "suggestions." While these are far from the doctor's orders, lesser restaurants would hardly dare to make such overtures for fear of arousing the suspicion that they were prompted by self-interest.

Money, of course, is kept discreetly in the background. Sometimes the prices appear nowhere on the menu, which is hardly an invitation to inquire about them, or they may appear only on the menu of the party's host. After the meal the check in nearly all restaurants is presented face down, but in these the handling of the money is carefully avoided. The check, the payment, the change, and the tip all travel on a tray. Cash registers are either nonexistent or inconspicuous. Credit cards increasingly facilitate a type of billing not unlike the doctor's. Mints, matches, and endless cups of coffee are offered to the "guests," who upon departure are likely to exchange thanks with their "host." (The owner of the exclusive shop may summon his subordinate to take the customer's money and wrap his parcel while he continues to chat with him.)

The care with which money is handled in these instances has many parallels where the sacred and profane are thought to be mixed. Obvious examples are contributions to the collection plate in church and the groom's or best man's anxiety about "slipping" the clergyman money (in an envelope, naturally) after the wedding. The latter is likely to be accompanied by the giver's profuse thanks, which are designed to convey the thought that the money hardly begins to compensate for the service rendered.

As an arch-symbol of the profane, money arouses a sense of incongruity and hence discomfort, not only when it accompanies the ideal of service but also when the relations involved are felt to be personal. Tipping provides some excellent examples of this combination.

Formally, even the most customary tips imply a recognition of special service — something personal beyond the minimal requirements of duty. That this occasions at least mild discomfort is evident from the rule that tips should be both given and received unobtrusively.

Tipping is also complicated by questions of status.[5] Our sense of status difference tells us when we may tip, so that it seems easier to tip the young boy who delivers our newspaper or medicine than the mature or elderly man. Should one tip the barber who owns his establishment, for

---

[5] Status here also refers to how those involved perceive it.

example, or the waiter or cab driver who happens to be one's friend or, perhaps more interestingly, the father of a friend? In her column of advice, Amy Vanderbilt cites some of the rules.

GIFTS FOR NURSES

Q: I do shopping for an elderly lady in a nursing home. I have a most difficult time finding Christmas gifts for her to give to people I don't even know. It is especially difficult with the nurses, for there are quite a number of them and she cannot spend a large amount of money on any one. I have suggested an attractive card with a bill enclosed, but have been told that this is socially wrong. Perhaps it is, but these days one tries to be somewhat sensible, and it seems to me the nurses would far rather have the money to spend as they like, or perhaps to combine with similar gifts.
A: I think your suggestion is excellent. One does not tip nurses; this is an offense to their professional standing and is frowned upon by their professional societies. However, a Christmas gift of money is not really a tip, and would be much more acceptable than some little gadget you choose without knowing the preference of the person to receive it. Money gifts at Christmas are a little "iffy." Money may certainly be given to employees; children love getting it; and sometimes it is the best gift for a relative who can really use it. But if there is any chance that offense might be taken, it is safer to send a gift certificate, or, of course, a gift itself.[6]

---

[6] *Ladies' Home Journal*, November, 1966.

Thus, the higher the status of the recipient, the more discreet and doubtful tipping becomes until it passes through this zone of mounting uncertainty into one in which tips begin to give way to gifts.

Thus, another major consideration affects the transmission of money — the question of status. As Amy Vanderbilt's advice indicates, sentiment generally favors the flow of money down the status hierarchy. This becomes especially apparent when the direction of the flow is reversed. The latter is made tolerable only by the feeling that something of immeasurably greater value has descended in return. The thanks which the doctor and clergyman receive may testify to the "inequality" of this exchange, but, as we have seen, they do not completely erase its "indignity." Not too distant parallels are the feelings aroused when wives support husbands and children parents.

Beliefs about personal relations raise problems similar to those which stem from the ideal of service and considerations of status. All three are closely connected — the first two because one's friends and relatives are supposed to have one's interest close at heart, and the last two because the protective and caring role of superiors often involves the downward flow of money. Combined, they create ticklish problems.

All three may deter the doctor from charging his friends, relatives, colleagues, and other professionals. Other combinations create those familiar dilemmas of everyday life in which we wonder how to repay the neighbor who has spent considerable time repairing our car or money entertaining our children or, in general, those whose "generous" gifts, gestures or favors we feel unable to reciprocate.

The most troublesome cases, of course, are when we dare not assume which of the two — friendship or business — was the other's main motive. If we do not offer payment, will he think that the love of money led us to take advantage of him in the name of friendship? On the other hand, will offering it give offense by implying that he acted out of mercenary rather than friendly motives or that we are treating the "favor" of an equal as the work of an employee?

A common way in which people try to get around the difficulty of deciding between money and thanks is by giving gifts. The symbolism and understandings surrounding gifts cleanse and transform the money and make it acceptable.

Among the considerations, therefore, that restrict or at least direct the flow of money are fear of ostentation, the ideal of service, the view of the relation as personal, and concern about status. Its alleged power to contaminate these ideals is what makes money "dirty."[7]

The connection between these ideals and the "cleanliness" of money shows up clearly in what was once called charity and is now called philanthropy. Charity, of course, is a classic virtue. But "it is better to give than to receive" not only because giving is considered morally ennobling, to say nothing of socially elevating, and, it is sometimes darkly hinted, a means of cleansing the money, but also because receiving charity is so often seen as humiliating and debasing.

Thus, the status gap between giver and recipient which, in the case of the buyer and seller, was so narrow as to be barely discernible, grows in the measure that the giver of money is defined as receiving less than an equivalent return. This principle extends beyond money payments, as the expressions of gratitude to the doctor and clergyman

---

[7] The late Clint Murchison, one of the world's wealthiest men, is reported to have said, "Money is like manure. When you stack it up it stinks, but when you spread it around it makes things grow." *Time,* June 27, 1969, p. 62.

indicate. The moral superiority of giving to receiving thus seems to run through social relations in general. (The reverse is equally true — the greater the status difference the less the giver is expected to receive in return.)

This principle becomes clearly apparent as we move out towards the ends of the continuum where God, in his majesty and goodness, gives everything of value to man, who is so base and insignificant that he can offer only gratitude, praise, and promises of obedience in return. On the purely human level one of the lowest places is occupied by the beggar, particularly the one who, in asking for himself, does not make even the gesture of offering pencils or a tune in return. In seeking "something for nothing" he upsets the people he approaches because whether they give or not, they feel put in the position of having to degrade him so openly.

This explains why the beggar and the priest have figured so largely in religious symbolism. The eastern religions have tended to combine the two roles, but in the Christian imagery they have represented mutually dependent polar opposites. The beggar, whose social position is so base, seeks only to satisfy his material wants and can offer nothing in return, while the priest, God's representative, out of compassion for the beggar gives him all that he has.

The sacred office of the priest offers our final reminder of the "contaminating" effect of money. To enter totally into the service of God, a man must renounce forever the "corrupting" attractions of money and sex. These similar images of money and sex are no coincidence. Both are seen as sources of enormous pleasure and thus as among the most powerful of motives but also as the essence of the profane or dirty. As we have seen, this combination restricts their expression with many barriers, legal and moral.

The "low" character of these alleged motives leads, of course, to denials of their importance, at least in one's own behavior. The strength of these disavowals varies, of course, with the spirit of the times. It is therefore curious that the twentieth century should have been so shaken by the "discoveries" by two nineteenth century, middle European Jews — Marx and Freud — that these hidden motives are what makes the world turn.

Leo in his study at home with Jamie
1965

III CORRESPONDENCE

1. Exercises in Futility: Complaints and Occasional Commendations

This section consists chiefly of my letters to the media: many letters to the Globe and Mail, the University of Toronto Bulletin, the National Post, other publications, and the CBC. The title has a double meaning. It refers primarily to my finger-in-the-dike response to the tidal wave of political correctness, and also to the black hole into which my letters to the Globe and Mail on that subject predictably vanished. My letters to the other publications usually did appear. The letters in each part are arranged chronologically. Unpublished letters are so indicated; those to individuals were not intended for publication. [LZ]

WONDERS

Alchemy is not dead, merely mutated. Instead of turning other metals into gold, it now promises affirmative action without quotas.

Leo Zakuta
2007

Reminiscences, Rants, and Raves

i. Letters to *The Globe and Mail*

The Globe and Mail, 19 February, 1963

My first venture

Children at the altar

Your feature article, "Children at the altar" (Feb. 14) was thoroughly irritating. Highly superficial articles of this type are so common that one ordinarily ignores them, but the prominence given to this article and its unwarranted claim to speak in the name of sociology make silence too costly.

No doubt some sociologists are frightened by the number of teen-age marriages; so, presumably, are some truck drivers, some sales clerks and some bankers. So what? The fears of all of these people, the sociologists included, have nothing whatever to do with sociology or with being a sociologist. Sociology is concerned with understanding why people act as they do. It provides no logical basis whatever for fear, dismay, hope or satisfaction about that behaviour, just as the study of, say, the dragonfly, cannot logically provide a pulpit for the zoologist.

Incidentally, perhaps one or several sociologists have used the term "defective population explosion" — I have never heard of it, but there are many sociologists and anything is possible — but why attribute this inanity to sociologists in general? As for the "good recipe for instant families," why was the kitchen sink overlooked?

Many other superficial and misleading statements in the article invite comment. However, I merely want to salvage what may be left of the reputation of sociology and sociologists after incessant maltreatment of this kind.

Leo Zakuta
Assistant Professor of Sociology
University of Toronto

Leo Zakuta

The Globe and Mail, 18 November, 1979

Propaganda?

Your column about depression in women ("Between the sexes: what gets women down," Nov. 3) made two main points:

1. "close examination of the myths surrounding the relationship between female biology and mental derangement reveals that they're often figments of the masculine imagination. ..." Instead of a "close examination," not a shred of evidence was provided on behalf of this dubious proposition. Why the "masculine" imagination" any more than the "feminine"?

2. The author's more important point was that the main cause of depression in women is subordination and dependence. "Because women have been encouraged to remain dependent, they rarely develop the feeling that they have the necessary inner resources to deal with life on their own ... marriage makes women submissive ... wives are encouraged to sacrifice their identities to their husbands and children, and depression is the result."

To support this equally dubious argument, statistics were cited to show an alleged increase in female depression since the Second World War. It must therefore follow that in recent decades women have been growing more dependent and submissive, and that their "identities" are becoming increasingly submerged. That certainly should be absorbing news to feminists as well as to everyone else.

When so many genuinely interesting changes are occurring in the everyday relations "between the sexes," it's a pity that a column with that title should consist of little but simple propaganda.

Leo Zakuta

The Globe and Mail, 8 May, 1985 (not printed)

Research?

Stephen Strauss's fine column (May 6) provided interesting reading. He cited a document called Treatment of the Sexes in Research, produced by the Social Sciences and Humanities Research Council, which informs us that "We are now aware that there is no value-free science. This realization does not mean we give up standards of scientific rigor and of objectivity."

Objectivity, it states, is an illusion, but it must be pursued anyway. And why not, since, in the next breath, we hear that objectivity is not only possible, it's easy. "I have not yet been given a solid, reliable example of bias against men even in the strongest feminist research," declares Naomi Black, a "member of the panel which screened the document." The secret seems to be to leave the research to the underdogs — women on relations between the sexes; blacks on race relations; employees on labour relations; and children on the family. The possibilities are endless. It's a comfort to know that our research is in such sure hands.

Leo Zakuta

Leo Zakuta

The Globe and Mail, June 15, 1987 (not printed)

Bewitched, battered, and bewildered

According to your editorial (Violence in the family, June 11), "the latest sobering probe into family violence comes from the Canadian Advisory Council on the Status of Women in its report, *Battered but not Beaten*. "Sobering" is the right word for the recklessness of the report's allegations and the carelessness of its procedures. We are told that "wife battering still hurts or maims as many as one million Canadian women a year" and that "Wife abuse encompasses more than physical blows and includes bullying, threats and controls that pose physical, sexual, economic or psychological danger to women and their children, friends and relatives." (June 10) Only the family pets are missing from this list.

How did we get such a nice round figure as a million? What constitutes battering? Is it any physical contact associated with anger or irritation? Were all reports accepted at face value? Whose reports were they? Were all reports by the same individual counted as separate cases? Only the reports of the alleged victims or were the accused perpetrators given their day in court as well? Anyone who assumes that the investigators must have overcome such difficulties knows little about how most of them work. Their usual procedure, especially if spurred by ideological commitment, is to dismiss such questions as irrelevant, secondary, and obstructionist. If it is often next to impossible to define physical "battering" and establish whether it occurred, the extension of battering to include bullying, threats, insults and the like takes the subject off into impenetrable mists. With that definition, breathes there a soul anywhere who has not been "battered"?

The kinds of punishment and "discipline" of women and children which were more customary in our patriarchal past have become much less acceptable today. Therefore we are probably witnessing more protest and talk about these events when they do occur rather than an actual increase in their occurrence. Nevertheless, within days, CBC Sunday Morning cited the figure of one million as a simple fact rather than as a report, and the next day the CBC announcer described the battering of women as an "epidemic," which the speaker who followed on Commentary naturally called on the federal government to stem. What "Battered but not Beaten" and similar "reports" chiefly prove is that anything repeated often enough becomes an unquestioned truth. Fold in a touch of hysteria and you have an instant epidemic.

Leo Zakuta

The Globe and Mail, 18 December, 1989 (only the first paragraph was printed)

Madness multiplied

As if the Montreal massacre weren't unbearable enough in itself, it has become a launching pad for an assault against men in general, to which your editorials, columns, and even cartoons have contributed. The latest and most revealing turn in this campaign is the exclusion of men from some memorial vigils. Who takes it upon themselves to pronounce these bans? Do such vigils belong to anybody other than injured humanity at large?

~~~~~~~~~

Six million Jews were killed in the Holocaust simply because they were Jews. Can anyone imagine gentiles being banned from the memorial ceremonies? As for the talk about "context" — anti-male propaganda masquerading as pop-sociology — the Nazi horror frightened Jews everywhere to their marrow. Nations were involved, not mere individuals. Were there editorials and speeches denouncing the gentile mentality?

Should there have been? Were Clifford Olson's string of gruesome child murders or the recent Mount Cashel disclosures evidence of a society that hates or "oppresses" (your word about men) children? Is preying on the aged a symptom of how the young (more generalizations) brutalize the old?

If the tirade that has been unleashed against men had been directed against, say, blacks, Asians, or women, you would have been flooded with protests invoking the anti-hate laws. But of course that would never have happened. Fear and fairness would have made you squelch such talk at the first foul whiff. But the current hysteria has swept these considerations aside for men. They may seem fair game, but targeting them is ignoble.

Leo Zakuta

In response to the Globe's having printed only the first paragraph of "Madness multiplied," Leo wrote the following letter. [AZ]

The Globe and Mail, 22 December, 1989 (not printed)

It is dangerous to write a letter to *The Globe and Mail*. Although my original letter (above) was not longer than most which appeared that day (Dec. 18), you exercised your "right to condense" by printing its first 4 sentences and eliminating the remaining 13, thereby distorting its message. That's not condensation, but butchery, which would seem mindless were it not that your paper apparently has unlimited room for male bashing, but so little for a defence against it.

Leo Zakuta

The Globe and Mail, 26 August, 1991 (not printed)

A sow's ear

Maxwell Yalden's letter (Shallow arguments on "liberty," Aug. 24) rejects "artificial quotas" and "reverse discrimination" but endorses "affirmative action." But that last term is only a euphemism for those other two phrases. Choosing or rejecting people on the basis of some category instead of on their individual qualifications is always discriminatory. And by any other name, it smells the same.

Leo Zakuta

The Globe and Mail, 28 December, 1991 (not printed)

Tales from the treadmill

"Terms of endearment that aren't" (Dec. 27) subjects the tired theme of how men debase women to yet another protracted flogging. "Most women, if not all, have been put in their supposedly rightful place with expressions like dear, dearie, honey, sweetie, doll" the author insists, without any sign of awareness of what everybody knows — that women use exactly the same terms [in speaking] to men. Ergo?

What matters is not this transparent silliness but the *Globe*'s predictable response to it — a feature article: a half-page spread plus large headlines and a huge drawing. No matter how feeble, the material in this genre finds generous space in your paper, whereas efforts, however brief, to expose this cant are usually stillborn. If this one appears, it will be an exception.

Leo Zakuta

The Globe and Mail, 6 April, 1992 (not printed)

Who knew Quebec?

It's odd that "25 authors and academics from English Canada" should have dissociated themselves from Mordecai Richler without indicating how they had been associated with him. Nor, judging from their remarks, could they have been intimately associated with Quebec in that era. Anyone who wanted to play their inappropriate game could easily find more than 25 "academics" and others who, like us, were born and brought up in Quebec and who would eagerly "associate" themselves with the validity of Richler's observations. The "25" have also managed to ignore the most compelling evidence about contemporary Quebec — the countless thousands of the English-speaking who have voted with their feet.
One point needs amplification. Many of Richler's critics accuse him of ignoring the Anglo-Saxon anti-semitism of that time, which, they say, was "just as bad." But was it? Many of the English in Quebec, reluctant to associate with Jews, tried to keep them out of "their" institutions — business, professions, universities and what not. As vile as that was, the French Canadian form was even more

dangerous — public rather than private, expressed in the media and in political movements. It involved incitations to action that in a different environment — Eastern Europe, for instance — led to pogroms. English anti-semitism would have kept the Jews in the ghetto, but the French form would not have let them live in peace even there.

Odd again that these 25 apparent "liberals" should decry Richler's talk about anti-semitism in Quebec. The wish to be "correct" rather than accurate leads people down strange paths.

Annette and Leo Zakuta

The Globe and Mail, 18 August, 1992 (not printed)

The Danegeld

Will our politicians ever realize that they can't buy Quebec's allegiance to Canada? Quebec's decision to leave or stay will not depend on bribes. Such inducements are worse than useless; they're dangerous, because they only encourage the recipient to raise the ante until it is too high to meet. When it is refused, both sides are inevitably hurt and angry.

Leo Zakuta

The Globe and Mail, 15 March, 1994 (not printed)

Shattered myths?

Re: "Unwed mothers vindicated: landmark data shatter myths" (Mar.14)

What an odd story that was — more like two contradictory ones. The first part elaborated on the headline. The froth included Dan Quayle, Murphy Brown, and a social work professor. But the actual report on the study's findings, which followed, told a very different tale, one which gave credence to those "myths" rather than "shattering" them.

E.g.,

1. A table showed that the unmarried mothers remained on welfare twice as long as the married ones.
2. Of teen-age mothers, 69% of the unmarried were on welfare in the decade compared to 43% of the married.
3. Among mothers who first gave birth after age 20, 56% of the unmarried were on welfare compared to 10% of those married.
4. "...the study found that many of the unmarried mothers never caught up with the married in education and income."
5. In 1979, 19% of the unmarried who had just had children had a high school diploma compared to 64% of the married.
6. By 1989, 39% of the unmarried mothers had graduated from high school compared to 77% of those married.
7. Poverty rates among the unmarried mothers were also significantly higher: 53% lived in poverty compared to 18% of the married.

And so it went. What "myths" the study may have "shattered" we are left to guess.

Leo Zakuta

The Globe and Mail, 2 November, 1996

Who's the foulest of them all?

Margaret Wente, meet former Quebec Superior Court Judge Jean Bienvenue. He said that in the depths of depravity men were no match for women. She simply reversed it. He deservedly lost his seat on the bench. And she? Guess.

Leo Zakuta

The Globe and Mail, 29 November, 1996 (not printed)

Response to Abella

Apart from its first and last sentences, Irving Abella's documentation of anti-semitism in English-speaking Canada in the 1930s and 40s (A few last reflections on the Roux affair, Nov. 21) was useful and instructive. His opening sentence read, "There was a sad irony to the spectacle of English Canadians sitting back after the resignation of Jean-Louis Roux as Lieutenant-Governor of Quebec and smugly enjoying the sight of French Canadians trying to come to terms with some genuine ugliness in their past." Obviously Mr. Abella did not enjoy that sight. Why should he assume that many others did? His last sentence said, "That (Canada's barring Jewish refugees after the last war), not parading down the streets of Montreal, was the real crime of this period." Both were crimes; neither diminishes the other.

His article's real problem, however, is not what it says, but what it does not say. In concentrating on the similarities in anti-semitism in Quebec and in English-speaking Canada, it overlooks important differences. Who even then were the English-speaking counterparts of Abbé Lionel Groulx, *Le Devoir* and Adrien Arcand? More significantly, it overlooks the great differences between Quebec and English-speaking Canada since then. Mr. Abella mentions "the Mackenzie Kings, the Frederick Blairs and the Vincent Masseys who closed Canada's doors to Jewish refugees." They opposed letting Jews in. Arcand and his associates wanted to throw out those who were in. Who are King's and Blair's parallels in the public life of English-Canada today?

The struggle of "French Canadians trying to come to terms with their past" is difficult precisely because the old feelings are still so widely entrenched. There is no better example, as others have pointed out, than the contrast between English Canada's reaction to Mr. Abella's book *None Is Too Many* and Quebec's angry denunciation of Esther Delisle's book. Those same feelings keep erupting in the remarks of public figures like Parizeau, Landry, Michel Gauthier and Pierre Peladeau, among others. Where are their current counterparts in English Canada? Similarities are important, but so are differences.

Leo Zakuta

The Globe and Mail, 31 December, 1997 (my title was "Was it murder?" but they published all the letters that day, including mine, under the heading "The Latimer case")

The Latimer case

Your editorials questioning Robert Latimer's sentence ("Latimer's sentence on trial," Dec. 2 and 3), are themselves questionable. Their first theme was that, in charging and sentencing, the law is not something to be bent or twisted on the basis of the accused's apparent motive: "Second-degree murder is murder, except possibly where the victim gives consent, never where the murderer claims a loving motive."

The facts do not support this sweeping assertion. As everyone knows, there's many a consideration between a killing and the charges that the Crown decides to lay. For instance, why did the Crown not charge Mr. Latimer with first-degree murder when there was no dispute whatever about his premeditation and even planning? Presumably it concluded that, given his apparent motive, it had no chance of obtaining a conviction that carried a prison sentence of at least 25 years before eligibility for parole. If so, the Crown considered motive from the start and bent the law accordingly.

The second theme was: "There is no such thing as an acceptable motive for setting out to take another person's life." This assertion is just as questionable. The law does find "acceptable motive" — killing the enemy, including civilians, in war, executing convicted killers (in many jurisdictions) and even killing in self-defence.

This is not to say that these acts are all alike, but only that, in the eyes of the law, killing — even intentional killing — and murder are not synonymous. Killing is the act; murder involves the judgment about whether that act was wrong and, if so, to what degree.

Accordingly, many question the justice of a murder charge at all in the Latimer case. If one believes that his action was not wrong or, even if wrong, so mitigated by his compassion and devotion, then second-degree murder is no more appropriate a charge than first-degree murder, from which the Crown understandably shrank.

All of this raises another issue — the law's ability to deal with such distinctions.

Leo Zakuta

The Globe and Mail, 20 June, 2001 (not printed)

Who created whom?

Joanna Manning and Mary Daly haven't got it quite right (A step backward for women, June 19). Ms. Manning wrote "In ... prayers God is invariably referred to as 'he.'" As theologian Mary Daly put it, "Where God is male, the male is God." To fine tune it, the order of Daly's two phrases should be reversed. It was best expressed in that old quip, "God created man in his own image and man returned the compliment."

Leo Zakuta

My letter consisted of the above paragraph. The Globe and Mail, as noted above, did not publish it. Nevertheless, I added the following passages to it shortly afterwards, but did not re-submit it.

The ancient world of our patriarchs is reflected in its legends, which speak to us across the ages. None speak more clearly or powerfully than those about the primacy of maintaining the male lineage. The dread of its extinction is symbolized in the twice-told tale of the willing sacrifice of the only son, as God puts Abraham and then himself to the supreme test.

    Thus Abraham submits to God's requirement that he sacrifice Isaac to prove his loyalty and devotion to God. And, in a later elaboration, God himself sacrifices his only son to prove his love of mankind and offer it a pathway to eternal salvation. Only an ultimate end could justify such terrible means.

The Globe and Mail, 22 October, 2001 (not printed)

Root causes?

The events of Sept. 11 have unleashed a torrent of responses which begin with "I don't condone that attack for a moment but. ..." Various messages complete that sentence. Most urge a search for "the root cause" of the attack or for "diplomatic solutions." Others warn against "escalating the cycle of violence." Still others identify "the root cause" as U.S. foreign policy and/or "poverty and despair." Here are some questions for these respondents.

1. Did you advocate a search for "the root cause" or for "a diplomatic solution" when Germany invaded Poland or annihilated the Jews? Or when Japan bombed Pearl Harbor? Or when the Ku Klux Klan fire-bombed black churches? Did you warn against "escalating the cycle of violence"?

2. Didn't U.S. foreign policy's most unforgivable failures occur in Central and South America or, in the eyes of some, in south-east Asia? Why are none of the terrorists from these places?

3. If "poverty and despair" are "the root cause," why do so few of the terrorists, their associates, and leaders seem to fit that model?

The search for "root causes" usually leads up a blind alley, and the words are a code for inaction, a ploy to deflect the anger of the injured and the outraged. The examples above show that when people genuinely abhor acts of violence, they do not look for "root causes" or "diplomatic solutions." They want vigorous measures to stop those acts, catch the perpetrators, and "bring them to justice." Can anyone recall pleas to "understand" a serial rapist? Will these apologists tell us that the rapist's victims brought it on themselves? That approach is a little like the joke about the two social workers who came across someone lying battered and bloody at the side of the road. "Quick," said one to the other, "we must find the person who did this. He must feel terrible."

Leo Zakuta

The Globe and Mail, 10 October, 2001 (not printed)

I submitted the following piece to the Globe and Mail on 10 October, 2001 for the "Comment" section. It was not printed. The version here has been updated.

Same-sex marriage?

Should same-sex marriage get official recognition? "Yes, now," said its advocates; "no, never," said the Pope, George Bush, and Ralph Klein; "soon, perhaps," said Jean Chretien and Paul Martin. "Let's see," said Stephen Harper, while many Liberal backbenchers and U.S. Democrats didn't know what to say. The sides lined up in battle array have left the state and church almost no escape. (That's what I wrote just a few years ago. In the meantime, provincial courts, the Supreme Court of Canada, and even Parliament seem to have found a path to "Yes." Some things do move quickly. This article does not take sides, but looks at how a "Yes" answer may affect us.)

Marriage is ancient and universal; every society has given it a place of importance. Like any custom, it is always embedded in webs of rules and understandings, some of which specify and prohibit whom and how many one may marry at any time. For instance, forms of polygamy, including polyandry (one wife and several husbands), have long flourished in many places. The deepest understandings, however, lie below the level of awareness and remain unspoken and seldom questioned. Few marriage rules are universal, but always and everywhere, as far as I know, the unspoken assumption has been that marriage can only be between the sexes. Until now.

Now that central principle is under attack. Having come all the way from "the love that dare not speak its name" to *marriage* itself in the historical blink of an eye, what may be next? Will it be opposite-sex couples, one of whom has a same-sex lover, or even same-sex couples with an opposite-sex third party? Indeed, such combinations probably exist already as new versions of the *ménage à trois*.

Larger questions come to mind. Is monogamous marriage itself still safe? Monogamy seems safer than marriage, although there are warning signs. Curiously, as some homosexual couples now want to marry, many more heterosexual pairs do not. (Are both eager to do what was once forbidden?) Will official marriage fade away or become mainly the province of the religious and homosexuals? And will monogamy also become optional? Is polygamy or even group marriage on the far horizon? Perhaps. Some lesbian couples have children, sometimes by the same father. If the father or fathers wish to remain involved with their children, might that set the stage for another protest that the one-to-one rule is too "exclusive"? For instance:

> And there is John ... (40) who is close enough to fatherhood to almost taste it. A mutual friend introduced him to a lesbian couple who were looking for a man who would be more than a sperm donor — an active father in their child's life

— and the threesome are now negotiating a co-parenting agreement. ... He is considering moving house to be closer to the mothers, who have become his close friends. The three prospective parents want an informal open-door arrangement that would allow the child to move from the mothers' home to the father's without scripting every step in a contract that reads like a post-divorce custody settlement.[1]

Here are a few more recent story headings from the *Globe and Mail*:

"Pregnant woman called him 'Papa,' sperm donor's court petition says" [nd, AZ]
"Man wants access rights as the father, while lesbian couple claim parent roles" (14 Sept., 2004)
"Same sex? Then why not legalize polygamy?" (Norman Spector, Op-ed, 27 Dec., 2004)
"Lesbian asks court to grant status as boy's third parent" (27 Sept., 2006)
"Boy can legally have 3 parents, court rules" (3 Jan., 2007)

Does it still seem so far-fetched?

Could surrogacy lead to the same possibilities for male pairs, a form of polyandry? Might plural unions become the preference of some heterosexual couples *with children* where one or both has found another partner? Plural unions may evoke less abhorrence than homosexuality itself did "just yesterday." Polygamy was never a remote idea even in Western society. Mistresses abounded, and bigamy and pockets of plural marriage are familiar. But same-sex marriage was beyond even the abhorrence surrounding

---

[1] Margaret Philip, "Gayby boom," *Globe and Mail*, 3 May 2003.

homosexuality; it was unimaginable, which is, of course, why no laws exist to forbid it. But that was then. And given how quickly the unthinkable can become the unstoppable, are any of these things inconceivable?

This is not meant as a catalogue of horrors, as in "See what may happen if we embark on the slippery slope of same-sex marriage." (Sociologically, it is neither a slope nor slippery.) The changes that took place during the sexual revolution of the last century and a half, hailed as "advances" and "liberation" by their advocates, almost always aroused widespread alarm and indignation. Many of these changes eventually became the uncontroversial currency of everyday life. Today's conventional family life and relations between the sexes (and generations) would have made the hair stand up on the necks of our not-so-distant ancestors. Will same-sex marriage and plural marriage go the same way? In the realm of the social, alas, prediction is futile. The only clear view is backward.

Official recognition, say the same-sex advocates, would make the pair eligible for all the benefits and entitlements of conventional couples. If so, that may bring another issue out of the shadows — how should such eligibility be determined? Until now, it has been geared to the traditional family organized around cohabitation and economic dependence within a household. But, as everyone knows, that family is becoming something of a shadow of its former self, as new forms of domestic life mushroom around it. So we find many non-sexual and even non-familial domestic groupings — single parent families, adult child and dependent parent(s), sets of siblings, but also friends and still other combinations — who live together in economic dependence.

An emerging issue is whether such households, or only those involving a sexual relation, should be eligible for benefits and entitlements. If the household prevails, these forms of assistance would become detached from marriage of every kind, which might further reduce the incentive to marry. While the household does not provide a clear criterion for the allocation of benefits and entitlements, a neat boundary disappeared once eligibility was extended beyond official marriage into common-law relations.

All of this raises another question. We usually try to explain important social changes by digging deeper. Thus, the growing indifference of heterosexuals to marriage obviously owes much to the altered position of women. That, in turn, clearly stems from the emergence of the more isolated and egalitarian nuclear family, and radical changes in the relations between the sexes and generations. These developments can, further, be linked to fundamental changes in the organization of society, such as the massive growth of cities, industry, and commerce, technological revolutions, and the like. But what underlying shift accounts for the sudden softening of feelings about homosexuality? None seems evident, except perhaps erosion of the traditional family and the rise of alternate forms. Maybe the winds of change can sweep across the face of our society without being accompanied by subterranean rumblings.

Leo Zakuta, Professor Emeritus, Sociology

The Globe and Mail, 18 September, 2003 (not printed)

Property?

A letter (History of marriage, Sept. 17) repeats a widespread misconception: "Until recently marriage was about ownership: the man owning the woman."

That idea confuses authority with ownership. Husbands and fathers (parents) did have considerable authority over their wives and children in our past, but they did not own them. Ownership involves the right to dispose of property by such means as sales, trades, gifts, or sometimes even destroying it. Husbands and fathers had no such rights. The letter cites the dowry as further evidence that daughters were the property of their fathers. That's illogical. If a father was selling his daughter to her husband, the money (dowry) should have gone in the opposite direction — to her father, not her husband. Sellers receive payments, not buyers.

Leo Zakuta

The Globe and Mail, 28 March, 2004 (not printed)

What threat?

Your editorial (Clarke's view of Bush, Mar. 27) began on the right track, but ended right off the rails. Its last sentence said: "Even if Mr. Clarke disagreed with that decision ("to take on Iraq"), in a sense Mr. Bush was only doing what he (Mr. Clarke) advised: acting pre-emptively against a gathering threat." What gathering threat? In every televised appearance last week, Mr. Clarke emphasized that there was no evidence that Iraq was a threat to the U.S.

Leo Zakuta

The Globe and Mail, 29 November, 2005 (not printed)

Hunting

The massive hunt for who or what is responsible for the black-on-black killings in Toronto continues. The hunt would be amusing if the situation weren't so tragic, because the name of the game is pin-the-blame, and the hunters place it on everyone and everything, except where it belongs. They blame the larger society for "systemic racism, segregation, and discrimination"; they blame governments for not providing more money for recreational centres, counseling services and the like; they blame the schools for the high dropout rates; and the police for the silence of the witnesses. Thus, their search focuses not on the black community, but on the outside society and its institutions, which allegedly create "poverty, hopelessness, and despair" in young black men, phrases which the hunters repeat like a mantra.

Where they do not search is in the black community. It is a curious form of denial. They do not blame the drug trade, the killers themselves, and the witnesses who protect them with their silence. The taboo against pointing to these groups is so strong that the hunters either overlook them or else regard them too as victims of the larger society, which somehow (how?) twists them into those shapes.

In the midst of all this come the reports of Rev. Rivers and his colleagues and their "Boston miracle." Rev. Rivers declares that his group's main goal was to break down "the wall of silence" that had allowed the killings to continue with impunity. However they did it, it seems to have worked. Their "miracle" refers to the dramatic decline in the black-on-black killings in Boston. Perhaps Toronto could learn something valuable from Boston.

The shooting at the funeral at the church may also have nudged the search in the same direction. The shock seems to have led to a closer look at the black community. A striking manifestation was the *Globe and Mail*'s editorial afterward (The many fatherless boys in black families, Nov. 26). The full significance of the absent fathers is difficult to ascertain, but what is clearly important is that the editorial dared to cross the forbidden line to examine the black community itself. Could the hunt be shifting its direction?

Leo Zakuta

The Globe and Mail, 21 December, 2005 (not printed)

Questionable "truths"

Every election campaign features "truths" that are far from self-evident. One is that politicians should confine themselves to "discussing the issues." But whatever for? Such discussions produce only a shameless shower of promises as the parties try to outbid each other. These promises constitute each party's platform, a device designed to hoist it as high as possible, perhaps even into office in a forthcoming election. So how can anyone take seriously the "discussion of the issues"? And when the election is over, that hoist is removed and disappears. The politicians find it easy to ignore what no longer exists and was only a device anyway. Nevertheless, many people are surprised and upset when that happens. In the first TV debate, we witnessed an amusing attempt to make the politicians promise to keep their promises.

Another unquestioned "truth" is that a high voter turnout is desirable. Again, why? Is there or can there ever be any evidence that the level of voter turnout has any relation to the quality of the ensuing government? Why shouldn't governments be chosen by those who care enough to vote? What can be gained by the efforts to drag in those who don't care to vote?

Leo Zakuta

The Globe and Mail, 12 September, 2006 (not printed)

Pap

The article, "Pull up terrorism by the roots" (Sept. 11), occupied three-quarters of your op-ed page with nothing but pap. It consisted mainly of unsophisticated criticism of the usual explanations of terrorism, but not until near the end did the writer disclose his own discovery of "the roots" — and quite conventional roots, indistinguishable from those which he had dismissed earlier. Be that as it may, now that "the roots" are supposedly known, how can they be "pulled up"? On that vital matter, the article said not a word. It's astonishing that it was given such prominence.

Leo Zakuta

ii. Letters to *The Globe and Mail* Columnists

To Steven Strauss, 16 December, 1990

I read both of your columns about David Suzuki with great interest and satisfaction. I've heard him often on the radio, and read many of his articles. Your remarks hit the nail squarely in the proper place. Were I not gun shy, I would have expressed this view in a Letter to the Editor. But the *Globe and Mail*'s butchery of my last letter is too fresh in my mind to risk putting myself in their hands again. However, I do want you to know that there are others who share your view and admire your courage in tackling such an icon.

Leo Zakuta

To Rex Murphy, 20 June, 2001

A belated note of appreciation for your splendid column (Voices from the twilight zone, June 9th). I wanted to write this as a Letter to the Editor, but other things intervened and it didn't get done in time. Nevertheless, I do want you to know how much I always enjoy your columns, and especially that one on the fractiousness in the Alliance and the NDP.

There are similarities in the two parties' woes. Their difficulties arise from their defeat in the last election. Just as in sports, political defeats elicit cries for the leader's head. The NDP doesn't appear to recognize how much the Alliance's looming menace cost it. Many a potential NDP voter was too frightened of the Alliance to do anything but vote Liberal.

Hard times bring the parties' purists to the fore. They seem to imagine that the political playing field is a level one — or else they don't care — and argue that pushing the party further away from the centre will gain it adherents. But the field curves downward as it moves farther from the centre, and the path which they espouse would bring both parties closer to the groups at the fringes who talk only to themselves. (Your remark about the Albanian Film Festival made me laugh out loud.) Maybe we will all gain if the zealots succeed and their parties become less audible and visible.

On a quite different theme, of the many remarks on the radio and TV on the night of Pierre Trudeau's death, yours stood head and shoulders above the rest. I wanted to write you then, but wasn't sure how to reach you in the absence of an e-mail address. If you have a copy of those comments, I would appreciate seeing it.

Leo Zakuta

To Jeffrey Simpson, 26 November, 2001

I enjoyed your column on the NDP in Sat.'s *Globe & Mail* very much, especially on the differences between opposition and government. One can almost say that when parties exchange office, they virtually exchange scripts. A platform, in any event, is just a device to hoist a party into office and, like most hoists, disappears when its job is done. And the stances, as you showed so well, are the careful one of those in office versus the carefree one of the opposition, who can say anything they think will please the public. 'Twas ever thus.

Leo Zakuta

To Ed Greenspon, 26 November, 2001

Your column on the NDP in Sat.'s *Globe & Mail* was brilliant. The unforgettable first sentence[2] said it all. Many

---

[2] "It's hard to know who poses the greater internal threat to the NDP .... Svend Robinson for promising to bring clarity

years ago I wrote a book about the CCF. Since then I have watched the NDP's thrashings about from a distance, through the media. But the media seldom get it exactly right. You did, so it was a pleasure to read.

Leo Zakuta

Greenspon's reply:

Thank you very much for your generous feedback, especially so from someone who knows what he's talking about.

To Heather Mallick, 16 March, 2003 (not for publication, LZ)

Bravo for that column (A kiss across the abyss, Mar. 15); it was exactly right. I'm a long retired sociology professor (U of T), with a long-standing interest in that subject, having taught courses on the family and relations between the sexes for decades. My central theme in all those courses was that for centuries, the sexes — and the generations — (in the West) have been growing closer, a bit like the converging movement of tectonic plates. One can see it in every area and activity — work, costume, speech, or what have you. ("The growing gulf," indeed!) Interestingly, the lower plate (substitute status group) moves faster than the other in this convergence. It's always thus when groups of different status converge, e.g., assimilation. But this is getting to be too much like a sociology lecture or paper instead of a brief e-mail.

---

to the party's positions or Alexa McDonough for continuing to sow confusion."

The book that you chose as a symbol of the change, *Pride and Prejudice*, was also excellent. I made the same choice when I taught, spending considerable time on it, and always giving my classes a major assignment to discuss the relation between Elizabeth and Darcy as a reflection and forerunner of the growing belief that romantic love was becoming viewed as a requirement for marriage. The main theme of that book, in my view, is that "love conquers all," especially the great barriers of social class. Darcy not only lowers his head and gaze to look at Elizabeth, as you say, but "incredibly," proposes marriage to someone so beneath his station because he is smitten by her intelligence and character. Even more "incredibly," Elizabeth refuses such a totally unbelievable "catch" because she considers his character defective. Not until she realizes how mistaken she has been about his character can she really come to love him, and their marriage transcends all the barriers.

Is the abyss between men and women still there, as you write? It depends on what one regards as an abyss. Compared to the past, or the traditional societies of the East and Near East, the gap now seems almost invisible, which many there find shockingly decadent and immoral. But though the convergence has traveled a great distance, it is still in progress, and far from complete. One of the many interesting consequences of all of this is that men and women, in and out of marriage, can be friends. That even applies, though less, to the generations. Enough! I could go on and on and already have, but your column inspired me.

Leo Zakuta

Heather Mallick's reply:

What a wonderful letter. I have male friends, and my husband is my closest friend. That's what Margaret said about Pierre, you know. They loved each other, but she never felt he was her friend. Your course sounds wonderful; wish I had taken it at U of T. Cheers,

Heather

To Suanne Kelman, 26 October, 2004

Dear Suanne,

That was a very good piece on Margaret Wente in last week's *Globe and Mail*. Annette and I are great fans of hers. Your remarks about the pretentious Margaret Atwood were the cherry on the sundae.

Leo

Unfortunately, I could not retrieve several admiring letters I wrote to Margaret Wente.

To William Johnson, 19 April, 2007

Your Columns

Dear Bill,

That was still another fine column in Tuesday's *Globe & Mail* — an impressive compression of much of Quebec's history in so short a space. So was your last column, calling for a clear statement by Quebec politicians of what they want. Not that any answer will be forthcoming, as you well know. None of them will dare to do so, even if they were so inclined, as long as the name of the game in all elections is simply the demand for "more." Nevertheless, the call to put up or shut up is useful: less, I think, for Quebec than for the rest of the country, whose willingness to give more may be less elastic than Quebec's demand for more. But it won't be soon. Annette, as always, sends fond regards.

Leo

This was the latest of a series of letters that I sent to Bill Johnson in praise of his columns. The others, alas, are irretrievable.

iii. Letters to the [University of Toronto] *Bulletin*

The Bulletin, University of Toronto, 22 January, 1979

Referees' letters will lose credibility

In the continuing debate about the right of students to have full and free access to their files, I have seen no reference to one practical consequence of such a policy — its effect on admission and fellowship procedures where letters of reference are required. The purpose of such letters is to obtain more information about the candidate than appears on the transcript.

As is well known, the referees almost invariably try to "help" the candidates by portraying them as favourably as possible and by avoiding any remarks that might conceivably be construed as "damaging." Although these practices limit their general credibility, letters of reference do have some value. However, if referees find it so hard to be frank even in confidential letters, they will be much less candid when they know that the student can see the letter.

Thus the limited credibility of these letters will inevitably diminish as candour does. Those who decide on admission and awards will therefore have to rely more heavily on the only other evidence available to them —

grades. The net effect of "open access" to letters of reference will almost certainly be to reduce their importance and increase the importance of grades alone.

Leo Zakuta

The Bulletin, University of Toronto, 7 January, 1980

Squeak

"Of Deans and deanlings" by David Rayside and Colleen Sheppard, Dec. 3, had several curious aspects — a full-page spread, no less, complete with pictures of the authors, and a front page teaser: "Something is dreadfully wrong with the office of the Dean of Arts & Science." But perhaps the oddest was the subtitle "A front-row view of an institution in decline." Front-row indeed! The article sounds as if the authors don't even know where the building is. They go on and on about the deans' alleged preoccupation with plagiarism and with the neatness of Sidney Smith Hall, two activities which are about as central to the dean's office as they are to most instructors, who also occasionally encounter plagiarism and a messy classroom.

To have cited such minor matters as typical and central, the authors must know astonishingly little about the deans' many and varied duties. Anyone is entitled to be heard, but *The Bulletin*'s overblown promises of a mighty roar couldn't turn this effort into anything more than a prolonged squeak.

Leo Zakuta

The Bulletin, University of Toronto, 24 January, 1983

Male and what created she/he them?

Is sexist speech an incurable disease? That sad thought was occasioned by the Jan. 10 *Bulletin*. It devoted an entire page to cure us of our "sexist" language only to demonstrate how deep and insidious it all is. The article began with a graduate student putting a "chair*man*" in his linguistic place by informing him that she was not a "lady" but a wo*man* (her words, my emphasis). Wo*men*, fe*male*, hu*man*kind — like a worm-infested apple, the article fairly crawled with such words. Indeed, its accompanying "Guide to the unenlightened" showed us how to use them instead of their "sexist" predecessors. (For instance, we are to say humankind, not mankind.) Surely, not wo*man*, but woperson. And, since injured sensitivities must be our first concern, perhaps we should think again about per*son*, regardless of its innocent derivation. What's to be done about hu*man*kind and fe*male*? Why not leave them and their ilk to the inventors of "chairperson" and "chair"? Anyone who can construct words that come so trippingly to the tongue ("The Chair abandoned itself to take part in the debate.") should be able to mistress this simple problem personfully. Will all now join in bringing these good thoughts to a close with the ancient refrain (1983 version) "Apeople."

Leo Zakuta

The Bulletin, University of Toronto, 15 June, 1987

News?

The social scientists' gift of discovering what everybody already knows was well illustrated by your full page story (Criminologists find news media reinforce dominant culture, May 25). The headline invites the question — what other culture would the media reinforce? (Or indeed attack, mirror, or what have you?) The authors also reveal and deplore — in the fancy language which usually bedecks much ado about very little — the media's preoccupation with "deviance." They must be the only ones who haven't heard the phrase: "When a dog bites a man, that is not news. But if a man bites a dog, that is news." It's also the first principle of sociology.

Leo Zakuta

The Bulletin, University of Toronto, 26 November, 1990

Old quotas, new quotas

President Robert Prichard's[3] Oct. 18 statement to Governing Council on the aftermath of the disruptions of Jeanne Cannizzo's[4] class at Scarborough College raises serious issues. His remarks are admirable, but I wonder what action the University will take to deter further classroom disruptions. In my experience, university

---

[3] John Robert Stobo Prichard was President of the University of Toronto from 1990 to 2000. [AZ]

[4] Jeanne Cannizzo was the organizer of the Out of Africa exhibition at the Royal Ontario Museum, which led to those disruptions.

administrations have been far freer with words than with deeds in support of academic freedom in the classroom. If the recent disruptions had been the work of white supremacists, would the president have responded by appointing "race relations advisors"? That response encouraged and legitimized the very behaviour which his words to Governing Council condemned.

The President's remarks about race and "racism," especially as magnified in public on Metro Morning by his race relations advisor, are ominous. They not only, in effect, blame the institution for the disruptions, but offer as a remedy a series of procedures which necessarily entail, among other things, a further return to the pernicious quota system that once permeated our universities. Besides their obvious unfairness to many individuals, these quotas were damaging to the institutions [themselves], because they placed other considerations ahead of academic qualifications. In the decades following the war, the universities became increasingly "blind" to those improper criteria, and the quota system steadily eroded and sometimes disappeared.

Now quotas are back and are spreading, this time openly, in the service of another ideology. But once the principle is accepted, it cannot be contained, because the number of groups who are "significantly under-represented" is potentially inexhaustible. Some of the current claims are highly persuasive, and others will doubtless become so. It is already easy to discern the beginnings of that endless line of claimants.

The contest between quotas and quality is not new. Quotas always exist in order to place other criteria ahead of quality. The universities have begun to lose a long struggle which they were well on their way to winning.

Leo Zakuta

Reminiscences, Rants, and Raves

The Bulletin, University of Toronto, 22 July, 1996

Say it as it is *(My title was "Dr. Pangloss' report")*

Behind the flowery administrative verbiage of the report on the School of Graduate Studies is a disturbing fact — much of the School's most important work will be gutted. "The new SGS," says the report, "is no longer a processor, checker, and gatekeeper" (Supplement, "Restructuring the School of Graduate Studies," June 3). These glib words dismiss and denigrate what were the university's efforts to maintain standards of graduate admissions and programs. Anyone with experience knows that turning "gate-keeping" over to the departments often guarantees a decline in standards.

Much better to have said plainly, "We are eliminating these important tasks because we haven't enough money." At least that would have made the cost clear. Instead, the report adopts the Panglossian stance that all is for the best in the best of all possible worlds–"We'll cut down, we'll save money, and we will be all the better for it." Queen's Park will cheer that message; painless surgery is its credo. And since money is the bottom line, why keep four associate deans when one or two could handle what remains?

Leo Zakuta
Associate Dean, SGS, 1972-76

The Bulletin, University of Toronto, 13 March, 2000

Thunder from afar

Although not yet president, Robert Birgeneau[5] has all by himself proclaimed that henceforth the University of

---

[5] Robert J. Birgeneau was President of the University of Toronto from 2000 to 2004.

Toronto will be committed to "diversity," a code word for affirmative action, itself a euphemism for a system of quotas and reverse discrimination. He also has a clear warning for those who don't share his view — shape up or ship out: "in meetings with the U of T administration, Birgeneau said, "I emphasized to them diversity is one of the high priorities that I expected everybody in a leadership position in the university to be committed to. If they weren't, they should find something else to do." (*Toronto Star*, Feb. 8)

Thunder from afar as the conqueror approaches. Rome must be nervous.

Leo Zakuta

The Bulletin, University of Toronto, 26 June, 2002

Diversity?

Paul Muter reproaches Professor John Furedy for objecting to the employment equity report (Diversity can increase excellence, May 21). "Professor John Furedy apparently fails to recognize," Professor Muter writes, "that there are at least two conditions under which increasing diversity tends to increase excellence" — the composition of police forces and the entry of blacks into major league baseball. The examples are fine; diversity helps where it's relevant. But is there any evidence that it's relevant in the university, which is what Professor Furedy wrote about?

In baseball, blacks were not merely discriminated against, they were barred outright from the entire structure of organized baseball. As a result, as every follower of baseball knows, a large pool of talent built up in the Negro Leagues. Is there any evidence that pools of talented physicists, economists and geneticists are denied entry into the universities or face barriers within them? Furthermore, now that the barrier to black players is long gone, diversity appears irrelevant in the teams' search for talent. Performance is what counts.

Does anyone suggest that medical research would be improved if the seemingly disproportionate number of Jews and Chinese in that field were diluted? In the same vein, the ranks of professional football, and especially, basketball players, consist entirely of males and mostly of blacks. Where are the proposals to achieve diversity and thereby strengthen these teams by hiring women and more whites?

What these examples show is that the issue is not diversity. That word is a euphemism and smokescreen for a patronizing program of social engineering that has little relevance to the universities.

James Robert Brown also takes issue with Professor Furedy (Diversity improves quality of research, June 10). His conclusion is emphatic: "A diverse collection of researchers actually improves the quality of research." But his long letter contains not a thing that supports that assertion.

Leo Zakuta

The Bulletin, University of Toronto, 24 November, 2003

Celebrating diversity?

President Robert Birgeneau's article on celebrating diversity involved more rhetoric than reason (Celebrating sexual minorities, Oct. 20). There is no reason to celebrate diversity or to deplore it. It is of no value in itself. It is obviously useful in such matters as policing and politics. But would professional football and basketball teams be stronger if women and more whites were added? Would medical research be improved if fewer Jews and Chinese were in that field?

But these are merely specific instances. To understand the issue of diversity, we must see it in its broader context. Immigrants and new ethnic groups enter societies in different places and move along varying paths. For instance, most concentrate in certain residential areas and occupations. In time they begin to disperse both residentially and occupationally, and move to new educational levels. The groups travel in various directions and at different speeds. Women too left the home and moved into the lower levels of white-collar work, and later, to more varied and higher occupational levels.

The paths of all these groups were blocked by those defending homogeneity of sex, race, religion, ethnicity, or the like. (The universities were no exception, especially in some of the most "prized" professional faculties.) These institutions injured not only those whom they kept out, but also themselves, by placing homogeneity above ability. The struggle to remove those barriers has been long and difficult, but now, instead of having a free flow of talent, new barriers have been erected.

The new barriers choose diversity above qualification. When special avenues are opened to those with lesser qualifications, doors are inevitably closed to some with superior ones, since places are always limited. That's why diversity no more warrants celebration than homogeneity did, awful as it was. Talent is what merits celebration.

Nevertheless, diversity can be welcome — when it occurs naturally. Examples such as the Chinese and the Jews show how feeble is the argument that affirmative action is needed "to correct historic injustices." The recent profusion of these groups in the universities owes nothing whatever to "affirmative action"; it owes everything to the dismantling of the barriers that blocked their path. That's why it's welcome. The old liberals sought to remove those barriers; the new liberals have erected new ones.

Leo Zakuta

The Bulletin, University of Toronto, 12 September, 2005

Missing

In her Forum article, Professor Charmain Williams devotes a full page to criticism of the faculty's apathy in dealing with "hate and intolerance" (Missing in action, Aug. 22). "I have put together a list of the top 10 reasons I have heard why academics can't deal with hate and intolerance at the university," she says. Her list seems to refer to the faculty in general, but does it apply to most, or only to some? Who knows? Have some faculty members tried to combat "hate and intolerance"? If so, how? Readers would be especially interested in the answer to the last question, but the article says not a word about what academics can do. So where are we?

Leo Zakuta

iv. Letters to *The National Post*

The National Post, 1 March, 2000

Doc Birgeneau *(My title was "(Im)pertinent questions")*

Dr. Robert Birgeneau has declared that, during his impending presidency, the University of Toronto will be committed to "diversity," a code word for affirmative action. Isn't the new president himself a white male? Wouldn't it demonstrate the strength of his convictions if he stepped down in favour of a member of some under-represented group? Wouldn't that give this whole movement an electrifying impetus and make him a pivotal figure in the university's history? Might he be reluctant to do so on the grounds that he was chosen as the best person for the job? If so, won't he be endorsing the primacy of the merit principle? And if here, why not everywhere? If we believe in "diversity," let's show that we mean it.

Leo Zakuta

The National Post, 17 June, 2002 (not printed)

Old taboos, new taboos

Robert Fulford's column on Mordecai Richler (June 15) was splendid. He touched other bases skillfully, but the column was mainly about Richler's barbed attacks on bigotry in Quebec. Fulford's words were doubly heartening because of their precision and rarity. Praise for this aspect of Richler's work has been regarded, at best, as in bad taste.

Another powerful voice of protest was Bill Johnson's as head of Alliance Quebec. And, like Richler, he was pilloried not only in Quebec, but far beyond its borders. My feeble efforts at protest, having been born and brought up in Quebec, consisted of letters to *The Globe and Mail*, none of which was ever printed. Taboos have always been with us. When the old ones faded, "political correctness" replaced them with new ones.

Leo Zakuta

The National Post, 27 January, 2003

Cowardice

Professor David Dewitt of York University's Centre for International and Security Studies says "it was decided that it was appropriate for the Centre to withdraw" from hosting a lunch with Daniel Pipes, of the *Middle East Forum*, because "there was enough unease around the issue of Campus Watch," an academic web site on Middle East issues (York professors shun Middle East scholar, Jan. 24).

To cancel a luncheon address on such cowardly grounds is totally inappropriate, especially for a university. The spokesman for York's Jewish students, Zach Kaye, had it right when he said: "If you disagree with (Mr. Pipes), then you challenge him and ask him to defend his opinions. You don't shut him up." Out of the mouths of babes!

Christine Furedy, professor emerita, urban studies, York University
Leo Zakuta, professor emeritus, sociology, University of Toronto
John J. Furedy, professor, psychology, University of Toronto

The National Post, 21 February, 2003 (not printed)

To go or not to go

If it is wrong, as the Canadian and other governments declare, for the U.S. to attack Iraq alone, why is it right if others join in? Will the forbidden weapons ever be found? Probably not, no matter how many inspectors. And what if they are found? All the talk — about weapons, inspections, UN Resolutions, collective vs. solo action, terrorism, and the horrors of war — obscures the primary issue, which is about the balance of probabilities. Is Iraq more likely to use those weapons if it is attacked than if not? My answer is Yes, which means, "Don't go."

Leo Zakuta

v. Letters to Other Publications

McGill News, Spring 1995

Minority limits *(My title was "The politics of rejection")*

Adopt Charles Taylor's defence of Quebec's language laws ("The politics of recognition," Winter '94) and many other limitations of minority rights can be justified. Applying his argument, Canada could curb certain manifestations of Quebec's nationalism, perhaps even those language laws, on the grounds that they threaten its survival as a nation. Taylor writes as if his political theory begat his support for the language laws. The reverse seems more plausible.

Leo Zakuta, BA '46, MA '48

SAFS[6] Newsletter, no. 25, April 2000

Imposed diversity: antithesis of a university

Despite the imperiousness of president-designate Dr. Robert Birgeneau's proclamation that the University of Toronto will be "committed to diversity," i.e., affirmative

---

[6] SAFS = Society for Academic Freedom and Scholarship.

action, his remarks betray considerable ambivalence or perhaps confusion. ("An Ivy League brouhaha," *National Post*, Feb. 26). The trouble began when the Dean of Science at MIT tried to support affirmative action by comparing the position of women and Jews.

"Dr. Birgeneau likened the position of women academics to that of the Jews after the Second World War, adding that 'when many academic institutions, both in Canada and the United States, were reluctant to hire Jewish scholars, MIT practiced absolute merit-based hiring, which meant that we brought to MIT people like Paul Samuelson and Noam Chomsky.'" His message: they were hired not because they were Jews, but solely because of their academic qualifications, and look how well it turned out. Sure, but where did affirmative action come in?

"So: Does he believe in quota-based affirmative action? 'I believe very firmly in merit-based hiring' he replied. 'We attained the top scientists in the world at MIT under my leadership by an unrelenting commitment to merit-based hiring, and in the current climate, in the current world we live in, merit-based hiring automatically produces a diverse faculty.'" Could it be any clearer? It turned out splendidly, but a ringing endorsement of affirmative action, it's not.

"That said, he also says he believes it's critical to 'aggressively search' for outstanding women faculty, and that he welcomes affirmative action and quotas as a 'temporary measure where it's necessary to correct egregiously bad historical behaviour and help ameliorate the effects of the environment for non-majority people.'"

So, Dr. Birgeneau tells us, "absolute and unrelenting merit-based hiring" did wonders for MIT. It recruited the best people; it "automatically produces a diverse faculty" and it overcame discrimination against Jews. (Could it not do the same for women, blacks and any other groups?) One might have thought, after all that, that he would be an ardent champion of the merit principle. But it seems it's not really that good after all. Something different is needed, something like "merit-hiring if necessary, but not necessarily merit-hiring." Mackenzie King's original phrase was designed to reassure both sides in an irreconcilable conflict of his support.[7]

Imposed diversity is as antithetical to the idea of a university as was the imposed uniformity of an earlier age. Both restrict access to talent.

Nevertheless, even if it's only confusion, Dr. Birgeneau's views are not merely harmless muddle. They can have dark consequences. "Dr. Birgeneau told the Post he was misquoted in the original article (*Toronto Star*, Feb. 8) when he allegedly said that those in leadership positions (at the U of T) who disagree with his views about affirmative action 'should find something else to do.' He tried to clarify matters by saying, 'I just do not want in my administration people who discriminate, that is, people who consistently favour one sociological sub-group over others.'" (Actually, there has been so little evidence of such discrimination in our universities in recent times that this sounds like a phantom foe or perhaps a straw man.)

But there it is: if you disagree with his views about affirmative action, you favour discrimination. That is, you're a racist, sexist, or whatever. To say that openly would be too patently absurd or even libelous, so it's turned into an insinuation or a smear. The universities — and they're not alone — are full of people so petrified by that

---

[7]   The original phrase, familiar to older Canadians, was "Conscription if necessary, but not necessarily conscription." Prime Minister William Lyon Mackenzie King, sometimes known as Wily Willie, faced a nation sharply divided by the conscription issue during the last world war. Most French Canadians were strongly opposed to it, while the rest of the country was just as staunchly in favour. So King devised a policy embodied in that deathless phrase.

smear that, sheep-like, they fall silently into line behind affirmative action policies. The media report the pathetic efforts of beleaguered department heads to prove the "diversity" of their staffs. As if it matters. A generation ago, another smear terrified the academic world into a similar sheep-like syndrome — the fear of being labeled a "reactionary." The faculty fell all over themselves to prove how democratic they were and how they believed in complete equality between teachers and students. That was a crock, of course, and it passed away, but not without leaving much damage in its wake. What threat will trigger the next outbreak?

Leo Zakuta

SAFS[8] *Newsletter*, no. 26, September 2000

The 15% solution

The plan is a marvel of simplicity. No wonder the CAUT BULLETIN[9] gave Prof. Chandrakant P. Shah's proposal so much space (Actions speak louder than words, April 2000). Its gist is that to attack "systemic discrimination . ... at least 15% of (university) faculty must be from visible (ethno-racial) minorities to maintain a minimal critical mass."

Academics, being notorious nit-pickers, will of course quibble with its elegant neatness. Some will say that the composition of faculties reflects such things as the different arrival times of groups in the country or on the academic scene, or wide differences among them in education and aspirations. A few, more cynical, may say the proposal reminds them of the natural law of levitation as a social panacea. But these are the words of nay-sayers and should be disregarded.

---

[8] SAFS = Society for Academic Freedom and Scholarship.
[9] CAUT = Canadian Association of University Teachers.

Still, any plan, however ingenious, raises questions. For instance, in confining itself to "visible ethno-racial minorities," isn't Prof. Shah's proposal also discriminatory? It excludes many groups which have strong claims to his protective circle, such as:

— religious minorities whose distinctive dress makes them clearly visible

— the disabled: they may be not "ethno-racial" but they're often visible

— gays and lesbians: although not "visible ethno-racial," why exclude them?

— women: they're hardly mentioned. Is it because, although visible, they're not a minority in society?

— the many invisible ethnic minorities which are seriously under-represented (right in Prof. Shah's own university). For instance, French-Canadians, Greeks, Italians, Portuguese, Poles, and Ukrainians. So, the percentage will have to be amended — 15% won't even begin to do the job. More like 65%–75%, if women are included.

More questions:
— Does the 15% apply to departments, faculties, or the university as a whole?

— If the 15% in a department or small faculty were women or Chinese or Hasidic Jews, would that be satisfactory? To whom?

— What's to be done with the groups so highly over-represented now to make room for these newcomers? Has Prof. Shah a plan for them too?

These quibbles aside, if the principle is sound, it deserves implementation. But why limit it to universities? If at least 15% is right for a university faculty, it must be right for every workplace in society. To achieve it we need, not a Commission or Committee — they only waste time and never do anything — but a Kommissar of Kultural Klassification, aka the kindly KKK, whose first step would have to be an "ethno-racial" classification of the entire populace (of what?) to establish percentages. (Just as in the university to implement the 15% solution). It can be done. There are famous precedents in the 20th century. It's an inviting prospect of a well-ordered society, almost reminiscent of Aldous Huxley's Brave New World.

Leo Zakuta, University of Toronto

Sociology [Dept.] News, 20 November, 2000 (not printed)

Research?

An ancient joke describes a sociologist as someone who spends much time and money to locate every whorehouse in town, when he could have asked any taxi driver. The latest issue of the *Sociology News* indicates that this tradition is alive and well at the University of Toronto.

One colleague "wanted to understand why ... married women with children were more likely to become self-employed relative to other women." It's hard to imagine that he didn't know why beforehand, but, if not, he could have asked any mother. The answer, "his work has determined," is "to fulfill the needs of their children and their perceived household responsibilities."

A prize-winning paper by Ph.D. students "examines the factors that predict whether a case (of domestic violence) will proceed to prosecution." The best predictor, they discover, is whether the victim cooperates with the criminal justice system. What's next? Will a large and well-funded study reveal that divorce and separation are more likely when the partners quarrel a lot or have lost interest in each other? There must be a Ph.D. thesis or two here. Nevertheless, the *Sociology News* is welcome and its format is pleasing.

Leo Zakuta, Professor Emeritus

Editor's reply, 28 November, 2000

Professor Zakuta, thank you for your comments. I agree with you whole-heartedly. The substance of some of the reported research was so obvious to me, I pressed the authors for more details, more information, but received none. Am I to presume that's really all there was to some of this research? May I assume that poverty is caused by a lack of money?

Still, I appreciate the articles I received from these contributors, and also that you enjoy the *Sociology News*.

Linda L. Gardiner, Editor, *Sociology News*, Dept. of Sociology

My rejoinder, 1 December, 2000

Thanks for your note. It was doubly welcome because when I told some friends (former sociology colleagues) about my letter, they looked at me as if I had just grown another head. They probably thought that with so many windmills about, why tilt at these? I think you're on to something. Poverty may well be caused by a lack of money resulting from — wait for it — insufficient income, too much spending, and the like. Ph.D.s and tenure have been awarded for less significant and less exciting findings.

Leo

U of T Magazine, Winter 2005

Birgeneau's conundrum (*My title was "Conundrum"*)

The two excerpts which highlight "The Birgeneau years" (*U of T Magazine*, Autumn 2004) undermine the article's main theme. The first excerpt, at the head of the story, expresses that point: "For U of T President Robert Birgeneau, excellence and equity went hand in hand." But the second excerpt contradicts the first. It says "Birgeneau argued that financial aid should be steered to those that need it most rather than those with the highest marks." That means that "equity" trumps "excellence." But if the financial aid were to go to "those with the highest marks," then "excellence" would trump "equity." So how can "excellence and equity" ever go "hand in hand"?

Leo Zakuta

Note to editor: I would have liked to add a sentence at the end, but I can't: They can't ("go 'hand in hand'") because it's cant.

The Toronto Star, 5 April, 2006

Working girls

Congratulations for publishing that long but superb article by Alison Wolf in the Saturday *Star*. It was a genuinely sociological piece, a rarity in that ideological wilderness, and shows how effective such an approach can be. If I were still teaching, it would be essential reading in all of my courses.

Leo Zakuta
Professor Emeritus
Sociology, Univ. of Toronto

vi. Letters to CBC Radio, CBC TV, and TVO

Radio Noon, 3 December, 1981

Bruce Rogers

I have just snapped my radio off, outraged by the misconduct of Bruce Rogers on today's Radio Noon. His behaviour towards Mr. Norman Sterling was appalling. I do not support Mr. Sterling's position re "freedom of information" legislation; in fact, I find his position indefensible. But that has nothing to do with his entitlement to a courteous hearing and treatment, especially as the invited guest of the program.

Mr. Rogers' conduct was beyond belief. For instance, instead of giving Mr. Sterling a chance to reply to the telling criticism delivered by Mr. Donald McDonald, Mr. Rogers kept interrupting, badgering Mr. Sterling with questions, and finally cut him off even though Mr. Sterling had not been given anything like the equivalent opportunity to state his case that had been given — entirely justifiably — to Mr. McDonald. A few minutes later, a caller (I believe it was the second one) was repeatedly abusive to the program's guest, with frequent reiterations about the "stupidity" of his views, plus several interruptions of Mr. Sterling's remarks. Mr. Rogers made one effort to keep the proceedings civil and orderly, and when that failed, he let the caller pretty much have his way. What was required was a clear and unmistakable reminder that a public debate, especially of this kind, requires civility and order. I have listened to Radio Noon often enough to know that Mr. Rogers is quite capable of delivering such a reminder **when he wants to**.

Instead, he concluded by thanking the caller — egregiously, in my view — for his contribution. I have the distinct impression that Mr. Rogers welcomed the caller's hectoring of the guest; after all, it was not that different from what Mr. Rogers was doing to Mr. Sterling himself. That partisanship was so intolerable in a program of this kind that I turned the radio off.

As I said above, I listen often to Radio Noon, and have been doing so for some time. Today's events were the large bundle of straws which broke this camel's back. The program has become increasingly difficult to take, simply because Mr. Rogers has obviously come to see himself as its "star." As a result, he shoulders most of the guests aside to a distinctly minor role while he argues with callers, interrogates them, answers their questions and generally acts as if he were the "guest expert." How can the CBC let these kinds of things go on?

Leo Zakuta

Sunday Morning, 27 March, 1983

A morning in the life of the CBC

The CBC has outdone itself this morning. Every hourly news report forecast "the possibility of **wet** rain" — they must have discovered something quite special. Then, the reading of Ned Myers' (?) diary was accompanied by all the ingenuity of a sound-effect storm, which succeeded only in making the reading virtually inaudible. Finally, the lead story in the 11 a.m. news reported that "Christians and Jews all over the world were celebrating Palm Sunday and the beginning of Easter Week." It's news to the Jews and, I imagine, to much of the astonished world. Two phenomenal scoops and it's still only 11.05 a.m.

Leo Zakuta

Morningside, 14 November, 1986

CLICK!

"And now for our regular panel.[10] Bob White is the ..." CLICK! Off went my car radio just a moment ago. I had stayed in the parked car, afraid to miss a word of Mr. Pitman's splendid musical letter to the university. Besides, as a regular listener to the CBC, and especially to Morningside, I was reluctant to turn off the radio. However, I've been doing it more lately, and have finally been irked into telling you why.

I always picture White, (Jim) Coutts, and (Eddie) Goodman (and their predecessors) as three buttons, say ORANGE, RED, and BLUE. Punch an issue — any issue — into the machine and out comes the totally predictable response — the NDP, Liberal, or PC party line. What famous names add to this dreary format eludes me. Dalton Camp, for instance, was tolerable until the Conservatives took over in Ottawa. At that instant, he too turned into a button, though the speed and thoroughness of the transformation was good for a few laughs. The only relief was Dave Barrett, who was funny and sensible as long as the ORANGE button was OFF.

Another recent CLICK! went to Chaviva Hosek and her colleagues on the panel on poverty. I endured their gratitude to the poor "for sharing their humiliation with us" because the subject seemed interesting. All I learned, alas, was how unfeeling this country is about poverty and, by contrast, how much the panel members cared. When this extended exercise in self-congratulation showed no sign of ending, my patience did. Not a word about why many were so poor. Was welfare or unemployment insurance inadequate? Were many ineligible for either? Were there

---

[10] The original panel was Dalton Camp, Eric Kierans, and Stephen Lewis.

other important reasons? The repeated assertions that we must banish poverty were mere huffing and puffing without any attempt to explain it.

The "dramas" with which Morningside concludes earned a permanent CLICK! Although most seemed pitched to a children's audience, my breaking point was their ethnic and sexual stereotyping (fancy that, on the CBC). What presumably made those images kosher was the misguided notion that conventional ideas were being stood on their head. Thus, elevated station guaranteed baseness of character. French-Canadians were therefore warm, wise, witty, and spontaneous. WASP women were redeemed a bit by being well-meaning, if blundering. But, as for the Anglo-Saxon men, at the social pinnacle, those bigots, who gave new meaning to the word "uptight," were beyond hope. A lot of that went a long way.

So, why turn on Morningside at all? For Margaret Visser, justly described as "incomparable," for Cuyler Young, for Maureen Forrester (this morning), and for the others who come to delight and inform rather than to harangue. (Some causes are aired so regularly that they sound like the sponsors' messages.) And for such unexpected pleasures as this morning's opener by Mr. Pitman. Now, if I could only have a copy of his poem. [see Reply to the English Writing Competency Questionnaire]

Leo Zakuta

Leo Zakuta

Mr. Pitman's poem

> Reply to the English Writing Competency Questionnaire (with apologies to Gilbert and Sullivan) by student no. M84095124

I didn't write the English writing competency test because:
I didn't think that, at my age, you'd doubt I had ability
To use the monarch's English with acceptable facility,
For I went to school in days of yore when Grammar was compulsory,
And lads who couldn't conjugate faced punishment expulsory.
My teacher pounded in the rules with emphasis definitive,
And made me swear a mighty oath to never split infinitives.
I learned my lessons very well and gained such erudition
That for forty years I haven't used a final preposition.
Many happy hours I swam in seas of punctuation,
And never mixed a colon with a mark of exclamation.
I learned to count the syllables in centaur and philosophy,
And many curious facts about the use of the apostrophe.

I quickly learned the penalties of mispronounciation,
And spelling bees I faced without the slightest trepidation.
I parsed convoluted sentences with ease that was astonishing,
And kept the genders separate thus to avoid admonishing.
I could name the numerous parts of speech and give their explanations,
And identify the dative case in Cicero's orations.
I picked out predicates so fast they thought it was a miracle;
Subjunctives gave me such a thrill that I got quite hysterical.
Gerunds, verbs and adjectives were intimate acquaintances,
But I must admit to some dislike of prodigal parentheses.
Demonstratives, I can recall, I used with ingenuity,
But never was I guilty of redundant superfluity.

Participles roused in me emotions that were amourous,
And prepositions, I opined, were infinitely glamourous.
Paraphrasing I adored, and lavished adulation
On synonyms and antonyms, and revered alliteration.

But, truth to say — and all men know I never tell a whopper —
I grew inordinately fond of nouns that were improper.
SV I sincerely hope that Grammar will experience revival,
For nothing's more erotic than a clause that's adjectival.
If still, in spite of all I've said, you question my ability
To compose a simple sentence with linguistical agility,
I'll take your test if you insist, but don't be diabolical;
Just let me pass lest I should grow extremely melancholical.

Radio Noon, Phone-in hour, 18 November, 1987

I used to listen to Radio Noon's Phone-in Hour regularly; now it's rare. I [herein] offer a suggestion that would restore me to a part-time basis. The shows consist of two distinct types:

1. **Informational**. The guests are experts on gardening, cars, personal finances, home maintenance, and other subjects. Except for the psychological counseling programs, which run to treacle, these are generally straightforward — interesting, informative, and sometimes even useful.

2. **Opinion and whatever**. These are harder to categorize. Their most common link is silliness, sometimes to the point of embarrassment. The opinion programs draw many callers out of the woodwork, whom the moderators have understandably found difficult to handle and whose profusion is irritating. The "whatever" type is represented by such programs as this week's (from the Royal Winter Fair). No one has any idea of what to do with the guest — David Peterson, Nancy White, and Knowlton Nash (today); so, callers are invited to talk about "anything." The result is just what one would expect. I have avoided this week like the plague; my remarks are based on many a past experience.

Presumably there is an audience for the second category (there's an audience for anything), but I have ceased to be part of it. But I do miss the informational type, and finding out what's on isn't always easy. My proposal (modest, I hope) is that you designate certain days of the week for the Informational programs. I, for one, would listen to these regularly and would give up the rest of the week contentedly to the other audience.

Leo Zakuta

Metro Morning, 3 April, 1989

Joe Coté's interviews

Your practice of repeating Joe Coté's interviews on successive days achieves new heights of boredom. If two days in a row are better than one, why not three days or a full week or...? The possibilities are endless. Even if the interviews were ok, that practice would be intolerable. But they're awful and the repetition is excruciating.

Still, I must admit, I've learned to defend myself. As soon as the repeat begins, I switch off the radio, try to guess the length of the interview, and leave a good margin of safety before turning it on again. It's innovative broadcasting all right.

Leo Zakuta

Reminiscences, Rants, and Raves

The CBC's reply:

 Canadian Broadcasting Corporation
Société Radio-Canada

```
                                       Radio 740
                                       509 Parliament Street
                                       Toronto, Ontario
                                       M4X 1P3

                                       April 11, 1989
```

Dear Leo Zakuta,

You make it sound as if our show is constant repeats. That is wrong. We sometimes repeat the last item in the show as soon as the program begins at 6:00 am. We do it because we think the interviews are worth hearing a second time. Audience research shows there are few people who listen at both times.

Of course, if you don't like it, you can turn it off. If you do choose to listen, you may actually be introduced to some new ideas that are worth understanding.

Sincerely,

Ken Wolff
Producer Metro Morning.

April 18

Dear Mr. Wolff,

Your bad-tempered message could have been reduced from 89 words to 5: "We know but don't care."

Leo Zakuta

Morningside, 18 April, 1989

Debate on the Charter

This morning's so-called "debate" on the Charter and the notwithstanding clause was a sorry business. Michael Mandel and Ann McLellan offered nothing but cant and, despite their superficial differences, essentially the same line of cant. Worse, both law professors spoke so badly. Stuart McLean couldn't cope with the fiasco or was unaware of its existence.

Leo Zakuta

Karen Levine, CBC Radio, 12 September, 1989

Lost innocence

I have seen and read "everything" about the Holocaust, many of them repeatedly. But I have never been more moved than by this morning's "Children of the Holocaust." I cried throughout and almost uncontrollably at the end. Thank you.

Leo Zakuta

Morningside, 7 Dec. 1989

Happenstance?

"We call it happenstance" said Mark Starowitz (?), the producer of The Journal, on Morningside, in reply to Robert Fulford's charge that Simon de Jong and the CBC had "bugged" Dave Barrett. I listened in mounting disbelief as no panel member challenged what first sounded like a slippery euphemism. But it wasn't even a euphemism. It was not "happenstance" but the very opposite. Planning is Happenstance can take its place proudly alongside War is Peace and Freedom is Slavery.

Leo Zakuta

Morningside, Oct. 20, 1990

Depression

What was depressing about this morning's panel on depression was not the topic, but how your panel treated it. On and on flowed the antiquated jargon, as insistent as it was empty, like the phrases mouthed by the Communist ideologues long after the world recognized their hollowness. All three panelists were stuck on a central assumption — that since depression is more frequent among the poor and unemployed, poverty and unemployment must be its causes. Maybe. But isn't the reverse also possible — that the overwhelming debilitation of depression leads to poverty and unemployment? What was startling was that in all that talk no one even considered that elementary possibility. (Nothing blinds one to the obvious better than being wedded to a doctrine.) Had they considered it, they could not have dismissed the "medical approach" with such utter disdain.

Leo Zakuta

Sunday Morning, 16 December, 1990

Centre Point

This morning's Centre Point (on freedom of speech on the campus) presented a thoughtful and balanced examination of a difficult and important issue. Having talked to Mary O'Connell several times during her preparation of the program, I was impressed by her industry, her effort to be fair, and her readiness to explore many aspects of this issue, all of which were manifested in today's highly successful program. It was one of which you can be proud.

Leo Zakuta

Morningside, 21 Mar. 1991

The manufacture of news

Dear Mr. Gzowski,

This morning you stated confidently and unhesitatingly — as if it were beyond doubt — that 1 in 10 Canadian women are abused by their men. Your circulation of this mythical figure is understandable because, since its initial appearance about 4 years ago, it has rocketed around the media and, despite the mixed metaphor, stuck like glue wherever it touched. Indeed, it has been escalating so that now we usually hear "1 out of 8 and even more."

    I have no idea what the actual figure might be, nor whether this ratio is high or low. But no one else knows either, or can know, which is what really matters. (I've enclosed a letter which I wrote when I first met that magical figure about why it's unknowable. *The Globe and*

Mail didn't print it.[11]) I'm writing to you because I have a professional interest in such matters, because you have many listeners, and because I know you like to get things right.

Leo Zakuta
Professor Emeritus, Sociology

Our correspondence follows.

Peter Gzowski's reply:

March 29, 1991

Dear Leo Zakuta:

Thank you for voicing your concern about the accuracy of our stats. I have enclosed a piece of background material which the producer of that piece provided for me. The one in 10 figure dates back to 1980, Linda MacLeod's first report for the CACSW, "Wife Battering in Canada: The Vicious Cycle."[12] A study by the Ontario Native Women's Association shows higher rates of abuse. At least 119 women were killed by husbands, ex-husbands, and common-law partners (NOT including boyfriends) in 1989.

Sincerely,

Peter Gzowski

---

[11] See "Bewitched, battered, and bewildered" in this volume.

[12] Peter Gzowski's reply to Leo included a photocopied page from Linda MacLeod, *Wife Battering in Canada: The Vicious Cycle* (Ottawa: Canadian Advisory Council on the Status of Women, 1980), which reported that that one in ten Canadian women living with a man experienced physical abuse in the course of the relationship.

My rejoinder:

Dear Mr. Gzowski,

The item above which you sent me recalls the Duke of Wellington's reply to the man who greeted him after Waterloo: "Mr. Smith, I believe." The Duke's reply: "If you believe that, you will believe anything."

Leo Zakuta

Sunday Morning, 21 October, 1991

Clarence Thomas — Anita Hill

Your treatment of the Judge Clarence Thomas — Anita Hill story yesterday was out of control. The "man-on-street" interviews, which opened it, represented only those who did not believe him, and the rest of the story either condemned him or was derisory. From long, though increasingly intermittent, experience with Sunday Morning, I hardly expected a balanced presentation of this event, but, even by your standards, this one was remarkable. And you wonder why the CBC has such a poor reputation.

Leo Zakuta

Reminiscences, Rants, and Raves

 Canadian Broadcasting Corporation
Société Radio-Canada

November 5, 1991

Leo Zakuta
44 Elm Avenue
Toronto M4W 1N5

Dear Mr. Zakuta,

    I disagree. Of the six voices featured in our man-in-the-street segment on the Clarence Thomas-Anita Hill story, two clearly believed Anita Hill had been harrassed, two clearly believed Clarence Thomas had been unfairly treated, one believed he did what was alleged but with Ms. Hill's cooperation and as a result of his ordeal would be a fair judge and one said it was simply everyday life in America.
    To suggest the rest of our coverage either condemned Judge Thomas or was derisory is absurd. Our principal coverage was an interview with a Yale law professor about the process of confirmation. The satirical song which followed was premised on the idea of three of the more morally suspect members of the senate casting judgment on Judge Thomas. It lampooned the spectacle, not the man.
    Finally, the CBC has an excellent reputation and the polls bear this out. Thank you for listening to Sunday Morning, though in future you might listen a little more attentively.

Sincerely

Michael Finlay
Executive Producer
Sunday Morning

7 Nov. 91

Dear Mr. Finlay,
    My complaint was that that program lacked balance and restraint. Your bad-tempered and discourteous reply confirms my view and suggests that a shorter leash may be in order. Your letter does no credit to the CBC, and I am sending a copy to the President.

Leo Zakuta

copy: Mr. Gerard Veilleux, Pres. CBC - (address unknown to L.Z.)

Sunday Morning's reply

Leo Zakuta

Morningside, 13 December, 1991

Dear Mr. Gzowski,

Thank you so much for intervening on our side in this morning's discussion of the Rape Shield Law. In the many years that I've listened to Morningside, I've never heard you take sides so strongly, so I know how deeply you must feel. Those feelings do you credit.

Sarah Binks,
Sweet Songstress of Saskatchewan[13]

CBC Radio, 18 August, 1992

Summerside, the 9 o'clock news, and other miscues

CBC Radio this morning has been disconcerting. On the 9 a.m. news, the announcer informed us that "Stalin's reign of terror resulted in the loss of thousands of lives." Thousands??? Everyone knows that it was not thousands but millions. It's no longer even a matter of dispute. What can be said about such ignorance by CBC news writers?

Then, at the start of Summerside, after Ian Brown interviewed a Yugoslav in London (?), he asked him to wait on the line while he interviewed another expert. Obviously, so that the first man could reply to the second's comments? Not at all. When the second interview was over, Brown bade both men goodbye. Why did he ask the first person to stay on the line? If the second interview took too long, why didn't Brown do something about it? The discourtesy to the first man was

---

[13] Alluding to Paul Hiebert's satirical novel *Sarah Binks*, which parodied the pretensions of academic, political, and literary cultural arbiters. [AZ]

incomprehensible. I have turned the radio off. That's more than enough for one morning.

Leo Zakuta

Fresh Air, 13 December, 1993

Tom Allen's straightforward, low-key manner is such a welcome relief from the sentimental excesses and parade of vanity that permeated Fresh Air for so many years. My wife and I called it Foul Air or Stale Air, but we tuned in regularly because it guaranteed additional sleep. Less sleep now — you can't have everything — because the content has improved considerably too, though we miss the breezy Sheila Shotten.

Leo Zakuta

Metro Morning, 12 January, 1994

Susan Huffs' (sp?) Commentary this morning on the Bobbitt case went beyond callousness and tastelessness as swiftly as the knife which so captivated her. It reached the gross and sick and remained there. The insanely angry we always have with us, but for the CBC to provide a platform for a giggling tra-la-la about a savage and dangerous act of mutilation shows a remarkable lack of judgement, even for Metro Morning. Can you just imagine what would be going on now in the corridors of the CBC if a male had been allowed to put on such a grotesque performance about a near-murderous act of rape?

Leo Zakuta
c.c.: Patrick Watson, Pres. CBC

Morningside in the Summer, 20 June, 1995

As a former academic, I listened with interest to the report on the Political Science Dept. at the University of Manitoba. Dr. Margaret Little was interviewed at length about her two charges of sexual harassment by some of her male colleagues and especially, [her charge] that the men in the department had created an "inhospitable climate" towards their female colleagues and students.

    She was followed by the Dean of Arts, who reported on the committee which he set up and on its findings. When he was asked about the views of the many male Political Science faculty members, he replied properly that they should speak for themselves and that he wouldn't presume to do so. And that was that. I had expected to hear their side of the story, but Morningside apparently considered it irrelevant. Not even a reference to having tried to interview any of them. Feh!

Leo Zakuta

Morningside, 6 October, 1995

Racism rampant

What would you do if a Morningside guest sprayed a stream of derogatory racial remarks on your program? Come down hard and instantly on them? Your listeners might think so, but not if they paid attention to your interview with several Canadian blacks this past Monday. The latter scattered derogatory statements about "whites" — not "some whites," but repeatedly about "whites" — as if they were seeding a field, without a murmur of protest from you. Apart from "racism" being offensive regardless of the source, it is patronizing to exempt certain groups from the same standard as all the rest.

Leo Zakuta

Reminiscences, Rants, and Raves

TVO (Please note), 15 January, 1996

Death of Yugoslavia

The Death of Yugoslavia was superb. It succeeded in making an enormously complicated story clear and comprehensible, all of which shows the great skill and intelligence of its creators. I'm not a fan of panel discussions as a rule, but the one which followed the final episode maintained the high level of the whole program. They were all very good; Janice Stein was excellent.

Leo Zakuta

CBC TV, Adrienne Clarkson Presents, 5 April, 1996

Debbie Filler — Punch Me in the Stomach

A belated expression of our delight in Debbie Filler's program. She brought her family to life with great affection and credibility. Our sole regret was that it had to come to an end. Please convey our appreciation to her.

Annette and Leo Zakuta

Metro Morning, 31 October, 1996

Commentary

Greg Malone's Commentary this morning was crude, childish and, above all, an embarrassment. My wife, who was listening too, said "That's on the CBC?"

Leo Zakuta

Metro Morning, Andy Barrie, 6 December, 1996

This morning you talked about the 16 women who were killed by "male violence." When you refer to the many children whom Clifford Olson murdered, do you say they were killed by adult violence? When you mention the millions of Jews whom the Nazis murdered, do you say they were killed by gentile violence? If you don't generalize in those instances, why do so in this one?

Leo Zakuta

Morningside, 7 April, 1997

The Morningside succession

If accurate, the report that Shelagh Rogers is not on the short list to replace Peter Gzowski is incomprehensible. She hosted Morningside so often, so long, and so superbly, that she is the obvious and natural successor. I remember with admiration, for instance, her handling of interviews with the mothers of schizophrenics. Instead of skating cautiously over the surface of this most delicate subject, and leaving the listeners with very little, she probed deeply and sensitively, and left her subjects comforted and her audience informed and moved. I can't imagine anyone else in Peter Gzowski's place.

Leo Zakuta

Reminiscences, Rants, and Raves

Sunday Morning, 25 December, 1997

A belated appreciation for A Life in Terezin on Sun., Dec. 14th. John Freund's low-key narrative made it moving beyond words.

Leo Zakuta

Metro Morning, 16 April, 1998

My wife and I have been regular listeners to Metro Morning for years. Part of it is the pleasure of hearing interviewing of the kind Andy Barrie did this morning with Transportation Minister Tony Clement.
    I don't like turning off the radio during the program, but now do so whenever your "political panel" comes on. Party representatives are deadly. They're like pushing buttons. Push each one and predictably, out comes the party line on the issue in question. The government supporter inevitably defends its action, and the opposition party speakers just as predictably attack it. The moment it's announced, the prospect of illumination, interest, and surprise vanishes. It's awful.
    What can explain the CBC's penchant for this kind of guaranteed boredom? Morningside featured such a panel for years. Is it a way of toadying to the political parties? If not, what else?

Leo Zakuta

Leo Zakuta

To **Max Ferguson** on his retirement, and his reply.

Max Ferguson 			13 Aug. 98
CBC
Box 500, Station A
Toronto M5W 1E6

Dear Max,

Please forgive the familiarity but we always call your program "Max", and, after almost 50 years, that sounds natural.

So much pleasure received for such a long time evokes great gratitude. It began in 1951 when I joined the legion of enthusiastic fans of Old Rawhide and his splendid cast of characters. It has endured over the decades. There will be a large void on Saturday mornings. Where will I ever hear those songs now?

Leo Zakuta

Leo Zakuta

Sept. 12, 1998

Dear Leo:

I'm working my way through an unexpected avalanche of mail and have only now arrived at your letter.

Your thoughtfulness in writing and generous comments on my past CBC work were much appreciated.

Sincerely,
Max Ferguson

Metro Morning, 9 September, 1998

This time: complaints

Yesterday morning's interview with Mr. Frank O'Dea was very disappointing. It was potentially important and fascinating. When Mr. O'Dea began to talk about the dramatic turnaround of his life, I waited with the greatest interest to hear how it was done, i.e., how he managed to overcome such enormous obstacles. Instead, Andy Barrie changed the subject to something much less interesting and significant. "I don't believe this," I said to my wife. Just at the critical point, he (Andy Barrie) turns away from what really matters. After a few minutes, Mr. Barrie returned to that moment when Mr. O'Dea talked about realizing that he had to take responsibility for his own life. I felt certain that Mr. Barrie had recognized his mistake and was about to correct it. Instead he did the same thing again, and the interview concluded without our ever hearing how Mr. O'Dea had managed such a dramatic "recovery" against such overwhelming odds.

This morning's program raised the interesting question of how effective the teachers might be in defeating the current government of Ontario in the next election. But, to answer that question, it turned to the most unenlightening vehicle possible, that useless panel of the representatives of the various political parties. The regular audience, of course, knew what their answers would be before they uttered a word. Another good opportunity to interest your audience missed.

Leo Zakuta

This Morning, 27 Sept. 1997

This Morning

It shouldn't be too difficult to rise above the level of Morningside. (Comparisons are unavoidable.) Yesterday's fascinating interview with Prof. Rubenstein will help, as will last week's engaging item about Housework. "Dramas" like PMO certainly will not. Phew!

Leo Zakuta

This Morning/Sunday Morning, 8 Nov. 1999

Charles Taylor on human rights

In yesterday morning's program about human rights, Michael Enright introduced Charles Taylor as the leading political thinker in Canada. That piece of puffery deflated rapidly during the interview. The first gaffe was stunning. Mr. Taylor correctly explained the 20th century's concern about human rights as a response to the extraordinarily repressive totalitarian ideologies earlier in the century. But he identified only two — Fascism and Nazism — and somehow ignored the first, most enduring, and most influential of these monstrosities, Bolshevism, even though its success was so influential in the rise of the other two.
    After that, the gaffes seemed trivial in a course that ran steadily downhill. One example will have to suffice. Mr. Enright asked what would happen if a university advertised for a male professor of mathematics. Mr. Taylor said rightly that the world would come crashing down on its head. "But what about the ads stipulating that a **female** must be hired"? Mr. Enright continued. "That would be different," Mr. Taylor explained. "That would be correcting a historical wrong." Need he be reminded that every totalitarian regime justifies its unspeakable acts as corrections of historical wrongs?

Finally, Mr. Taylor was an odd choice for a program on human rights. As a vocal advocate of Quebec's language laws, he has supported the suppression of some rights of English-speaking Quebecers. And on what grounds? Naturally, to correct historical wrongs and because protecting the rights of a majority justifies some suppression of those of a minority. With such a view, anything goes, including human rights.

Leo Zakuta

Sunday Morning, 2 January, 2000

Blather

Blather reached its purest form throughout the first part of today's Sunday Morning.
If pretentious garbage's to be strewn,
You can't improve on Marshall McLuhan.

Leo Zakuta

This Morning, 2 Jan. 2001

Why?

Why was this morning's discussion of the brain curtailed so senselessly? The Halifax psychiatrist wasn't permitted to get into schizophrenia and Alzheimer's, though those topics were fascinating and important, and he talked about them so lucidly. Suddenly we were told that there was no more time, and he was cut off at 9:50, so that another dumb song, which could have been played at any time, came on to fill the gap until the 10 o'clock news. And, with time apparently so short and the topics so important, all that Ralph Benmergui wanted to talk to him about was God. What's the matter with you people?

Leo Zakuta

Sounds like Canada, 22 September, 2003

Youth voting

This morning Shelagh Rogers and Bernard St. Laurent spent much time bemoaning "the failure" of so many young people to vote. Why? It was all based on the unproven and unexamined assumption that voting is a good thing. It presumably ensures better government. Is there a shred of evidence to support that? Not voting is also an opinion. Your commentators spoke approvingly of Australia's law compelling people to vote. What's the point of persuading people who are not interested or have no opinion to vote?

Further, is there any evidence that their votes would materially affect the outcome of elections, since they might well reflect the general pattern of the ballots? If that were not so (and who could ever tell?), mightn't one argue that it's unfair for those who don't care to distort the votes of those who do?

Leo Zakuta

Metro Morning, 9 January, 2006

Rev. Rivers

What a mess you created between 7-8 this morning. We were promised Rev. Eugene Rivers (of Boston) "for the hour," so we listened eagerly. "For the hour" indeed! I doubt that we even got 10 minutes of him. He was interrupted constantly by

–weather reports
–traffic reports (frequent and identical)
–a long sports report
–Andy Barrie talking too much and often "correcting" Rev. Rivers, although he obviously understands much less about these issues (black-on-black killings) than Rev. Rivers does.
–Rosemary Gartner's useless contribution (I'm a sociologist.)
–the phone-in questions. There wasn't time for many of these, which was just as well. Their contribution was minimal. The first question was about "the power of prayer," which made for a really sophisticated discussion. Were the questions screened?

The constant interruptions disrupted the continuity of the few remarks that Rev. Rivers was permitted. Alas, he sounded so sensible and knowledgeable.

Leo Zakuta

Fresh Air, 19 November, 2006

Supermarket Saturday

Yesterday's program concluded by asking for more e-mail. I am complying as a long-time listener to Fresh Air and a veteran supermarket shopper. The program was long on promises and short on delivery. In the first hour the host kept telling us that "the entire program would be devoted to supermarket shopping." But perhaps one-third of it was, none in the first hour. The segments that did deal with the subject were mostly peripheral; there was nothing about the experience of shopping in a supermarket, which one would have thought would be central. E-mail from listeners was invited repeatedly but only two e-mails were used. One of these was about a woman whose water broke while shopping in a supermarket. Since that could have happened anywhere, it was completely irrelevant. I will pass over Longo's self-promotion because it was more interesting than the other segments. The host made sure that we knew that supermarkets lured people in to spend more money and time than they intended and that supermarket shopping was somehow beneath him. If so, he was the wrong person for the job. In all, it was thin fare padded with lots of music, news, weather, and whatnot to fill out the three hours.

Leo Zakuta

2. Personal Letters

i. To Jim Richardson, President, Canadian Sociology & Anthropology Assoc., 19 May, 1983

Prof. J. Richardson
President, CSAA
Concordia University
Montreal

Dear Jim,

The attached letter suggests that I write you to, in effect, explain my absence from the CSAA's rolls. I've had such requests periodically and, while I usually feel a reply would be futile, writing to you is different.

Many years ago — I think it was during the "October Crisis" of 1970 — the Association began to take political stands. I considered any political role inappropriate for such an organization. I might have stayed if there were some prospect of changing it, but the tide was running overwhelmingly the other way. The CSAA was especially vocal in the chorus of Canadians First, which I despise as narrow-minded and harmful. (I'm old enough to remember the unpleasant odour of America First in the 1930s.)

I've been remote from the CSAA and things may be different now. But as long as the vast majority of our colleagues regard sociology as a latter day replacement for the old moral theology, I'm happier to maintain that distance from the collectivity, whatever feelings I have about the particular individuals.

Sincerely,

Leo Zakuta

ii. Exchange of letters with my friend Myer Katz + attached memo

Letter from Myer Katz, 12 Dec., 1989

Dear Leo,

I received the attached during my absence and knew you would be interested. In fact, I will suggest that, even though you are retired and not a "male staff in the school," you become a corresponding member of any group that is formed. ...

Myer

Attached memo from the Director of the McGill School of Social Work, undated. (Myer had been his predecessor in that position and was still a member of the faculty. The memo is about the "Montreal massacre" at the University of Montreal.)

> From: (The Director)
> To: Male staff in the School
>
> In the aftermath of the U de M massacre I find myself wanting to meet with other men to talk, initially, about the event in terms of its wider meanings for the relationships between men and women.
>   Perhaps we should consider an on-going group here? Or perhaps some of you are members of a men's group — I am now and have always been skeptical. Now, I am forced to begin to see this possible role in counteracting some of the terrible consequences of masculine culture. Please let me know what you think.

My reply to Myer Katz, 16 December, 1989

Dear Myer,

Thanks for your letter and the enclosure. I accept the group's expected invitation with alacrity. Surely they won't reject a former academic (sociologist, yet) and McGill graduate (twice), who has advocated equality for women for at least half a century ('twas mother's milk to me).[14] As a corresponding member, I already have my first message for my new colleagues — the slaughter made me feel sick but not guilty. Nevertheless, I am eager to learn how our collective snivelling will make one woman safer.

Leo

iii. To my friends Chris and John Furedy, 16 March, 2000

McGill in the 1940s

Dear John and Chris,

...

Your reference to the "*numerus clausus*" law in Hungary reminded me of something not entirely different here, at McGill. (I don't know whether you're familiar with it.) When I was in high school in Montreal, and for many years before, McGill had an admission requirement of 75% for Jewish students vs. 60% for others. Admissions were based on province-wide exams known as Junior Matriculation. The most interesting aspect of the whole thing was how open McGill was about that "regulation";

---

[14] My mother had been a strong feminist as long as I can remember.

they made no attempt to hide it. Not only did all the Jewish high school students in Quebec know about it, but so did our teachers, who talked about it openly. In my high school, which was predominantly, but not exclusively, Jewish, none of our teachers was Jewish. But most, if not all, made a great and open effort to drill us, so that we could overcome the 75% barrier.

In my Junior Matrics, I managed 742 out of 1000 (74.2%), because my maths were dreadful. My Principal offered to write a letter to McGill asking them to waive the 75% restriction. I declined, not on the basis of any principle, but because tuition fees at McGill were $250 while those in Grade 12 (= 13 in Ontario) were only $100, and the difference was large to my family at that time. From Grade 12, one entered 2nd year at McGill, and that was easy because so few students took that route that they didn't bother to put up barriers.

Once I got in, naturally there wasn't a trace of any of this attitude in the faculty, except for one pompous old ass from PEI who first became a dept. head, then the Dean of Arts & Science, and later a cabinet minister in the Diefenbaker govt. How it was manifested was a funny story which I'll tell you some time. (It didn't involve me.)[15]

---

[15] Two stories, both about the same professor. He taught a course on Shakespeare. The class was huge, held in Moyse Hall, then the largest classroom and meeting hall at McGill. He lectured from the platform; the "lectures" consisted of reading the plays in a monotone and making occasional comments about some passage. One of these was that Othello could not have been a black man since Desdemona had fallen in love with him. The other was in response to a presumed disruption. He stopped and addressed a rather swarthy student: "We let you in here and this is how you behave." The student was Syrian (from my high school). What was the professor thinking? Not a murmur in class about either episode.

Entrance into medical school was even more difficult for Jews. Very few got in no matter how good their marks were; most of those who did were the sons of doctors. All of that lasted until the war was over. What swept it all aside without even a puff of smoke was the return of the veterans, funded by government money.

When I look at McGill in recent times, I conclude that "they" were right about putting up the barriers. They doubtless said, "If we let them in, they'll probably overrun the place." When you see who the Principal (president) is now and the Deans of the various faculties, including medicine, you can see how prophetic they were. If only they had lived to see it.

Leo

iv. To my friend Brian Bixley, 22 March, 2003

Iraq: to go or not to go

... You[r letter] pointed out the sanctimonious posturing of Bush and Blair as they wrapped themselves in morality, ideology, and patriotism, shedding belated tears for the poor Iraqis, on the one hand, and, on the other, expressing fears about the close links between Saddam Hussein and Bin Laden. The other side's main flaw is naïveté and silliness, at best, wrapping itself around the pathetic UN. Chretien's final (?) position is a good example: if the U.S. succeeded in buying the votes of Guinea, Cameroon, Bulgaria or the like, that would justify (Canada joining) an attack. France and Germany seemed to be saying something similar, e.g., let's-continue-to-talk-to-them ("diplomacy") and let's-give-the-inspectors-all-the-time-they-need. Both seem equally pointless. Talk to whom?

Saddam Hussein? How can you talk to him when he's choking with laughter? As for the inspectors, they could be offered a lifetime contract with a huge prize if they ever find anything. Fat chance!

My position, I would like to think, is not ideological, just sensible. Is the Tiger of the Euphrates more likely to use these forbidden weapons if he is attacked than if not? The answer, I think, is yes, though one can't be certain. For over a decade (since Gulf War I) he hasn't used them or attacked anyone outside Iraq. Nor do I think he's likely to. The faintest move would give the U.S. the excuse it seeks to pulverize him, and he knows it. In the end, the U.S. couldn't find such an excuse, so it invented several — links to Bin Laden, the sufferings of the Iraqis, and so on. But if S.H. is cornered and feels all is lost, then I think the danger is greatest. And Bush & Blair and their henchmen are now beginning to say just that.

So I think they should have just let him be, a far from satisfactory solution, but more reasonable than the others. Now, of course it's too late for that, and we have to hope for a quick and decisive outcome with as little bloodshed as possible. After that, who knows?

Leo

v. To Beryl Donaldson Langer, 5 December, 2005

Excerpt from a letter to my friend and former star student, Beryl Donaldson Langer, 5 December, 2005. She teaches sociology at La Trobe University in Melbourne.

Sociology *(The title was not in the original letter.)*

Now we come to your "RESEARCH NOTE: Consuming Anomie" *(which was enclosed)* and I must tell you why I disagree with your approach. Your disapproval of consumer capitalism is clear, as it has been in your previous papers which I've read. (A defense of consumer capitalism would have been just as unacceptable.) You feel that it's harmful, to children anyway. (You will probably say, "Hold it right there. I never said 'harmful'; that's a value judgement." Only for the sake of the argument, I will reply, "Your objection is sustained," and let's follow the line of your reasoning.) You write, "The life world of consumer childhood — a 'world of peer evaluation, based on goods, media characters, and product knowledge' — can be seen as inherently anomic, a world in which desire is endless, satisfaction fleeting, and sufficiency unattainable. Every turn of the environment–product cycle presents children with a new universe of toys, games, clothes and collectables that make the things they already have, however plentiful, inadequate to their 'needs'" (p. 261). The evidence for this assertion is presumably elsewhere; it's not here. I can think of many exceptions, but we'll let that pass.

The very next sentence, Durkheim's Dictum [my term, LZ], is used to clinch that argument. To "pursue a goal which is by definition unattainable is to condemn oneself to a state of perpetual unhappiness." Alas, that's utter nonsense. I would have called it pure bullshit were it not so rude. Worse, it's not true. One might equally say it can guarantee a state of perpetual happiness. Nearly everyone, the happy and the unhappy, endlessly pursues goals which they know are unattainable. A few throw themselves enthusiastically into the quest for universal peace and brotherhood, even though they know they can't attain it. But, more prosaically, the rest of us keep pursuing goals which we know we can't attain — to be a much better teacher, plumber, lawyer, and policeman; a much better mother, father, wife, husband, son, daughter, and friend. We want our children to be what we know they can never be, a futile hope which they reciprocate. We want our health to be better than we know it can be and our favourite team to win every game. We want ... we want ... we want. Man's reach does exceed his grasp. Perhaps that's human nature. It's certainly a central part of living. Mostly we make some degree of peace with our failings and go on.

All of this brings us back to the beginning. Consumer capitalism certainly does feed into our manifold wants, though in ways that are so diverse and far-reaching that they are not susceptible to easy generalization. Are those effects (of consumer capitalism) good or bad, harmful or beneficial, or both? Those judgements are moral, not sociological.

I've always had a maxim that if one asks "Should it be?", then one cannot simultaneously ask, "Why is it?" It's as if they were two linked doors — open one and the other closes. Annette just walked in and saw what I was doing. "This has been difficult," I said. She replied, "If you didn't think she was so great, you could never have done that." To which I say, "Amen."

Leo

Reminiscences, Rants, and Raves

IV TRIBUTES TO LEO

> **ZAKUTA, LEO**
> On October 18, 2008, of a mesothelioma, at the age of 83. Husband of Annette, father of Jamie and Silvie, brother of Ken, brother-in-law of Bea Zakuta and Sylvia Lustgarten. Taught sociology at the University of Toronto 1952 - 1985. A secular service will be held on Friday, October 24th at 1:00 pm in the Music Room of Hart House at the University of Toronto, followed by a reception. Visiting will take place at the Manulife Centre, 44 Charles St. W, Toronto, apartment 3209, Friday evening from 6 p.m. and Saturday from 12 p.m.

This obituary, written in advance by Leo himself, appeared in the *National Post* and the *Globe and Mail* on Monday, October 20, 2008.

1. Memorial Service for Leo Zakuta[1]

October 24, 2008

1:10	Abba Lustgarten	Welcome, biography of Leo Zakuta
1:20	Silvie Zakuta	
1:30	Jamie Zakuta	
1:40	Jacob Lustgarten	
1:45	Margie Golick	
1:50	Margaret Cockshutt	
2:00	Norm Dyson	
2:05	Abba Lustgarten	Announcements (visiting, table of materials, reception)
2:20	Stephen Ain	Leo's "Last Words"
2:30	Reception	

---

[1] Planned program for the memorial service as prepared ahead of time by Abba Lustgarten, who organized the memorial. The actual program did not correspond to the plans exactly, as we decided to include remarks emailed in by friends who could not attend in person.

Leo and Annette on their deck at home
Toronto, c. 2000

i. Abba Lustgarten

Good afternoon. I am honoured to welcome you all this afternoon as we remember and celebrate the life of Leo Zakuta. On behalf of Annette, Jamie, and Silvie, I would like to thank you for participating in this ceremony and for the caring, friendship, and support that you have shown for Leo in so many ways. Special thanks to those who have traveled from afar to be with us, and for the kind messages of condolence from those who could not be with us in person.

Leo was my uncle. I first met him when I was a young child, and have grown up with his presence in various ways for my whole life. So, I feel privileged to give voice to some of my own reminiscences of Leo, and to introduce a number of the people that were closest to him, who will share their thoughts and feelings here today.

Since my uncle's death, a thought has been with me that I feel certain is shared by many or all of us gathered here, namely: if there was one person in the world who I could pick to eulogize a cherished friend and family member, to speak with insight, warmth and wit — it would be Leo. On numerous occasions, through letters, poems, and particularly, speeches at moments like this, we have been thankful for the thoughtful clarity of his voice.

And so, how specially poignant that he is not here to help us out today. But that is not completely true. Always supremely organized, right to the end of his life (and, I would add, bold and courageous), Leo carefully considered and expressed his wishes for today's proceedings.

Specifically, the room we are sitting in — the Music Room — was his choice, here at the University of Toronto, where he spent such a big part of his life. His choice to be cremated, the absence of religious ritual, and the specific invitation of today's speakers, are all according to his plan. He even typed up a document of his last words, which we will read soon. Leo's hand is guiding us — and yet, I will really miss hearing his voice.

We have all been thinking a lot about Leo lately, and I expect that some of you have thoughts, feelings, and memories that you may wish to share. Please take a moment to consider if you wish to share a brief reminiscence out loud. Later in this service, there will be an opportunity for you to do so. Now, I'd like to present a brief biography of Leo.

Leo Zakuta was born in Montreal on August 27, 1925. His parents, Keile and Hershel Zakuta, had come to Canada in the 1920s from the shtetl of Svislocz in Russia. His father worked as a carpenter and his mother was a teacher in the Jewish orphanage. The family struggled through difficult times during the Depression, when Leo was just a young child. Later on, after the Second World War, his father formed a partnership with his brother-in-law, and from then on, they thrived and prospered.

After attending Strathcona High school in Montreal, Leo went to McGill and eventually got his doctorate in sociology from the University of Chicago. His first teaching job (for one year) was in Winnipeg. Soon after, in 1952, he got a position to replace another professor at the University of Toronto (U of T) for a one-year term. He slightly extended this — for 33 extra years.

For many years he taught undergraduate courses on subjects like sociology of the family and relations between the sexes. He loved teaching, and preferred to mark all his students' assignments himself, always turning down the help of teaching assistants, and writing his own copious notes on his students' papers.

In 1956, while teaching in Toronto, he returned to see his family and friends in Montreal. Over the summer, he reconnected with a girl he had met years earlier, while working as a camp counselor. This, of course, was Annette. By the time he returned to Toronto in September, he was a married man.

He was appointed associate dean of the School of Graduate Studies, and served two terms, discovering that he also had a penchant and enthusiasm for the administrative side of academic life.

In 1963, Annette and Leo adopted Jamie, and then in 1964, Silvie was born. Their large old house on Elm Avenue, and especially the long driveway — perfect for ball hockey — and the jumbo-sized back yard, were a perpetual centre of activity for neighbourhood children (and one of my favourite places to go).

At the age of 59, Leo was offered early retirement, which, to his wife's surprise, he accepted, but he continued to write on various topics, remaining active in academic life. It was at this time that his interest in tennis turned from enthusiasm to obsession.

Leo and Annette have maintained a lively and warm circle of friends and family throughout the years, many of whom are sitting here right now.

Three years ago, in 2005, Leo and Annette moved out of their house into an apartment high atop the Manulife Centre, where Leo was able to return after his hospital stays, and remained until the end of his life.

I would like to share a couple of personal reminiscences of my uncle Leo.

In Leo's office at home hangs a tribute poster made for him by his tennis buddies, on which the letters of his name "L" "E" "O" are associated with the traits leadership, equity, and organization. This poster got me thinking of other L-words that could epitomize fundamental parts of Leo's character. As I began to think of these, I had the feeling that Leo would enjoy and approve of this kind of exercise.

It turns out that there are quite a few: "love," "learning," and of course "leadership," but there are two that stand out for me: "language" and "labels."

And, associated with each of these is an object that when I see it, always makes me think of Leo, and beyond that, always makes me chuckle.

So, first: language — Leo's learn-ed love of language. Communicating his ideas in his work and interpersonal relationships was clearly important to Leo, but way beyond this was a joy and playfulness with words that is evident in the myriad poems, limericks, letters, tributes, and in fact, eulogies that flowed from his pencil, typewriter, and eventually, his word processor. He was keen to share all of these widely, and they are available to any of you if you are interested. Now and in the future we can visit Leo through his words, as I have done in the past few days.

One of my favourite language-related memories is of a bumper sticker Leo had on his car. In ludicrously ornate print, it shouted: "ESCHEW OBFUSCATION." Paraphrased in normal English: "Don't use fancy and confusing language!" Every time I see a bumper sticker — any bumper sticker — I think of Leo, and I have to smile.

The other L-word is labels. Most of you will be familiar with Leo's habit of labeling everything around him. Maybe the word 'habit' is a bit of an understatement. "Life-long obsession" might be closer. In particular, he loved to tag almost anything with little plastic sticky labels. For most people, this technology went out of use somewhere around 1970 or so, but that was of no importance for my uncle. It worked for him.

Please don't think of this as an aversion to new gadgets — consider that Leo was the first person I knew to own an electronic calculator! So why, then, was he so taken with labels? Could it have something to do with his Yiddish name, by which his mother originally called him? The name is none other than — Leybl! Coincidence? Well, yes, I guess — just a curious coincidence.

My theory for his labeling fervor is this: Leo, probably more than any person I have known, seemed to have a clearly-thought-out conception of everything around him. He always seemed certain and committed in his opinions, and could tell you exactly how he saw things. Perhaps, since in his mind, everything so clearly had its place, he just wanted to make it clear for the rest of us. I think it was delightful the way this systematic approach to life extended to everything from academic discourse to keeping track of tennis balls, to sorting garbage, to preferred flavours of ice cream.

Whenever I see one of those little stick-on plastic labels, I think of Leo and again, I have to smile. (Of course, nowadays the only time I see them is when visiting the Zakutas.)

By a strange coincidence, I also still have a machine for making those little plastic labels, and over the past couple of days, I have made a bunch that say "Leo Zakuta." They are in a beautiful bowl made by Annette. I encourage you to take one home with you and stick it onto some appropriate object, where in the years to come, you will remember my uncle 'Leybl,' and smile.

While I didn't see him that often in the last few years, Leo really was one of my favourite people, and I will miss him.

ii. Silvie Zakuta

When I thought about what to say about my father today, there were many things that I could have spoken about. But there were a few that really struck me, and I wanted to share those with you today.

The thing that struck me most when I thought of my dad was how devoted he was to me, my brother, and my mom. He had no end of time for us, infinite patience, and such a great desire to help. As an example, when I was growing up, I used to get the most excruciating headaches — it seemed like all the time. I would wake up in the middle of the night crying. Whenever I had a headache, my mom gave me medicine and went back to bed. At that point my dad always took over. He pulled up a chair next to my bed and played word games with me for hours, in order to distract me until I fell back to sleep. And it always worked.

Sometimes it took a short time, sometimes a long time, sometimes what seemed like all night. He never told me that he wanted to go back to bed or even that he was tired or sleepy. He never said that he had a lot to do the next day or that he had to be at work early. He always stayed with me as long as it took for me to get back to sleep, without any complaint or even a hint of impatience.

When I thought about what to say today, I was also struck by how much pleasure my dad derived from my pleasure. We shared an awful sweet tooth and a passion for anything chocolate. Throughout my childhood and adulthood, no matter what he was eating, if it was sweet, and especially if it was something chocolate, he wanted me to have some of his. He was not just willing to share desserts that he loved with me, as many people might be, but insisted on it.

It didn't matter to my dad how little he had or how much he was enjoying it. In fact, the more he enjoyed it, the more he wanted to share it with me. When he thought the dessert was really good, he wouldn't take no for an answer. My father got so much more pleasure from my enjoyment of those sweet things than he would have gotten from eating them himself.

The last thing that struck me when I was thinking about speaking today was that my father was the one that I really needed to help me prepare. He was such an accomplished writer and speaker. He was so smart and self-assured, and so interested in helping me.

When I was a child, he was not just prepared to spend the time he felt necessary going over things that I had written for school, but he really wished to do so. He would spend long periods of time making sure they were perfect. I think he would have been just as happy to continue this with me as an adult, but I wouldn't let him.

At the beginning of my Grade 7 year, when I had just started at a new school, there was a public speaking contest. Each student had to write her own speech and present it to her class. I didn't know how to begin to write mine and had no clue as to what subject might be interesting or appropriate — and the thought of presenting it terrified me.

My father suggested that I write about people's use of jargon in professional writing and call it, "The Use and Abuse of the English Language." He said that once I had written my speech, he would go over it with me. I liked the subject and I found the promise of his help reassuring.

I wrote the speech, and my father went over it with me word by word. There were no computers in those days, so each draft had to be separate and completely rewritten, according to my dad. We prepared draft after draft, and each time the speech improved a little. By the time we were finished, it was at a professorial level.

Each class had to choose one student to give her speech in front of the whole school. By no fluke and to my horror, my class picked me. Although I know it was unfair to my classmates in retrospect, it was a great learning experience that I never would have had were it not for my dad.

That was just one example of the many, many things that he worked on with me and taught me about writing and speaking and so many other things throughout my life. I was so lucky to have been taught so much with such enthusiasm and skill by my father. More importantly, I was so lucky to have had Leo Zakuta as my father.

*Leo, Silvie, and Annette at Silvie's law school graduation
Queen's University, Kingston, Ontario, 1991*

iii. Jamie Zakuta

A Eulogy for / Tribute to / Celebration of ... Leo Zakuta, my Dad

Dad was caring and devoted and an extremely generous man. He always made time for his loved ones and friends, no matter what the sacrifice or inconvenience to himself. Over the last few days I've had difficulty choosing just a few anecdotes that show his fine qualities, because there were so many.

   I think a good place to begin is with a story about hockey — one of several passions Dad and I shared. When I was 8 or 9 years old, Dad decided to coach my hockey team. Aside from the obvious organizational commitments, this included standing behind the bench on many frigid evenings on which one's feet took 20 painful minutes to defrost after the game — and he wasn't skating with us to keep at least somewhat warm.

Although every kid wants to be on a winning team, my father valued equal participation and learning much more than victory. An illustration of this was in his naming of the forward lines on our team. There were no 1st, 2nd or 3rd lines, but instead red, white, and green, thereby eliminating any indication of one line's superiority over another.

I can recall many games when we were trailing by one goal with little time left. Most of the kids were clamoring, myself included, for Dad to send out the best five players for a chance to tie or win the game. But he would simply motion to the next line whose turn it was to play the final minutes, win or lose. I remember frequently being upset and embarrassed by this, but looking back, I realize how tough it must have been for him to do that and how great it was that he did.

Speaking about Dad would not be complete without a tennis tale or two. Alongside sociology, writing, and his family, tennis was Dad's other passion. As some of you know, a framed poster which his tennis gang made for him hangs in his study at home. It uses his name as an acronym for "leadership–equity–organization" (L.E.O.). This in itself speaks volumes about the kind of man he was, but I would like to add a couple of personal stories.

Some of you will remember Bill Alexander, a tennis friend of Dad's, who was a real maverick. Years ago, when Dad and Bill were in their late fifties, they relished the opportunity to challenge me and my friend to tennis matches. We always figured our twenty-something legs and superior reflexes would guarantee us victory. However, Bill and Dad often won. How did they do it?

They had a very clear strategy — some deftly-angled shots but mostly infinite patience, which often lured us into beating ourselves. These two professors gave us a real lesson in tennis and life!

My father also taught me something else which I'll

always remember. When I was younger I often came to the tennis courts looking for a competitive game of singles. Dad would always invite me to join his gang if I had no one to play with, yet I usually turned him down. As the years passed, I began to accept his invitations more and more often. I came to really look forward to joining his gang in their love of the game, camaraderie, and enduring friendship.

Aside from his passion for teaching and sports, my father was quite an organizer and inventor. When the addition to our home on Elm Avenue was completed in 1971, Dad was faced with what he saw as the daunting task of remembering which switches operated which lights.

One day, my father bought a label gun and went crazy with it! My mother discovered, to her horror, that every switch had a name like "MEZZ," "BSMNT" and "STRS." The family would have figured out which switch corresponded with which light, but Dad was not taking any chances.

Around the same time, my dad nailed two large pegboards on the sides of the basement stairs and organized them with every imaginable item. When my friend James opened the door, he was awestruck, and exclaimed that it resembled a couple of aisles at Canadian Tire. My father liked to come up with practical solutions to mechanical problems — solutions that were quirky and inventive.

One story from his final months illustrates this well. During his third trip home from the hospital this past difficult year, he was strongly encouraged by his doctor to use his walker to rebuild his overall strength. He always had a cowbell attached to his walker to alert my mother when he needed help. But he didn't want her to come running if it was not necessary — she had enough to deal with! At times he felt confident moving around on his own. So he devised a way to muffle the bell with a cork and attached it to the clangor. That way with a couple of simple twists, he could activate or silence the bell as needed.

I'd like to mention a couple of things that happened during Dad's final months. On a beautiful late August afternoon — Dad's last birthday — we headed to the tennis courts to visit his gang. I pulled into the park and Dad struggled from the car to his walker and then struggled with his walker through the gate to the courts. Somehow his friends knew he was coming and had placed a chair at the back of the court for him.

His physical abilities were almost gone, but his enthusiasm never waned. He cherished that time with his friends, just watching them play. He smiled so much that day, never having hit a ball.

Because of my father's keen interest in politics, he was determined to vote even though he knew his days were numbered. He insisted that I take him to the polling booth, which involved pushing him in his wheelchair with his oxygen tank attached. As it turned out, that was four days before he died.

Something else I'll miss terribly about Dad — throughout our adult life, we always talked sports. Even during his final weeks, he never lost interest in watching them. He still phoned me, or if he was too weak, asked Mom to, in order to check the times and channels of the games that day. Most notably, the CFL, which he still preferred to its over-hyped American counterpart.

Over the past months that Dad was sick, the three of us began each day at my parents' apartment, to be with him. He referred to us as his "team." My conversation with him often opened with a discussion of the previous night's games. Just 10 days ago, on the eve of the Montreal Canadiens' 100th anniversary, he asked me if I had seen the fluky goal that tied the game. He was still cheering Les Habitants right to the end — they did win in overtime that night.

As a final thought, my dad really enjoyed literature and poetry. One of his favourite poems, and mine, was the "Rubaiyat" by Omar Khayyam. I'd like to end with a stanza which we both particularly liked:

There was a Door to which I found no Key:
There was a Veil past which I could not see:
Some little Talk awhile of ME and THEE
There seemed — and then no more of THEE and ME.

iv. Jacob Lustgarten

Last Saturday morning my uncle Leo passed away peacefully, at home, with his family present. He had for the last couple of years fought pretty hard against a formidable illness. It wasn't that he wanted to leave, but it seems he ran out of alternatives. Just a week earlier he had expressed disdain for a doctor who advised him that he may only have weeks to live.

Our families had been close all of my life, and before, but I got to know Leo particularly well during the last part of my father's life. Leo was an absolute rock of support as we struggled with my father's gradual loss of strength and independence and, in the last few months, Leo faced a very similar process.

Like many of my generation, I am running low on Elders and perhaps not far from becoming one myself. Leo was a great sage, with strong insightful opinions on many issues ranging from education and politics to driving and even parking, one of his pet peeves. I will really miss his meticulous instructions.

Reminiscences, Rants, and Raves

44 Elm Avenue in Toronto
Zakuta home from 1961 to 2005

When I was quite young, we moved to Toronto from Montreal, and my whole family moved in to 44 Elm for a short time. It became a second home to us as I went through high school and university. Some of us saw a little less of Leo during the "tennis years," when his intrepid ensemble pursued the sport year round, outdoors. Others are doubtless better qualified than I to comment, but it is my understanding that Leo contributed not only his athleticism but his full administrative expertise, acquired during a career as a professor and high-ranking officer at the University of Toronto.

Leo, Annette, Jamie, and Silvie in the family room at home

For the most part, I saw the family side of Leo, but over time I got glimpses of other areas. I always sensed he was not only a great family man, but to many, a very important friend in need, to others a critical mentor and educator.

There are many special qualities that are uniquely Leo, and these will stick in our memories as part of his legacy. Among them: his absolutely unequivocal and fearless support for any underdog he felt deserved it; his love and joy of time spent with family and friends; his love of ice cream ... every flavour!

v. Margie Golick

Because Leo himself crafted many apt tributes to friends and relatives and colleagues, living and dead, it is intimidating to try to pay homage to the master of the precise word, the man who shunned sham and pomposity, but who had no trouble expressing his admiration and affection.

Leo was many things to many people — son, brother, husband, dad, teacher, mentor, colleague, tennis buddy, grocery shopper, and pal. I can vouch most knowledgably for his role as a friend. I was one of many — part of the Montreal connection that includes Vivian Rabinovitch (we hung out with Leo and his friends Lenny and Lou at college more than sixty years ago); Rose and Myer Katz; Morrie and Ruth Rohrlick; and Marianne and Howard Stein. We knew him before Annette did, and some of us knew Annette before Leo did.

Leo was outrageous and funny in those days, I remember much levity and laughter and irreverence and a lot of raucous good fun, especially outdoors in summer and winter. I have forgotten most of the specific incidents of sixty years ago, but I do remember a bunch of us at a

Laurentian lake skinny dipping at midnight, disrobing in the pitch dark — and Leo gleefully producing a flashlight. And I remember on cross-country skiing outings his prowess at writing his name in the snow.

In spite of living many miles apart we remained close friends — so comfortable with each other that there was still a bit of the teenager in us when we were together. All that raucous behaviour predated his time at the University of Chicago. When he came back to Montreal a full-fledged sociologist with a PhD and a book in the works, he was much more serious and subdued and ready to settle down. Without missing a beat, he found Annette — undoubtedly the prettiest girl in Montreal — and married her six weeks later.

He went off to teach at the University of Toronto, and I gathered from our conversation at that time that he loved teaching but was less enchanted with academic rituals and politics.

We Montrealers tended to visit Toronto more than Leo and Annette came to Montreal. We had children and grandchildren here. But no matter how many dance recitals or Purim plays we had to go to, we always spent time with the Zakutas. Leo did more than his share to keep the friendship alive. His generosity equaled Annette's. Hers is very visible because her many gifts of pottery over the years have prominent places in all our homes. Leo offered services. And companionship; and often advice.

In my case he offered a chauffeur service — meeting me at the station or taking me to the station whenever my own family members were not available. He made me feel it was so little trouble that I always felt free to ask him or to take advantage of his offers, which were, of course, contingent on his tennis schedule.

He loved his tennis buddies. Everyone who knew him knew of his incredible loyalty and devotion to his friends. He organized reunions for members of his old Montreal gang, and we were all touched at his care and concern for his friend Leonard Levine through his long illness.

Jamie and Silvie learned well from their dad and were always at Leo's side during his illness.

I was dazzled by his prowess as a grocery shopper. He would advise me on the best brands of cookies and the best flavours of ice cream, which he always had available to serve to me in his kitchen on Elm Avenue or on the 32nd floor of the Manulife.

His generosity to his friends took other forms too. Many of you were probably recipients of his printed and collated memoirs; his tributes to his friends and colleagues in prose and verse; and his wonderful rants, "Exercises in Futility" he called them — letters to editors and broadcasters expressing his pleasure and displeasure at their products. He had a love-hate relationship with the CBC, and let them know it.

This sharing of his accumulated thoughts with friends was a generous gift. I suppose I didn't realize how incredibly special it was until the other night, when I read through all three volumes. He has left us access to this wonderful family history, an account of his remarkable parents whom he adored — and a written record of his thoughtfulness, warmth, kindness, and loyalty to friends as well as his impatience with fools, intellectual fads and pop sociology, injustice, and bad grammar.

He came to tributes in verse rather late in life, but had a real flair. I was the recipient of two of his poems. One was written twenty years ago for my 60th birthday. It was long and funny and full of compliments and insults and send ups and reminiscences and — something that would cheer the heart of any old lady — the notion that he still remembered me in my prime. Here is my favourite couplet:

Who could have pictured a woman serene
In that feisty young filly of seventeen?

And I loved his hymn to moving. I never thought that he could leave his beautiful house on Elm Avenue with equanimity. But he knew that to everything there is a season. The move to a high rise apartment spawned a poem that began:

> No more planting, no more weeds
> No more mowing, no more seeds
> No more gardeners, no more leaves
> No more roofing, no more eaves. ...

I, too, write verses for friends and family on special occasions. And Leo always admired my poems — no matter how foolish. And now I have a big regret: that I never wrote a poem for him or about him. I'll have to console myself with *trep verter* — that's a Yiddish expression for the words you think of on the steps when you are on your way home; the words you should have said when you had an audience. Here are my *trep verter* — much too little and too late:

> Whether dropping his pants
> Or writing his rants
> In elegant prose
> To friends and to foes
> There was no one like Leo
> He did it Con Brio.

Leo, Buddy Boltuck, and Bernard Goldstein
Lake Michigan, 1949

vi. Margaret Cockshutt

I first met Leo in 1973. He was then a professor of Sociology and since 1972 the Associate Dean of Division II in the School of Graduate Studies. As such, he was the Chairman of the Division II Degree Committee. The Committee members' role was to uphold the academic standards of the graduate school, and at the same time to seek occasional exemptions from a standard for a particular student in their departments. Leo was in the unenviable position of being the Chairman and at the same time a strong advocate for the School's standards.

Last spring Leo asked me to speak at this gathering and to tell this story. In 1972, before I was a member, there was apparently a heated Committee discussion of one issue. Leo didn't tell me what he said, but it must have been something like, "This is the position and I am the graduate school." One of the Committee members was Ted, one of the good guys whom Leo respected. Ted turned red with anger and said, "No, you are not." Long pause. Then Leo said, "You are absolutely right. I won't make that mistake again," and he told me this spring, "I never did make that mistake again."

I've thought a lot about why this incident made such an impression on him. I think he then found his balance in chairing the Committee and letting members fight the battle for him. When I joined the Committee in 1973, I found the meetings were usually intense, with members struggling to make convincing arguments even for a sometimes weak case, and then other members objecting strongly. Leo presided over all with fairness, a firm hand, and wisdom in presenting the standards while he also knew when their slight relaxation would be possible. Rather like trying to take a group of recalcitrant cats for a walk.

One year there were three or four members who were highly regarded academic heavyweights. At one meeting I had a heated argument with one of them and won my point. As we were gathering up our papers at the end, Leo said to me, "Well, Dave Schultz, that was quite a performance." Leo was quite surprised that I knew that Dave Schultz was the toughest member of the Philadelphia Flyers hockey team. We became close friends from then on.

In 1976, my term was up as my department's Coordinator of Graduate Studies. After I returned to my regular teaching duties we saw each other at occasional academic meetings, and talked to each other frequently about our individual problems with students or colleagues or the University bureaucracy.

Leo retired in 1985, and when I retired some years later, he suggested that we have lunch together every few weeks. We did that for many years, and discussed our interests — he was multi-faceted in his interests: tennis (his passion for the tennis club); our shared interest in watching the

Wimbledon, U.S., and Canadian matches on TV; baseball; the theatre and reading plays; and his interest in watching hockey and football. Always we returned to discussions of past and present University of Toronto events and people — they had played such a large part in his life.

He was a clear-sighted analyst of people — understanding their foibles and weaknesses, recognizing and appreciating their strengths. He was warm and generous in his appreciations, witty in expressing his judgments, a caring friend.

The world is emptier without him.

vii. Norman Dyson

Norm, visibly moved, read parts of emails that Judy Hellman and Deborah Heller had sent him for the occasion. [AZ]

Dear Annette,

Enclosed is the documentation that you wished. I am virtually computer illiterate, so kindly tolerate my typing, etc. There were a few comments that I discarded in the interest of staying within the time limits.

The only one worthy of resurrecting was to be made just before the reading of Judy's and Deborah's e-mails:

> Recently, on the court, I commented to John Weiser that playing in Leo's gang not only was a great physical workout, but had a spiritual quality to it. John quickly replied, "Yeah, I agree and I expect to experience both every time I play." (Coming from John, the comment resonated.)

Looking forward to carrying on Leo's legacy if it ever gets above zero.

Warmest regards to you, Silvie, and Jamie,

Norm

viii. Judy Hellman

Subject: My thoughts about Leo
24 October, 2008

I feel heartsick to find myself so far from Toronto that I am not able to share this moment of loss but also of celebration of Leo's life with Annette, Silvie, and Jamie, as well as the other members of Leo's "tennis family."

As an undergraduate, years ago, I was required to take a course in political theory and, with a bare minimum of enthusiasm, I read my way through what we were told were the great classics of political thought. What I retained from this exercise in forced labour was the following:

Most of the great thinkers agreed that "man" was imperfect, although they didn't agree on just how imperfect man might be. But the great thinkers also thought that man could be made more perfect and could manage to live in harmony with others if the right arrangements were put into place. This, my professors told me, is what government is supposed to be — a series of arrangements that force us to be our best selves.

I never found any of this to be persuasive until I met Leo and entered his tennis world. It was in that context that I saw that when someone like Leo (even as he denied that this was the case) put in place a series of regulations about inclusiveness, about ways that people of varying abilities could play quite happily together, and about how there was to be no fuss or discussion as to who was to play with whom, much less any discrimination by gender or age — in effect, he had had set out governing principles that provided a context in which we could all be our best and most generous selves. For this, and for giving me the gift of tennis (an activity I had lost along the way to adulthood), I will always be in Leo's debt.

There are dozens of other gifts that Leo also gave: the example of his long, loving marriage to Annette; the special treat of playing as his partner when Silvie or Jamie was also on the court; the luminous September day when he persuaded me that I could play tennis on Yom Kippur and my parents, in the next world, would never know; or, perhaps the most important, the example of his enthusiasm and joy in doing the things he most enjoyed in life, almost until the end.

Like the rest of you, I will miss Leo more than I can possibly say. I will especially miss that moment when Leo would look across Rosedale Park and announce with delight: "Oh, good! Here comes Sheila" — or Don, or Peter, or Norm, or any of the rest of us — but especially when he would say, "Oh, good! Here comes Judy."

Judy Hellman

ix. Deborah Heller

Subject: Leo's death
October 23, 2008

What do I have to say about Leo other than, as I said last night, that he was a wonderful person? Yes, I can be more specific.

He was not only the hub and initiator of the group that still bears his name, but the glue that held us together. More important is that he made playing with his group a welcoming and joyous experience. I might begin by saying that long before I ever played with his group I had the happy experience of being partnered with him in one of those round robins that used to be organized by the Rosedale Tennis Club. At the time, this was an experience I found excruciatingly anxiety-provoking. But Leo was remarkably accepting and even reassuring. I could scarcely serve at all in those days, and his response as my partner was to say, appreciatively, "You know, nothing is harder to return than a soft serve."

Later, when I joined his tennis group, I was always grateful for his unfailingly kind remarks — both when one flubbed and also, on those blessed — if rare — occasions when one did something surprisingly successful and he pretended to find one a fearsomely tough opponent. I think his kind and generous approach to tennis was an enormous help in taking the angst out of tennis for me and, though I can't speak for others, possibly, for all of us.

Best,
Deborah Heller

x. Chris and John Furedy

Subject: Thinking of you and the memorial
Oct. 22, 2008

Dear Annette, Silvie, and Jamie,

We are grieving with you for Leo. We are sending the attached note in case it might contribute to the memorial on Friday, although we realize that probably the whole event is tightly scheduled and packed with words that family and friends want to express.

With love,
Chris and John

> Many of you may know that in the past two years, Leo gathered together various letters that he had written to newspapers, the CBC, the University of Toronto *Bulletin*, and to friends. Leo called this collection "Exercises in Futility." The title had a double meaning, [alluding] to his "finger-in-the-dyke response" (as he put it) to the surge of political correctness, and to the seemingly black hole into which his letters to the *Globe and Mail* disappeared.
>   Leo may have thought that his stand against political correctness was futile, but we have to say that it was inspirational to us and numbers of others who shared his concerns. Perhaps Leo did not realize this: he was the highest level university administrator to speak out against political correctness and the erosion of freedom of speech. He did so with clarity and rationality, and often irony and humour. Many a coward must have shuddered inwardly.
>   Thank you, Leo, for this and so much more,
>
> Chris and John Furedy
> Sydney, Australia
> October 22, 2008

xi. Stephen Ain

In line with Leo's wishes and instructions, his "Last Words," which he had written in June, 2008, four months before he died, were read aloud by his cousin, Steven Ain.

Last Words

I have always wanted the last word. Even as a boy in arguments with my mother, I insisted on the last word, and I shouted abusive last words at the bigger boys who had just beat me up even though I knew they would beat me again for these new last words. So here I am speaking to you for the last time from the great beyond.

This message is mostly about people. First, Annette. We did not have a good marriage; it was a great one. When I married Annette, I hit the jackpot. It did no harm that our family backgrounds were almost identical. Our families knew each other and had mutual friends and acquaintances. We understood each other's home life and could also speak Yiddish to each other. Our beliefs, tastes, and ideas about how to live were almost identical, so it was only natural that we became extremely close.

No words can describe her devotion and support for me in my illnesses, though she will minimize her role. Don't believe her. She was in my hospital room all day every day. When I told my doctor she was "my lifeline," he replied, "I know." Her best moments came when I became despondent and believed that I would never see home again. She kept telling me how mistaken I was and how the doctors had many other resources if I were really in trouble. That helped.

After I came home from the hospital, she spent endless hours bandaging, re-bandaging, and treating my wounds (from a fall), and seeking more and better care, all without a trace of complaint. She checked me so frequently that

Jamie renamed her "the hummingbird" after the only creature that can hover. She displayed the same devotion during my subsequent stays in hospital and at home. Words fail me.

Next, the children. They were always at the centre of our lives. Jamie was a brilliant student and athlete. We had a rough passage with him, but it has turned around completely and our relationship is mutually helpful, affectionate, and respectful. He is my very close friend.

We share a strong mutual interest in professional baseball, hockey, football, and tennis. When we played tennis together as doubles partners, I used to cite the old joke about the elephant who crossed the swinging bridge with the flea on his back. When they had crossed, the flea remarked, "We sure shook that thing, didn't we."

Silvie was also a brilliant student. She became a lawyer with her own practice and developed a really satisfying niche of her own. She has a very supple mind and she's thoroughly circumspect about confidentiality and which cases she takes on. No fiddling with the rules. She is soft-spoken, but anyone who thinks that's a sign of weakness will soon find himself badly mistaken. She's tough.

Her devotion to me while I was in the hospital was much like Annette's. Her office was just down the street from St. Mike's, so she was often there, usually with some treat for me. She felt she couldn't do enough for me.

Now for my doctors. Gina Shochat was skillful, efficient and caring. She may have saved my life on at least one occasion, and kept a close and watchful eye on me throughout. She was always available, which gave me a strong sense of security throughout my illness. She is a great doctor and a true friend.

Dr. Dale Dotten (of St. Mike's) had the same qualities. He knew how to walk that fine line between honesty and empathy. Eventually we became friends, bonded by… what else? First, professional baseball and football

(Stephen Jay Gould and George Will), and then many other things. A learned man, he was also the one who picked the New York Giants even before the 2008 NFL playoffs began. And the smiling cheerful faces of the nursing staff in the Hematology Ward.

I have asked three friends to say a few words about me. First, Margie Golick, a good friend since 1944, as smart as a whip and a super-achiever. Then Margaret Cockshutt, a close friend since about 1972, whose intelligence, strength, and humanity I greatly admire. I also wanted someone to speak on behalf of our tennis group. I have asked my friend Norman Dyson to do so, especially because he has had so much experience addressing the public in his long and distinguished career as a lawyer and a judge. He joined our group in the late 70s along with Peter Goering, so I sometimes referred to them as "new boys."

To all my other friends, a fond farewell. There is no time to name everyone and a great fear that I may inadvertently forget some, so I must do this collectively.

That is all I have to say except for a brief footnote.

Footnote

This footnote is not about people but pursuits. The activity which I most enjoyed was, of all things, sociology. I admit it's an odd and perhaps surprising choice, because I did so little sociology after my retirement. Why have I chosen it over tennis? Perhaps because I was never better than a so-so tennis player, since I lacked the fine hand-eye coordination required for real success. However, I thought, rightly or wrongly, that I did have a real capacity as a sociologist. I found it surprisingly easy to spot the main weakness in a piece of research, a proposal, or a paper at a meeting.

I also liked to write. When I did, I revised endlessly, eliminating words and trying to find the best phrase. I enjoyed the process and had infinite patience for it. But the best combination was writing about sociology.

I am now writing a series of essays on that subject entitled Essays on Inequality. The first one, "Till Death Do Us Part?" was written much earlier than the others. Three others have followed, and I am now working on a fifth, entitled "The Tomboy and the Sissy: Riding the Social Escalator," which is an examination of upward and downward mobility. I hope to include one further essay entitled "Social Sciences: Hard Facts Rest on Soft Foundations."

I am eager to complete these essays. But I have no idea how much remission time I may have and whether I will be able to. I know what Annette is thinking about my writing my "Last Words" and asking that they be read here today — "control freak until the very end." Now that SHE has had the last word, I must pull up my symbolic shroud and say a final goodbye.

2. Unveiling of Plaque in Honour of Leo at Rosedale Park

*Gathering at Rosedale Park to unveil the plaque at courts 7 and 8
Rosedale Park, Toronto, October 2009*

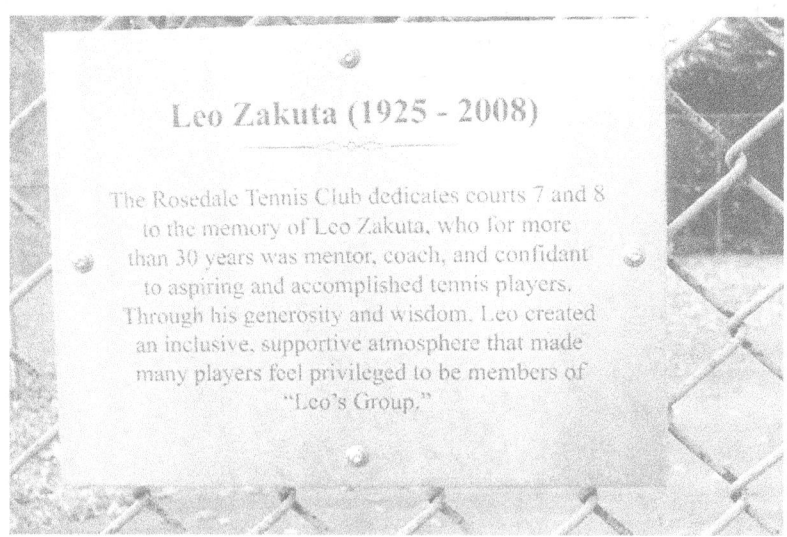

*Plaque installed by Rosedale Tennis Club in honour of Leo
Rosedale Park, Toronto, October 2009*

i. Sean Miller

I was very lucky to have played most of my tennis throughout my life here at Rosedale Park. As we all know, it is one of the most beautiful, quiet, fun places in this world, and it also had Leo.

As a kid growing up, Leo always made me feel like I was Bjorn Borg. Whenever he walked by while I was playing I would hear, "Wow what a shot," "Unbelievable hitting," or when we chatted at the club house, he would tell me what a joy it was to watch me. I knew that my abilities were just a little better than any tennis hacker out there, and I was just a kid, but it didn't matter; because Leo always knew how to make you feel like you were special and someone he cared about.

I know this will be said a number of times today, but his passion for this great game and (as my dad would say about Leo) his amazing ability to bring so many wonderful characters to play in his tennis community and make everyone welcome, was incredible. Whenever my Dad wasn't showing up, Leo would always want to know where he was, if he was okay, if my family was okay ... and then once he felt satisfied that there was nothing to be concerned about, he would make it clear to me to tell my Dad, "to get his butt out there ASAP."

Dad really thought Leo was a super guy. Dad was never a regular, but whenever he did go out and play with the group, he would tell me excitedly how much fun he had had, how well he had played, and then he would inevitably go through the same routine of asking himself why he didn't get out there more often.

Another special guy and an original member of Leo's tennis posse was Bill, who I know you all loved and whose early death was a real loss. One of the fondest memories I have of the group was watching Bill playing hard and serious out there on the court, while always having a cigarette butt hanging out of his mouth. I was fortunate enough to develop a relationship with Bill, and he always used to tell me how much that tennis community had meant to him over the years, how much work Leo would always put in to make it successful and reliable, and what a warm and caring person Leo was.

When I would be playing ball hockey with my buddies in the Rosedale rink in super-cold late fall or early spring, it really felt like home looking up on courts 7 and 8 and seeing Leo and the gang playing tennis with winter jackets, hats, and gloves. My hockey friends found that pretty funny, but I also know they were extremely impressed with that kind of passion and dedication.

I really miss Leo around here. The place feels a lot emptier without his big heart. To me, he'll always be the King of Rosedale Park.

ii. Judy Hellman (read by Anne Lenchak)

I have the impression that Leo never contemplated a time when he wouldn't be out on the courts, four seasons of the year, whacking a tennis ball. And because he didn't waste time projecting a world in which he wasn't playing tennis, I think that he never shared my secret concern about what would become of his group when he could no longer provide the catalytic force to make tennis "happen," not to mention performing the concrete tasks of monitoring the conditions of the courts, taking custody of the nets, raking, sweeping, shoveling, and leaf blowing, introducing new players to the old established players (often more than once!!) and particularly important for folks who cycle over from far away — patiently responding to telephone inquiries on the likelihood of decent weather and a basic minimum number of players.

Under the circumstance, I think that Leo, who always denied that his contribution was as central and indispensable as it was, would be unsurprised and very pleased that we have, somehow, managed to carry on his traditions and that we have kept playing in the beautiful pickup game that he established. It's true that we have slightly altered some of Leo's established patterns of rotation in and *out* of the game. But all of the fundamentals that Leo instilled in the rest of us by his good example are still in place.

Last autumn I wrote, for the occasion of the celebration of Leo's life, that Leo was for me a perfect example of what my political theory profs had meant when they talked about the "perfectibility of man." The idea is that human beings are imperfect, but that they can be made more perfect and can manage to live in harmony with others if right arrangements are put into place. This — my professors told me — is what government is supposed to be: a series of arrangements that force us to be our best selves.

Leo, through example, set out rules of inclusiveness about ways that people of varying abilities could play quite happily together and how there was to be no fuss or discussion about who was to play with whom, much less any discrimination by gender or age. And in this way, Leo had set out governing principles that provided a context in which we could all be our best and most generous selves.

And so we have carried on, faithful to Leo's principles, which we have fully embraced as our own. Deborah and Don and Norm, among others, have assumed Leo's task of liaison with Richard, who has been very responsive to our desires to carry on our famous pick-up game. We have taken to phoning one another to build a quorum of players on any given day. And I can say that my own contribution has been to take up Leo's practice of scanning the horizon — even as the ball is hit to me — to check out who else might be on her or his way across the park to join us.

I know that I share with everyone else the sense that every day that we are out here playing is a continued gift that Leo has given us.

iii. Peter Goering

Tennis — A Spring Incident

Some years ago, as March rolled around, the days became warmer, the light lingering longer and the winter snows disappearing, Leo decided to see if our outdoor courts, at Rosedale, could possibly become playable again with a little clean-up and tidying. So this one early spring day, Leo, on his own, arrived at the courts armed with his trusty broom and shovel to attempt cleaning up and drying the court surface.

Two nets were already in place, having been put up in the late fall in case playing off-season became possible, a practice we (and Leo) had pursued for many years. With some effort and supported by the warm sun and drying breezes, Leo managed to clear one of the two courts by removing snow patches, dispatching puddles, and tidying the surface of stray leaves or other debris.

The next day, some of us (including myself) were called by Leo to be made aware of the successful court cleaning, and tentatively set a day and time to play. The weather cooperated, and a day later four of us turned up at the appointed time to play our first outdoor game since early winter. To our great surprise and dismay, the cleared court was occupied by a couple (whom none of us knew) who were enjoying the fruits of Leo's labours, ignoring us as they played.

Leo politely introduced himself and indicated that he had cleared the court to make it playable and that we had arranged to use it that afternoon. As the four of us stood there, the couple continued to play still ignoring us and indicating in an off-hand manner that these were, after all, public courts. Leo then, in a calm voice, suggested that his shovel and broom were available for them to use to clear the second court.

They continued to ignore us. But when Leo gently suggested that the nets were his property (pointing out the name and address marked on the upper band), they still ignored him. With considerable aplomb, and not saying another word, Leo then lowered the net and waited.

Nothing ruins a tennis game as much as not having a net in place! The couple retreated and without uttering an angry word — and amid gales of laughter — packed up and left, leaving our group (with a properly re-installed net) to proceed to play.

The action speaks volumes of how Leo, over the years, managed awkward situations without a confrontation. I'll always fondly remember that incident.

iv. Barry Sessle

Musings

I had the pleasure of joining "Leo's Group" in 1978; I was introduced to the Group and its inimitable Leader at Rosedale Tennis Club by Bernie Hemrend, who was sorry that he could not attend today's ceremony. My experience of Leo from the outset was similar to that expressed by so many others today. He was very welcoming, inclusive, friendly, and (often) accommodating. He was also concerned about the well-being of others in His Group. Examples of this last feature that have not been mentioned today, were his repeated warnings to his fellow players, first, to avoid stepping on the ginkgo's smelly fruits when the tree (overhanging courts four and five and the outside pathway) was in season, and second, to avoid putting close to our clothing any newly-labeled tennis balls (labeled by him, with his marker pen that he retrieved from the depths of his tennis-paraphernalia-containing bag) for fear of the marker ink soiling our tennis clothes, which, of course, were always *très haute couture*!

And clothing reminds me of what I think was, for me at least, one of the funniest happenings in Leo's Group. It occurred 15-20 years ago, when Leo and Annette were still living on Elm Avenue. Leo had accidentally fallen down the basement stairs while visiting his brother in the Eastern Townships in Quebec, and had injured his lower back. However, this "minor" injury didn't keep our intrepid Leader away from the Club for too long, and soon we were welcoming him back to join us on the tennis courts. Leo felt that before getting down to playing tennis, we all first had to see the living proof of his mishap. Thus, those present were able to witness first-hand the extent of the injury since Leo turned his back to us, dropped his tennis shorts, lowered his underpants and displayed some very large purple patches in his lumbo-sacral area. The propriety of Rosedale Tennis Club was, however, not shaken to its foundations since (if I recall correctly) this all happened on court six, well out of sight of most club members present that day; nonetheless, they may have been puzzled by our howls of laughter, with Sheila Smith leading the way, resulting from this vintage Leo act.

v. Peter Moon

Annette — as promised.

This is based on an e-mail I sent to one of the group who was in Argentina when the unveiling took place, a phone conversation with someone who was at the event, and my memory.

Leo was Leo, and whenever his name crops up, it brings a smile to my face. During the unveiling, there were a lot of smiles all around. He was that kind of man.

Peter

~~~~~

I am not sure I should say what I am about to say, it's likely to get me killed on an occasion like this. But here goes.

What nobody has said is that Leo was a control freak. He was, and I should know, because in my own way I am something of a control freak myself, as some of you know. But Leo did control our games in his own way, as everyone who played with him knows.

Sometimes it drove me mad. I wanted to get on with the game but Leo, being Leo, would play tennis at his own pace and in his own highly sociable way. Time and again, he would see someone he knew walking past the courts, and he would stop play to wander over to the fence with a smile on his face to chat to them. "Oh, look who's here," he'd say to those of us who wanted to get on with the game. Or he'd stop or delay play to ask who'd seen the game — baseball or football or whatever — on TV last night. And whether we had or not he'd lead a discussion about what he thought were the turning moments of that game. And if it was tennis, he loved to tell us what John McEnroe had said.

I would fume and sometimes I'd still be fuming when I got home, and sometimes I'd still be fuming while I was in the shower. And then I'd start to laugh at myself because it was just Leo being Leo, and me being me, and I could never stay mad at him for very long. Nobody could. How could you possibly remain angry with such a uniquely pleasant control freak?

I haven't played tennis for a couple of years, the army keeps me too busy, but Leo still pops into my mind when I am watching tennis on television, and sometimes even when I am in the shower.

Another thing he'd do, as you all know, was he'd take control of the balls before we could get started and he'd sit over there with a magic marker marking the balls. But he would take forever to do it while he held court on whatever subject was of interest to him at the moment, usually sport and usually something he'd seen the day before on television. And he'd hold onto those balls for what seemed to be forever while some of us wanted to get on with the game. He'd release them, slowly, one at a time. While he held the balls he had control.

Well, that was Leo. He could be aggravating and controlling but he was always Leo — charming, delightful, and the one who held our games together. And he loved tennis.

He really was a good man, a decent man and, well, a good Canadian. What is being done here today is, I think, a wonderful thing for a wonderful man.

vi. Shirley Harris

My name is Shirley Harris, and this is how I came to know Leo. I had been a member of another club in the city, and had not had a particularly good time while playing there. It wasn't exactly inclusive. My friend, Richard Nicolson, who is the director of tennis at Rosedale Tennis Club, suggested that I come over to Rosedale Park, join the tennis club, and play with Leo's group. I didn't take him up on the suggestion for a while (much to my chagrin). Then one day, I decided to join Rosedale and find out about Leo's group. I called Leo, introduced myself and told him I would be coming over to join the group. He was delighted.

When I arrived at the courts where we play, I instantly felt a shower of warmth wash over me. Immediately, I felt part of the group. That was the wonderful thing about Leo and the group. They took anyone and everyone, regardless of their ability. From that moment on, I went regularly (sometimes seven days a week). It was so much fun being part of that group of avid tennis players.

Leo and I had quite a bit in common. We both loved baseball and CFL football. We used to sit and talk about things on the way to our cars after tennis was over for the day.

I adored Leo — everyone in the group did.

PS Annette, hardly a day goes by when I don't think of Leo. He was one of my very favourite people in the world. And — even though I only knew him for four years, it was as if we had known each other for a lifetime. I have kept his name on my call/name display on my telephone. The last time he called me was July 24th, 2008 at 10:47 a.m.

I miss him so much. He was such a great friend. My life was enriched by his kindness and generosity. I have chronic fatigue syndrome and fibromyalgia now, and so have not played tennis for a long time. There isn't any particularly good way of treating the condition. It's just a hit and miss kind of thing. If I ever get over it, I will go back to Leo's Group and play again.

vii. Deborah Heller

To: leozakuta@rogers.com

Years before I started playing with Leo's group, I had been struck by a *New Yorker* cartoon that etched itself into my memory. It showed two men against a background of raging hell fires, inhospitable crags, and demons at the ready with pitchforks. The caption — obviously the helpful explanatory words of an habitué to a newcomer — read: "It's like tennis; only there's no net, no balls, no racquets. ..."

I had viewed this cartoon with a painful sense of recognition. Tennis *can* feel like a descent into hell. By contrast, the great thing about playing with Leo's group was that it changed all that. Leo made tennis *fun*. He created a welcoming atmosphere of acceptance and tolerance, in which any potential sense of strong competition was nipped in the bud by the frequent rotation of partners. Hell fires and demons faded as tennis became a true pleasure, fostering a sense of camaraderie and community.

viii. Richard Nicolson

To: leozakuta@rogers.com

I am so sorry for the delay. I sent you an email a few days after the dedication, but in a rush I misspelled the address. I didn't notice that it bounced back until I got your voice message. My speech was as follows:

> It's a stunning fall day, the sun is shining and it's about 15 degrees. Leo would have hated it!!!! He played much better in snowy, 2-degree weather, half-snow-covered courts. The Rosedale Tennis Club is the best club in the city, and the reason for that is members like Leo. Leo has helped create a truly inclusive environment. As my good friend Shirley Harris can attest, Leo included all comers into his round robin group without prejudice. In the 7 years that I got to know Leo, every encounter was warm, friendly, and filled with the excitement of playing another day of tennis on courts 7 and 8. I'm sure that Norm and the rest of the group continue to honour Leo's memory by playing tennis at Rosedale, inviting and accepting new members to participate. I miss Leo very much. ... I am a better person for having known him.

Richard Nicolson
General Manager, York Racquets Club

ix. Annette Zakuta

Thank you so much to everyone who came here today to honour Leo. I'm sure you know that this would have meant so much to him. I especially want to thank Sean Miller for dreaming up this very creative idea of a plaque on courts 7 and 8, Norman Dyson for making it happen, and Peter Goering for all his wonderful photographs of "Leo's Gang." I would also like to thank Don and Deborah, and Lou, and Sheila, and Judy, and Haneko, and Ann, and Barry and Laurie and all the others in the group for being as devoted to Leo and the game as Leo was to them and the game.

On behalf of my family, I want to thank you all for this extraordinary honour.

x. Norm Dyson

After the unveiling, many of those who had attended went to Rose and Norm Dyson's house for a reception. Norman played his guitar while everyone sang the following song, which Norm had written for the occasion.

SO IT'S "PLAYER IN" FOR LEO
(to the tune of 'Brush up your Shakespeare')

Verse 1:
We've had a great day at court seven
We hung Leo's beautiful plaque
We're still trying to copy his effort
And the way he covered our back.

Chorus:
So it's "Player in" for Leo
He loved to hear that call
For every time it sounded
He knew it was tennis for all!

Verse 2:
He loved to joke and to *kibitz*
But his tennis was a serious game
You played your best and your hardest
But when finished we were all the same.

V FAMILY DOCUMENTS

1. The Zakuto Trail

i. *Yiches*[1]

Ever since I can remember, I have known the name Abraham Zacuto. We heard that he was a famous scientist in Spain whose accomplishments brought him into association with Christopher Columbus and played an important part in his explorations. Vasco da Gama was probably mentioned, but I'm not sure. Later, when I told my friends about my "famous ancestor," I replied to their questions and challenges about the connection rather facetiously. I had learned, I said, that although we cannot choose our descendants, we can choose our ancestors. I

---

[1] (Yiddish) untranslatable, perhaps the counterpart to *naches*: the satisfaction one gets from one's descendants. *Yiches* is the prestige one gets from one's ancestors, though ordinarily more recent ones.

added Mark Twain's story that Adam and Eve and the Garden of Eden had been located in Hannibal, Missouri, his hometown. When asked how he knew, he replied that in the thousands of years since, no one had ever been able to disprove it. That usually ended the discussion.

I thought a connection was likely, but far from certain. The difference in spelling was irrelevant; our name had been spelled in so many ways, nearly always with a "c" rather than a "k." I never thought to ask my father how it became "k." Perhaps it was as simple as the spelling of an immigration official, but I'll never know. Over the years I gathered bits and pieces (I can hardly remember which) which seemed to support our connection with Abraham Zacuto, but I didn't pursue it systematically.

The next major occurrence was the advent of Stanley Wax (a second cousin in Miami), who was something of a genealogist and who took all of this seriously. Stanley got my brother's name and business address, and wrote to him. Ken, knowing that I was more interested in the subject than he, directed Stanley to me, and so we began a somewhat one-sided correspondence in 1990. What made it one-sided were his efforts to enlist me in his avid pursuit of information about the recent family, which was numerous, scattered, and of little interest to me. What I cared about was the past — the more distant the better. Nevertheless, he kept stating boldly — as if there were no question about it — that we were all descendants of Abraham Zacuto. So there was further support for that belief.

Through Stanley I met my Boston cousins the next year. I had only the vaguest idea of their existence. My father may have made the odd offhand reference to them, which failed to register with me. Relatives, other than those closest to us and his mother and full sisters, were of little interest to him. He had probably hardly even known his older siblings; they were much older and of a different mother. In any event, Stanley had written to the Boston family about us, and they contacted us when they were in Toronto and suggested that we meet. My initial (private) reaction was much like my father's, but I could not refuse. (I was reluctant to meet more "observant" Jews of my vintage.) No one knew our exact relationship, but I arrived with a family tree. The meeting was a splendid surprise. (We quickly established that we were first cousins; their mother was my father's half-sister.)

They were thoroughly congenial and appealing, and we had much in common. They were educated, sophisticated, and secular, and we took to them instantly. We spent much time with one couple, Lillian[2] and Hyman Goldin, in Spain in 1992, especially in Andalusia.[3] And the verbal lore about Abraham Zacuto had also been part of their Kantrowitz heritage growing up. This too seemed like further support.

Then came the "Lineage" chart (in 2000) from Steve Weiss, a distant relative and a committed genealogist. It

---

[2] Lillian Goldin's maiden name was Kantrowitz; her mother's maiden name was Zakuta. Lillian's mother was apparently a half-sister of Leo's father (from his first marriage, because she was so much older than Hershel), though I'm not certain. [AZ]

[3] The Spanish government invited Jews from all over the world to "return" to Spain in 1992 to mark the 500th anniversary of their expulsion. The project, called By My Spirit, received little publicity in North America, but much in Europe. Nevertheless, Stanley Wax enthusiastically organized a Zacuto contingent to participate in the Spanish ceremonies. Annette and I joined it. Unfortunately, like Moses failing to reach "the promised land," Stanley died shortly before we all left. His wife and granddaughter did come, however, as did a good portion of the Kantrowitz family, and others. The whole venture was a great success, and we were welcomed in two splendid ceremonies in Toledo. At one, we unfurled a large banner, made by one of the Goldin sons, which proclaimed "Descendants of Abraham Zacuto."

seemed to remove most of the remaining uncertainty, though perhaps not all. I had always assumed that the 18th and first half of the 19th centuries were a "black hole" as far as records were concerned, because the Germans must have destroyed everything. But Steve Weiss wrote me the surprising story that the Zacutos had remained in Amsterdam until about 1800, so they are recorded in the 18th century archives.

Still, I have some questions. What could have possessed them to leave Holland shortly after 1800 to make their way to a small village in Eastern Europe? Or did they? Were some Zacutos already there? If so, when did they get there, from where, and where did the migrants from Holland go?

Furthermore, my great-grandparents are identified simply as "Koppel" Zacuto,[4] doubtless because their names and dates (of birth and death) are unknown. However, I have a full list of their children, grandchildren and further descendants. One of their children was my grandfather, Arieh Leib, who must have been born by the mid-19th century. I know surprisingly little about him–I don't recall my father ever mentioning him. (He would almost certainly have disapproved of my mother's family. Her father was as close to being a secular Jew as one could be in a shtetl.) What I do know is that he was poor, very devout, and lived on the outskirts of the shtetl. And even that came from my mother. The 19th century still has its mysteries.

---

[4] Leo's original read "Koppel" (i.e., a couple) Zacuto. Leo was under the incorrect impression that "*koppel*" meant "couple," but in fact it is a Yiddish diminutive of "Jacob." [AZ]

Leo Zakuta

*Leo and Annette at the Zakuto reunion
Salamanca, Spain, 1992*

ii. Lineage

From Steve Weiss (May 2000)

1275	Castile, France (1st generation).
1306	Arrived in Spain.
1440?-1515	**ABRAHAM BEN SAMUEL ZACUTO**, 6th generation; astronomer, geographer, doctor, mathematician.
1473	Published navigational tables (University of Salamanca); associate of, and collaborated with, Columbus and da Gama.
1492	Left Spain for Portugal.
1497	Left Portugal for Tunis; made his way to Jerusalem.
1575-1642	**ZACUTUS LUSITANUS**, great-great grandson of Abraham Zacuto, aka Manuel Alvares de Tavara. Born in Lisbon, doctor and medical writer.
1625	Came to Amsterdam; took the name Abraham Zacuth; died in Amsterdam.
1614	Enrique Zacuto, later Moses Zacuto. arranged for his son Diego Nunez, age 20, to be taken from Lisbon to Amsterdam, where he became **MORDECHAI ZACUTO**. (The family was named Nunez in Portugal.) Remarries his wife in a Jewish ceremony in Amsterdam.
1617	Mordechai and his brother (unnamed) arrive in Posen.
1620	Expelled by the Jewish community; family remained in Posen until about (or later)1630.

1612-97	Rabbi **MOSES ZACUTO**, son of Mordechai, kabbalist, poet, dramatist; went to Posen to study Kabbala; adherent of the false messiah Sabbetai Zvi; died in Mantua.
1622-1702	Seven Zacutos buried in Hamburg, Germany.
1810?	A Zacuto who had been born and married in Amsterdam died in Shislevitz (Svislocz).
1831?	**Koppel Zacuto**, born in Shislevitz.
1860?	**Arieh Leib**, his son, born in Shislevitz.
1894-1986	**Hershel (Harry) Zakuta**, son of Arieh Leib, born in Shislevitz, immigrates to Canada, where in 1924 he marries Keile Ain, born in Shislevitz.
1925, 1927	**Leo** and **Kenneth Zakuta**, sons of Hershel, born in Montreal.
1956-62	**Sharon, Sandra, Michael, Arnold**, children of Ken, born in Montreal (26th generation).
1963, 1964	**Jamie** and **Silvie**, children of Leo, born in Toronto (26th generation).
1990s	**Louis** and **Kayla** Zakuta, children of Michael (27th generation).

In the course of his research, Leo found material on eminent members of the Zacuto family in various secondary sources, examples of which follow. [AZ]

iii. Abraham Zacuto (b. Salamanca, Spain, ca. 1450, d. Portugal, ca. 1522)

(1) Barry Levy [Jewish Public Library], *Planets, Potions, and Parchments: Scientific Hebraica from the Dead Sea Scrolls to the Eighteenth Century* (Montreal: McGill-Queen's University Press, 1990)

Abraham ben Samuel Zacuto of Spain, Portugal, and Jerusalem, 1452-c. 1515

Abraham Zacuto studied astronomy at the university in Salamanca and became one of the leading astronomical consultants to the Spanish and Portuguese explorers. He was personally involved in the travel preparations of Vasco de Gama, and Columbus made extensive use of his charts. Zacuto is credited with constructing the first copper astrolabe; his astronomical tables, which were sought by many sea captains, improved upon the Alphonsine Tables, the best in existence until then. It is reported that Columbus used Zacuto's prediction of an eclipse to intimidate the natives he met, a story popularized in Mark Twain's *A Connecticut Yankee in King Arthur's Court*.

In addition to his many astronomical contributions, Zacuto composed *Sefer Yuhasin*, an important historical work first published in Constantinople in 1566. Part *VI*, which contains an outline of the history of the non-Jewish world, includes much information on the history of science.

HaHibbur HaGadol on astronomy (which also circulates under at least a half-dozen other titles) was written at the request of Zacuto's patron, the bishop of Salamanca, and has enjoyed tremendous popularity. It was translated into Spanish, and an abridgement was translated into both Latin and Spanish by Joseph Vicinho, one of Zacuto's students. An Arabic translation was also made, the Spanish version was transliterated into Hebrew, and a revised Latin translation was published in 1496.

(2) Meyer Kayserling, *Christopher Columbus and the Participation of the Jews in the Spanish and Portuguese Discoveries,* translated by Charles Gross (New York: Hermon, 1968 [reprint of 1894 edition]), 46-50.

Abraham Zacuto

At its sessions, which were held at Valcuevo, near Salamanca, Columbus presented and defended his project. Among others, there participated in this conference the astrologer Fray Antonio de Marchena, who always championed Columbus's cause, and the Jewish astrologer Abraham Zacuto, who, by his important contributions to his branch of knowledge, materially promoted Columbus's undertaking.

Abraham Zacuto, or Çacuto, was born in Salamanca about the year 1440, and was commonly called Zacuto of Salamanca. His ancestors came from South France, and, as he himself informs us in his celebrated chronicle, they remained steadfastly loyal to their religion in spite of all persecutions. He devoted himself to the study of mathematics, and especially astronomy, and won the favour of the Bishop of Salamanca, who allowed him to attend the university of that city. Here he became professor of astronomy, and many Christian and Mohammedan disciples revered him as their teacher. His chief astronomical work was the *Almanach Perpetuum* with tables of the sun, moon, and stars, which, as his pupil Augustin Ricci informs us, was prepared between 1473 and 1478, at the request of his patron, the bishop, to whom it was dedicated. It was translated from Hebrew into Latin and Spanish by his pupil Joseph Vecinho, or Vizino and was printed at the press of Magister Samuel d'Ortas in Leiria. Owing to its wide circulation, it went through several editions during the author's lifetime. ...

Zacuto's *Tables* always accompanied Columbus on his voyages, and rendered him inestimable service. To them, in fact, he and his crew once owed their lives. On his last voyage he had visited the coast of Veragua, the name of which is still perpetuated in the title of his present descendant, the Duke of Veragua. In its rich mines he found plenty of gold and precious stones. After leaving Veragua a terrible hurricane greatly injured his only two surviving caravels, rendering them unseaworthy. After he reached Jamaica he was in a desperate plight. The ungrateful Francisco de Porras had stirred up a conspiracy against him; Columbus himself was prostrated by illness; the natives were hostile to him and threatened his life; the few sailors who remained loyal to him were disheartened, and exhausted by hunger. The admiral and his followers anticipated certain death.

Thereupon he resorted to an expedient which is characteristic of him and of his time. By means of Zacuto's *Tables* he ascertained that there would be an eclipse of the moon on February 29, 1504. He then summoned certain caciques, or native chiefs, and told them that the God of the Spaniards was very angry with them because they did not give him and his sailors sufficient food, and that God would punish them by depriving them of the light of the moon, and by mercilessly subjecting them to the most pernicious influences. When night arrived, and the moon was invisible, the caciques and their followers raised a doleful wail, and, throwing themselves at the admiral's feet, they promised to provide him with plenty of provisions, and implored him to avert from them the impending evil. Columbus then retired on the pretence of communing with the Deity. When the thick darkness began to vanish, and the moon began to appear, he again came forth, and announced to the expectant caciques that their contrition had appeased the divine wrath. The full light of the moon soon beamed forth, and Columbus's object was attained; he encountered no more hostility, and obtained an abundance of food. ...

iv. Zacutus Lusitanus (b. Lisbon 1575, d. Amsterdam 1642)

Hendrik Brugmans, History of the Jews in the Netherlands (Geschiedenis Der Joden in Nederland), edited by Hendrik Brugmans and A. Frank (Amsterdam: 1940), 655-56 (translated for me by Karl Helleiner). [LZ, 195?]

Abraham Zacutus Lusitanus of Lisbon and Amsterdam (1575-1642)

Abraham Zacuto, also called **Zacutus Lusitanus**, great-great grandchild of the famous astronomer of the same name, is doubtless the most important of all the Portuguese Jewish doctors in the Netherlands. Born in Lisbon in 1575, he graduated at 18 from the famous university at Siguenza as a doctor of medicine. After that he practiced in Lisbon for 30 years. Out of fear of the inquisition, he left Portugal and went to Amsterdam, where he joined the covenant of Abraham at the age of 50; he died Jan.1, 1642. In his practice with his female patients, he used a Dutch woman as an interpreter, through whom he won their complete confidence. Besides being a famous practitioner, he was also a man of science who published many things. His most important work is a book, originally in six parts, *The Principles of Medical History*, which contains the observations of the most famous physicians of ancient times and those of his contemporaries, as well as his own. In addition: *The Admirable Practices of Medicine*, in three parts, a manual for the bedside and [manual] of prescriptions for young physicians. An English version was published later.

Zacutus corresponded with many famous contemporaries, among others Frederick, the Elector of Palatine, and his wife; De Castro, professor at the University of Padua, etc., etc., dean of the physicians in Rome. ...

Several writers praised his character, but others called him conceited and haughty. It is possible that he had difficulties adjusting to the new environment, with its liberal opinions and style of life, due to his lofty origins, and education and training in the conservative Spanish atmosphere. Whatever the case, Zacutus was highly respected by the Jewish physicians. Benito de Castro, the personal physician of Christina of Sweden, says of him, "O fortunate period which we praise because of your merits, that such a scholarly person has come from Spain" and "Greetings, glory and fame of the medical profession. Have as always affection for me."

v. Rabbi Moses Zacuto (ca. 1620-1697)

J. Melkman, *"Mozes Zacuto en Zijn Familie,"* Studia Rosenthaliana 3 (1969), 145-55.[5]

---

[5] I received a copy from the archives in Amsterdam, sent to me by Stanley Wax. I was lucky enough to have a Dutch colleague, Jos Lennards, who was willing to translate it for me. Even so, I found deciphering the translated text difficult, because each person had both a Portuguese and a

Moses Zacuto and his Family in Amsterdam

Until recently little was known about the youth of Moses Zacuto, Hebrew poet, dramatist, and kabbalist who lived in Italy during his later life, and died in Mantua in 1697. Except for one autobiographical item, our only source was the funeral speech of his pupil Benjamin Cohen of Reggio, and some questionable data. To make matters worse, his biographers drew far-reaching and even mistaken conclusions. Most scholars agreed that he was born in 1625 and was so captivated by mysticism in his youth that he moved to Poland to study the Zohar. Only one biographer presented clear evidence that Moses Zacuto was born around 1612, but his arguments were wrongly rejected. Nobody doubted that he went to Posen to study the Kabbala, although the Sephardic world then had many more kabbalists than did the Ashkenazic, and Posen was hardly known as a centre of Kabbala.

In an earlier publication, we have referred to the inaccuracy of these beliefs and have shown that the Jewish historians' portrait of Rabbi Moses Zacuto is completely distorted. New important material in the Municipal Archives of Amsterdam provides a much clearer understanding of his early environment and the wanderings about which he complained. These documents also illuminate the economic history of the Marranos, but that is beyond our present focus. We will only review in chronological order the documents pertaining to Moses Zacuto.

1. May 14, 1614. Enrique Zacuto, a Portuguese broker, arranged with the skipper Pieter Franz to take his son, age 20, named Diego Nunez, from Lisbon to Amsterdam. Enrique Zacuto, whom we will encounter later as Moses

---

Hebrew name, and one important figure was not named. [LZ]

Zacuto, was the grandfather of our Rabbi Moses Zacuto. Was Diego Nunez also Mordechai Zacuto, the father of our Moses? We know that the Zacuto family was named Nunez in Portugal, for one of Enrique (Moses) Zacuto's daughters lived in Lisbon as Isabel Nunez as late as 1637. Establishing the identity of Diego Nunez is not easy, however. We can find only two sons among Moses Zacuto's heirs: Abraham and Mordechai. That could imply that the young man of 20 is Mordechai, Moses' younger son, but two other documents call this into question. One indicates that Mordechai was married before coming to Amsterdam, whereas Diego appears to be a bachelor. The other seems to allude to a younger brother of Mordechai in Posen. Perhaps there was a younger brother who died before his father; no document registering the passage of Mordechai and his family to Amsterdam exists.

2. 1615. According to a note in the receipt book of the Sephardic community Beth Jacob, Mordechai Zacuto remarried. When Marranos returned to Judaism, they remarried to make the marriage legal in Jewish law. This usually took place soon after arrival. We can therefore assume that Mordechai Zacuto arrived in Amsterdam in 1614 or 1615, already married. His son Moses may have been born by then.

3. March 25, 1616. Simon Rodrigues da Costa, alias Jacomo Ruiz da Costa, transferred insurance policies to Enrique Zacuto to discharge his debts to him. This is our first evidence of Moses Zacuto Sr.'s financial transactions.

4. Nov. 17, 1616. A commercial transaction involving diamonds between Moses (Enrique) Zacuto and his son Mordechai, as one party, and Manuel Cardozo de Milao (alias Manuel Taxeira), agent of Alvaro de Nijs of Hamburg and Daniel de Hollande (alias Gomes Rodrigues

Milao), as the second party. This transaction shows that Moses Zacuto and his son had connections with the most important Marrano families whose business extended to many countries.

5. Feb. 15, 1618. Document in Portuguese. Samaria Vides de Galilea, age 50, declared that about 6 months earlier he was in the warehouse of Mordechai Zacuto in Posen in Greater Poland and noticed that he carried a particular type of wool. This statement shows that Mordechai Zacuto already lived and had a textile business in Posen in 1617. Why this declaration was drawn up is not clear, but it tells us that the Zacuto family was attempting to establish a firm foothold in Poland. Early in the 17th century Jews were active in the import and export of commodities in Poland, and the demand for textiles in Western Europe led Enrique Zacuto to send his son to start a business in Posen. For a resident of Galilea to act as a witness in Amsterdam for a business in Poland illustrates the frequency of international connections among the Portuguese Jews.

6. Sept. 22, 1618. Settlement of unpaid account between Nunez Homem and Enrique Zacuto for insurance of ships between Lisbon and Angola and the West Indies. This transaction also reveals the family's international trade.

7. Dec. 10, 1618. Enrique Zacuto boarded out his son Mordechai to Nicolas Benoit for 120 Carolus guilders to learn the polishing of rubies, sapphires, etc. This indicates that Mordechai's initial attempt to establish a foothold in Posen had failed. Whether his family accompanied him during his short stay there is not clear.

8. April 15, 1620. Enrique (Moses) Zacuto transferred to Francisco Nunes Homem a debenture against Manuel Mendes de Castro. This transaction shows that the Zacutos

had connections with Hamburg, where de Castro was an agent for, among others, firms from Amsterdam.

9. Aug. 6, 1620. Declaration by Manuel Pimentel, age 25, at the request of Enrique Zacuto, that he and Abraham Bezamerro and Mordechai Zacuto had visited the city of Posnania, where he witnessed the arrival at Zacuto's place of "certain cloths" sent to him by Enrique Zacuto. Thus, two years later, the family apparently again tried to start a business in Posen; this venture of Mordechai's lasted longer.

10. Dec. 3, 1620. Declaration by Jacob Lucas, cloth salesman, on the request of Enrique Zacuto on behalf of his son Mordechai, that in 1619 he had received 48 pieces of white cloth for Mordechai, which he sent to Jan Cornelis "cloth dyer" to be dyed.

11. Document in old Dutch: untranslated. This notary deed shows that Enrique Zacuto also had business connections in India, especially in Goa, where there was a Marrano colony. He had an agent in Lisbon as well, which shows how far-ranging his business was.

12. Aug. 1621. Moses Zacuto gave his cousin Isaac Zacuto, of Venice, the right to collect outstanding claims against Abraham Abarbanel, also of Venice. This followed the usual practice among Sephardic families of choosing relatives as agents. Moses Zacuto's business appears to have extended to the great centre of Sephardic Jewry, Venice.

13. March 29, 1623. On Nov. 2, 1622, Diego Martina Bendia, Portuguese merchant in Amsterdam, sold to Moses (Enrique) Zacuto, sworn Portuguese broker, 38 pieces of cloth which are in the possession of Francisco Dias Nunes in Danzig. Other documents confirm that Francisco Dias

Nunes of Lisbon is an agent in Danzig for Portuguese Jews from Amsterdam.

14. Decision by the Jewish community of Posen. [Hebrew document, followed by a Dutch translation.]

> Mordechai and his brother, sons of Moses Zacuto, tried to represent themselves as tradesmen (in Posen), which was forbidden to strangers, and tried to get the same rights as the residents. But the city's Kahal [communal leadership] decided they were not qualified to do so, and could only remain there a month, during which they were not allowed to trade with non-Jews [lit., the non-circumcised], but were only permitted to sell to Jews. The Kahal issued an ordinance on June 15, 1620 warning them not to go to any market in Lublin without the Kahal's approval. They disobeyed, but the Kahal did not take timely action against them. The Kahal then decided that from then on they could not reside in the town, but would have to leave and not return, except for the markets, at which times they could stay a night or two. If they disobeyed again, they would be fined 1000 zloty and forbidden to trade. The fine would go for the building of the shul in Swierzenc.

This document from Posen's community annals is important. The leaders of the Posen community regarded these Portuguese Jews as competitors whom they were not prepared to tolerate in their midst. Even though the royal privileges stipulated that Jews should suffer no annoyance and be allowed to engage in business freely, the Jews in Posen were less tolerant than the non-Jewish majority. We may assume that the regulation adopted in 1620 was also aimed at Mordechai Zacuto, who was based in Posen by 1617.

The wording of the above text suggests that the decision was taken only after a long and difficult discussion. While the Kahal initially permitted a stay of a month, and allowed them to go to the Lublin market if it granted them permission to do so, it then restricted their stay in Posen to the times the market was held. Both brothers were told to leave the city at once.

What is the date of this decision? Baron says 1620, but that is obviously wrong, as is apparent from the document. The decision itself states that the ordinance of 1620 was not executed, and the elapsed period would not be held against the brothers, i.e., no fine would be imposed for the unenforced ordinance. We don't know how long the 1620 ordinance was a dead letter, but other documents show that the family lived in Posen as late as 1630.

What was the identity of Mordechai's brother who was also told to leave the city? When Moses Sr.'s inheritance was divided, there appeared to be only two sons: Abraham and Mordechai. Perhaps Abraham was the brother whom the Kahal did not name. It may have regarded Mordechai as the principal, since he had lived in Posen longer. However, Abraham, age 40, was older than Mordechai, and it seems unlikely that Posen's Kahal would mention the younger brother instead of the older. Possibly Diego Nunez, who was fetched from Lisbon in 1614 (see #1), was not Mordechai, but an even younger brother who worked for him? If so, perhaps he died before his father's inheritance was divided, leaving no wife and children.

15. March 23, 1629. Mordechai Zacuto, son of Moses (Enrique) Zacuto (deceased), acting as a legal agent for his brother Abraham and his sister Simca Zacuto, declared that he received payment from Juan Gonsales for debts owed to his father. Mordechai was thus settling his father's business affairs in Amsterdam. Simca, as we know, lived in Posen then; perhaps Abraham was there too.

16. 1629. Simca Zacuto, daughter of Moses Zacuto, sent a request from Poland to the Dotar society in Amsterdam to participate in a draw of dowries for Sephardic girls. This shows that the family had not yet left Poland in 1629 and Simca was about to marry.

17. Feb. 25, 1630. Again Simca requested an allowance from the Dotar, but now from Hamburg, where she was marrying (had married?) Abraham Coen.

18. Abraham Zacuto succeeded his father Moses Zacuto as a member of the Dotar brotherhood.

19. March 5,1637. Legal decision in a lawsuit initiated by Abraham Zacuto on behalf of himself, his brothers and sisters, all children of the late Moses Zacuto, and Isabel Nunes' two legal children, as plaintiffs, against Abraham Franco Mendes as defendant. The plaintiffs were the sole heirs of Antonia (Isabel Nunes' sister), who died a few days ago. She had left some pieces of furniture paid for by Philip Pelt in exchange for two promissory notes sent from Hamburg by Manuel Rodrigues Isidro to Bento Osorio. All these merchants were among the best-known Sephardim.

20. March 22, 1637. Moses Zacuto's six children divided Antonia Nunes' inheritance:

1. Abraham Zacuto
2. Isabel of Lisbon
3. Mordechai Zacuto's heirs
4. Sara Atias, widow of Haham Isaac Atias
5. Rachel Atias of Aleppo
6. Simca, wife of Abraham Coen, of Hamburg

21. Nov. 19, 1637. Isaac Nahar signed the receipt for Antonio Nunes' inheritance in the name of Mordechai Zacuto's heirs in Amsterdam and Hamburg. (Some of Mordechai Zacuto's under-age children apparently lived in Amsterdam while Rabbi Moses Zacuto was one of the Hamburg heirs.) Isaac Nahar (from Naar) was a well-known physician and Rabbi in Amsterdam. In 1666 the rabbinate sent him on a visit to Sabbetai Zvi. For a few years he was Parnas of the Talmud Torah, one such year being 1637.

These documents clarify Moses Zacuto's early environment and his written statements. The Zacutos were a true Marrano family; in Portugal they were named Nunez. While some members departed for Amsterdam, where they re-adopted the name Zacuto, others stayed behind. But the two branches of the family remained in contact. Moses Zacuto's grandfather, whom we met as Enrique and as Moses, lived in Amsterdam by 1614. He must have been a remarkable businessman.

Kellenbenz's description of the economic activities of the Sephardic Jews in general applies fully to this family. Its members represented the family business in various places, including Lisbon, Hamburg, and Venice. Interestingly, Moses Zacuto Sr. was one of the few Portuguese who also attempted to penetrate Eastern Europe and even stationed two of his sons in Posen. The opposition of the local Jews undermined this attempt. But the business already appears to have been declining, like those of so many Portuguese families, which peaked after a generation. Nothing remained of Moses Zacuto's worldwide business: his daughters married rabbis and his other son, Abraham, showed no sign of economic activity. We have seen that while the firm was exporting cloth to Poland, Mordechai was learning how to cut diamonds, and he and his father was active in this sphere.

All of this shows that Rabbi Moses grew up in a well-to-do family of Marrano origin. The grandfather's drive to expand moved his sons from one place to another, which explains why Rabbi Moses (his grandson) studied at several locations in his youth, as his pupil Benjamin Cohen of Reggio relates. Now we can understand why he studied in Posen where his father had a cloth warehouse, although it is harder to establish exactly when he was there. A traditional interpretation holds that he was among the first pupils of Rabbi Saul Levi Morteira. If so — and there is no reason to doubt Rabbi H.J.D. Azulai's assertion — he probably did not accompany his father during the latter's first stay in Posen (1617) or at the beginning of his second stay. According to Franco Mendes, Morteira began teaching at the Talmud Torah in 1616, but did not sign a contract until 1621. Rabbi Moses would have been too young to have been Morteira's pupil in 1616. The lamentation which he dedicated to Morteira after his death demonstrates that he saw himself as his pupil.

Presumably Mordechai allowed his son to come over when it seemed that the 1620 ordinance would not be enforced. It is impossible to tell when the family left Posen, though certainly not before 1629, when Rabbi Moses' aunt was still living there, but it was surely before 1637, by which time Mordechai was dead. Did Rabbi Moses go straight from Posen to Hamburg, where we find him in 1642? Perhaps, but he may have returned to Amsterdam before settling in Hamburg.

Given the confusion created by the name Moses, let us note that the family had additional branches in the 17th century. We are certain that several families lived in Hamburg; our documents show that one cousin lived in Venice. But we also find family members in Zamosc (Poland), among whom is "Mojzesz," which indicates how common this name was in the family.

These Zacuto family members are buried in the Hamburg cemetery:

No. 1526	Moses
No. 1527-383 (17 Dec. 1622)	Moses
No. 1528-384 (6 Jan. 1624)	Gracia, wife of Moses
No. 1529-443 (20 Oct. 1682)	Esther, daughter of Isaac
No. 1530-444 (27 July 1684)	Moses, son of Isaac
No. 1531-454 (18 June 1694)	Esther
No. 1532-463 (10 Nov. 1702)	Gracia

The buried include at least 3 Moses Zacutos. One of the first was probably Rabbi Moses' grandfather, which means that he must have died by 1623.

Encyclopedia Judaica

Zakuto, Moses ben Mordecai

Zakuto, Moses ben Mordecai (ca.1620-1697), kabbalist and poet. Zacuto, who was born into a Portuguese Marrano family in Amsterdam, studied Jewish subjects under Saul Levi Morteira. ... He moved to Italy, remaining for some time in Verona. From 1645 he lived in Venice and served for a time as a preacher under Azariah Figo. Afterward, he became one of the rabbis of the city and a member of the Venetian yeshivah. Between 1649 and 1670 he was proofreader of many books printed in Venice, especially works on Kabbalah. He edited the *Zohar Hadash* in 1658, and also wrote many poems for celebrations and special occasions. ...

After the apostasy of Shabbetai Zevi he turned his back on the movement and joined the other Venetian rabbis in their action against Nathan of Gaza when he came to Venice in the spring of 1668. ...

In 1671 he was invited to serve as rabbi in Mantua, but he did not go until 1673, remaining there until his death. He enjoyed great authority as the chief of the contemporary Italian kabbalists and corresponded with kabbalists in many places. He never realized his desire to settle in Erez Israel. ...

R[abbi] Zacuto's published exoteric works include his commentary on the Mishnah, *Kol ha-Re-Me-Z*. A collection of halakhic responsa was published in Venice in 1760. A commentary on the Palestinian Talmud is lost. His major activity, however, was in Kabbalah. ... He went over the entire corpus of R. Luria's and R. Vital's writings and added many annotations under the name *Kol ha-Re-Me-Z*. ... R. Zacuto wrote at least two commentaries on the Zohar. ... R. Zacuto arranged tikkunim ("special prayers") for several religious ceremonies according to Kabbalah. These were often reprinted and had great influence, especially on the religious life in Italy

A major part of Zacuto's poetry is devoted to kabbalistic subjects, such as his poems in the book *Hen Kol Hadash* (Amsterdam, 1712) [and] in *Tofteh Arukh* (a description of hell: Venice, 1715). Besides this he arranged voluminous *collectanea* on kabbalistic subjects. The first was *Shibbolet shel Leket*, on all the books of the Bible (Scholem, *Kitvei Yad be-Kabbalah*, 1930, p. 153, para. 107).

2. The Ain Family

i. Svislocz in Our Time[6]

It is 36 years since I left my native shtetl, Svislocz. During all these years, most of which were painfully hard, in the new land, I never longed for the country where we were considered strangers — humiliated, persecuted, and hounded. On the other hand, my shtetl, Svislocz, where I was born and spent the loveliest years of youth, has remained deeply ingrained in my heart.

Keile's parents — Zisel and Aaron Ain, Svislocz, 1923

Neither time nor distance has dimmed the memories or severed the ties of closeness and friendship with my *landsleit* all over the world: I always remember our shtetl, Svislocz, with love, respect, and pride. Despite terribly

---

[6] Keile Zakuta, "Svislocz in Our Time" [Yiddish], *Svislocz Yizkor Book* [Hebrew and Yiddish], (Tel Aviv: Gutenberg, 1961), 81-87; translated by Leo Zakuta with the help of Emanuel Goldberg in Dec. 1990.

difficult economic and political conditions, the shtetl progressed and developed in every way, and stood at the forefront among many *shtetlach*, both near and far. As far back as the 1890s, Svislocz was known as 'Little Warsaw.' Both in outward appearance and in industrial and cultural development, Svislocz represented a city in miniature.

Keile Ain (top row, 2nd from left)
with her students and other teachers
Hebrew caption reads: Hebrew public school, Svislocz
Svislocz, c. 1920

Svislocz was one of the very first shtetls to awaken from the deep slumber and backwardness into which Jewish life had sunk. The motto of the Haskala (Enlightenment) epoch — Be a Jew at home and a man of the world outside — struck deep and fruitful roots in Svislocz. A small group of *maskilim* conducted a difficult but successful struggle against the backward *balebatim* of the shtetl. The first Hebrew school was founded, the reformist cheder where Hebrew and the national language [i.e., Russian] and elementary general studies were taught. Soon, even the *talmud torah* began to teach the national language one hour a day. A library was also founded. Progressive Jewish parents — the more prosperous, naturally — began to send their children to *gymnasias* (high schools), which existed only in the largest cities. A very few even reached the universities. On the holidays, along with the yeshiva students, the gymnasiasts returned to the shtetl and paraded in the streets in their uniforms with brass buttons and badges on their caps. With what respect and envy the ordinary children in the shtetl regarded those students!

The Jewish youth of Svislocz quickly became educated; they read and developed in every way. Jewish young men entered the leather factories, learned trades, and began to earn money and become self-supporting. Strangers who were leaders of and agitators for various parties, appeared in the shtetl, and, under their supervision, various political groups were started. The young people read and studied the illegal literature--which was widely disseminated--in earnest. They agitated [for reform], held discussions, and participated in secret gatherings, very often falling into the hands of the terrifying Russian police.

The youth in Svislocz become revolutionary — daring and ready for sacrifices. They even organized demonstrations with red flags, revolutionary songs, and the shtetl's police, including the chief, were forced to go along with the demonstrators. But a wave of house searches and arrests soon followed. One such night became etched in my memory — the terrible scene at our neighbour's house, the ripped bedcovers and pillows, the overturned and broken cupboards and chests where they searched for illegal literature, and the despairing cries of the parents and children when a young son was led away, an innocent boy shackled in chains.

I was seven years old then. The very next morning I resolved to review my own books to see if they were kosher. My prayer book was the first victim. I threw it into the burning oven because it was missing the first page with the imprint, "Permitted by the censor." Among the first victims of that terrible time was Peretz Bernstein, a young man born in Svislocz, who was beaten to death by police thugs in the Grodno jail. We must also note the resolute and courageous conduct of the young people of Svislocz during the time of the pogroms, when the terrifying cry "Beat the Jews and save Russia" spread throughout Russia.

Hershel Zakuta
Svislocz, 1923

Passport picture of Keile Ain
Svislocz, 1923

When the organized pogroms reached our district and the peasants appeared in the market with axes and sacks ready to kill and rob, no pogrom occurred in Svislocz despite the heated incitement and the peasants' readiness to carry out the savage slaughter. The pogromchiks sensed that it would not be easy. Jewish self-defence had been organized in the shtetl, and its members had resolved not to let themselves be slaughtered like sheep.

I recall clearly one gathering place of the self-defence group. Some of the arms that had been prepared to be used in defence were hidden in the chicken-coop under the oven in my grandfather's small house (in a poor district). Even though I was still a child, the dreadful fear and the oppressive atmosphere in which the whole shtetl was enveloped have remained forever in my memory. Even now I shudder when I hear church bells ringing, because that was often a call for a pogrom.

The large wave of Jewish emigration in that period included a substantial portion of the young people of Svislocz. The year 1910, when the great fire wiped out three-quarters of Svislocz, and the next few years of homelessness, poverty, and epidemics, were difficult ones for the shtetl. But Jews are resourceful. Svislocz was rebuilt with more attractive, comfortable, and modern homes. It had barely caught its breath when the dark storm clouds of the First World War approached.

The 1914-1918 period was very difficult — years of suffering and struggle: the Russian mobilization when so many young men went off to war; the Russian retreat in 1915; the robberies and killings; the German invasion, with the fear and danger of the frontline positions; the plague and the long bitter suffering under the ruthless heel of the German army. Those were years of bitter and terrible struggle for daily existence, for a piece of dry bread, for a garment made from a sack.

The cultural and spiritual life of the shtetl was even more difficult. The schools and libraries were closed. All meetings and gatherings were forbidden. The young people didn't study or read. There was a danger that a whole generation would remain backward and might become demoralized. But the Jewish spirit prevailed. Despite all the prohibitions and dangers, Jewish and Hebrew libraries functioned in secret, and people studied and read until late at night by the light of a tiny oil lamp.

I remember how my mother used to call me 'the girl with whiskers.' The whiskers were produced by the soot from that oil lamp. We waited until evening for a newspaper or telegram, which arrived on the last train. Later, when one could subscribe to newspapers, four of us would share one paper, because we lacked the few pennies [to buy it individually].

I recall very well the deep joy, the exaltation, and the timeless hopes engendered by the Balfour Declaration. The Zionist Centre was soon founded, and various factions crystallized: the general Zionists, right and left Young Zionists, left and right Labour-Zionists. Other groups reorganized simultaneously: Bundists, Populists, and Communists — seven or eight parties in a shtetl of 4,000 to 5,000 people. In fact, things became quite lively and cheerful, especially after the German withdrawal.

I remember the endless discussions and debates that took place at the Zionist Centre. They kept splitting into right and left when it came to a vote — both in the groups themselves, and in the community; and later, in the Polish parliament. The shtetl was electrified. I recall how I kept trying to persuade my mother not to vote with my father for the general Zionists, but for the workers' list instead. The atmosphere in the house was explosive, but I never found out for whom my mother had voted. She was a strong believer in the secret ballot. But I was sure that the success of the workers' list owed much to the votes cast by my mother and the other mothers.

The summer of 1920 is deeply ingrained in my memory: the Bolshevik-Polish war, especially the Polish army's retreat. The hated Poles, from whose anti-semitism Jews had suffered so much, experienced a .great defeat in Svisloсz, and barely managed to escape from the advancing

Russian army. With what excitement, impatience, hope and trust we — particularly the young people — awaited our Bolshevik liberators!

1 recall so well the night when the victorious Bolshevik soldiers marched into our shtetl to the strains of the "Internationale," and the wonderful speeches in the marketplace. With what joy and hope we heard the speeches about equality and freedom! Oh my, how naively we believed them. Disillusionment, however, came quickly and bitterly. The liberators showed their true colours; drunk with power and with an unquenchable thirst for revenge, they lorded undisturbed over the shtetl. They did not take long to shatter our beliefs and our hopes. We quickly realized that despotic power, wild revenge, and bloody tyranny would not bring equality and freedom. How debased, senseless, and misleading those words of the "lnternationale" sounded. We could hardly wait for liberation from "the liberators"; the scene became even darker.

We Jews went from the frying pan into the fire. We knew very well what awaited us at the hands of the arriving Polish victors. The wild anti-semites even wanted to make the Jews of the shtetl the scapegoats for their horrible defeat at the time of their the previous withdrawal. If not for the American Commission, which accompanied the Polish army to prevent pogroms, the Jews of Svislocz would not have got off so lightly.

The difficult economic situation, the new evil decrees, and persecution by the Polish anti-semites made Jewish life intolerable and the future hopeless. In 1923 I left Svislocz — left everything that I loved, everything that was so dear to me. The parting was hard and my homesickness painful. I never forgot my shtetl, neither the weekdays with the great worry about earning a living, nor the beautiful, serene and exalted days of the Sabbaths and holidays. Along with the deep mud before Passover and the sad, grey days before Rosh Hashana, I have not forgotten how lovely our shtetl was in the spring, when the orchards bloomed alongside corn fields with blue corn flowers that we wove into garlands, or the wonderful and lovely summer nights when the moon bathed the large marketplace with magical light, as if it was watching over the sleeping shtetl.

It is not forgotten — not the thickly-treed orchard nor the paths in the little forest near the [train] station where the young people strolled, sang, played, carried on romances and dreamed. Some dreamed of a national home in Israel; some of national autonomy in exile, and some of the communist revolution. The ideals differed, but all the dreams were of a beautiful and bright future.

Oh, what a dark, dreadful, and pitiless future awaited the Jewish youth. The young lives were cut off, and the Vishneviker Woods became a mass grave for their fathers and mothers.

Our shtetl was burned and wiped off the earth [by the Nazis and their collaborators]. Our murderous neighbours, like wild beasts, waited in vain to inherit the Jewish homes with the Jewish goods and property. Not a trace of the shtetl remained. At the Jewish cemetery only desolate winter winds mourn the lonely and abandoned gravestones.

My shtetl is dead, as are all who were near and dear, but their images all live on in my heart.

Keile Zakuta
Montreal 1959

ii. Letter to Keile Zakuta from her Father, Aaron Isaac Ain[7]

Svisloçz 18/6/1923

My dear daughter Keile,

We received your telegram from Danzig today. I am writing you this letter while still under the oppressive weight of your departure. It pains me greatly that we parted as though it would be forever. You didn't open your closed heart even though you were about to leave, and I am also to blame for that, which distresses me even more. We haven't yet received any letters from you since you left on your journey. We're very anxious, because as you say, you didn't have a chance to calm down until you got to Warsaw. It bothers us very much; we would be comforted if we knew that you were at peace.

My dear daughter, I beg you not to worry about us. We will bear our loneliness and be consoled by the fact that your journey will take you to a goal and a purpose, which is better than no purpose at all. I hope that your journey will bring you fulfilment. I am very happy that you finally listened to us and took the baggage with you. We received the telegram from Danzig on Tuesday morning. We didn't know what to think — with every train, we expected you to come back. We impatiently await a letter from your journey, and hope to learn how you felt in beautiful Odessa with Chanale, and whether you had any unpleasantness [there] with them.

We are all well. For the last few days, Yosefke has been more at ease, he's at home more, and that makes us happier than before. Please forgive me for this letter. I absolutely

---

[7] Translated collaboratively from the Yiddish by Annette Zakuta, Sylvia Lustgarten, Vivian Felsen, and Nessa Olshansky-Ashtar.

cannot hold myself back from expressing my thoughts in writing.

Be well, my dear daughter, and be at ease. I wish you good fortune in your new life. Believe and hope, look to the future without despair. Write us about everything.

Your loving, forlorn, and lonely father,
Aaron Isaac

P.S. Yosefke is at school now, and the mail leaves before noon. We don't want to wait for him. He is writing a second letter, but his letter isn't finished yet.

Iguana Books
iguanabooks.com

If you enjoyed *Leo Zakuta: Reminiscences, Rants, and Raves* ...
Look for other books coming soon from Iguana Books! Subscribe to our blog for updates as they happen.

iguanabooks.com/blog/

If you're a writer ...
Iguana Books is always looking for great new writers, in every genre. We produce primarily ebooks but, as you can see, we do the occasional print book as well. Visit us at iguanabooks.com to see what Iguana Books has to offer both emerging and established authors.

iguanabooks.com/publishing-with-iguana/

If you're looking for another good book ...
All Iguana Books books are available on our website. We pride ourselves on making sure that every Iguana book is a great read.

iguanabooks.com/bookstore/

Visit our bookstore today and support your favourite author.

www.ingramcontent.com/pod-product-compliance
Lightning Source LLC
Chambersburg PA
CBHW070306230426

43664CB00015B/2649